Praise for **ACHILLE MBEMBE**

Winner of the Gerda Henkel Prize
Winner of the Ernst Bloch Prize

Praise for **NECROPOLITICS**

"Mbembe refreshes the debate in a Europe consumed by the 'desire of apartheid.' This is a man who is not afraid to throw national history, identities, and borders out the window. French universalism? 'Conceited,' asserts Mbembe. . . . In the style of Édouard Glissant . . . he doesn't limit his geography to the level of the nation but expands it to the 'Whole-World.' He dreams of writing a common history of humanity that would deflate all the flashy national heroism and redraw new relations between the self and the other. In a France and a Europe that are even afraid of their own shadows, one can clearly see the subversive potential of Mbembe's thought. His latest book, *Necropolitics*, draws the unpleasant portrait of a continent eaten up by the desire of 'apartheid,' moved by the obsessive search for an enemy, and with war as its favorite game." —Cécile Daumas, *Libération*

"[Mbembe's] new book . . . is a precious tool to understand what occurs in the North as well as in the South. The analyses of this faithful reader of Frantz Fanon are irrevocable: war has become not an exception but a permanent state, 'the sacrament of our era.' . . . One of the biggest challenges we have to face, Mbembe warns us, is to defend our democracies while including this 'other' whom we don't want if we are to build our common future."
—Séverine Kodjo-Grandvaux and Michael Pauron, *Jeune Afrique*

Praise for **CRITIQUE OF BLACK REASON**

Winner of the 2015 Geschwister-Scholl-Preis
Winner of the Le Prix FETKANN! de la Mémoire 2013

"Achille Mbembe speaks authoritatively for black life, addressing the whole world in an increasingly distinctive tone of voice. This long-anticipated

book resounds with the embattled, southern predicament from which its precious shards of wisdom originate. . . . Mbembe sketches the entangled genealogies of racism and black thought on their worldly travels from the barracoons and the slave ships, through countless insurgencies, into the vexed mechanisms of decolonization and then beyond them, into our own bleak and desperate circumstances."
—Paul Gilroy

"Achille Mbembe has placed the discourse of 'Africa' squarely in the center of both postmodernism and continental philosophy. Every page of this signifying riff on Kant's *Critique of Pure Reason* is a delight to read. African philosophy is currently enjoying a renaissance, and Mbembe is to its continental pole what Kwame Anthony Appiah is to its analytical pole. Every student of postmodernist theory should read this book."
—Henry Louis Gates Jr.

"With *Critique of Black Reason*, Achille Mbembe reaffirms his position as one of the most original and significant thinkers of our time. . . . His voyages in this book through a painstakingly assembled archive of empire, race, slavery, blackness, and liberation . . . produce profound moments of reflection on the origin and nature of modernity and its mutations in the contemporary phase of global capital. A tour de force that will renew debates on capital, race, and freedom in today's world."
—Dipesh Chakrabarty

"*Critique of Black Reason* constitutes an important move in bringing together francophone and anglophone postcolonial thought and is a timely demonstration of the reinvigorating potential of both critical thought and translation."
—Hannah Grayson, *Postcolonial Text*

"We are familiar with the experiences of slavery, colonialism and apartheid, and the historical narrative through which each has unfolded. What Mbembe has done is to tie them all together in a bundle, under the rubric of black reason, that now serves as the genealogy of much of contemporary black experience and the history that has shaped black people's view of themselves."
—Gabriel O. Apata, *Theory, Culture, and Society*

"Incontrovertible reading on the complex dynamic between race and belonging in twenty-first-century societies. . . . Brilliant and pioneering. . . ."
—Dominic Thomas, *Europe Now*

NECROPOLITICS

THEORY IN FORMS

A series edited by Nancy Rose Hunt and Achille Mbembe

NECRO-POLITICS

ACHILLE MBEMBE

Translated by
STEVEN CORCORAN

Duke University Press
Durham and London
2019

Politiques de l'inimitié © 2016 Editions La Découverte
English translation © 2019 Duke University Press
All rights reserved
Printed in the United States of America on acid-free paper ∞
Cover designed by Matthew Tauch
Typeset in Arno Pro by Tseng Information Systems, Inc.

Library of Congress Cataloging-in-Publication Data

Names: Mbembe, Achille, [date] author. |
Corcoran, Steve, translator.
Title: Necropolitics / Achille Mbembe ;
translated by Steven Corcoran
Other titles: Politiques de l'inimitié. English
Description: Durham : Duke University Press, 2019. |
Series: Theory in forms | Includes bibliographical
references and index.
Identifiers: LCCN 2019009527 (print)
LCCN 2019016270 (ebook)
ISBN 9781478007227 (ebook)
ISBN 9781478005858 (hardcover : alk. paper)
ISBN 9781478006510 (pbk. : alk. paper)
Subjects: LCSH: Fanon, Frantz, 1925–1961. | Political
violence. | Decolonization—History—20th century. |
Democracy. | Postcolonialism.
Classification: LCC JC328.6 (ebook) | LCC JC328.6 .M3913
2019 (print) | DDC 320.01—dc23
LC record available at https://lccn.loc.gov/2019009527

CONTENTS

ACKNOWLEDGMENTS

This essay was written during a lengthy stay at the Witwatersrand Institute for Social and Economic Research (WISER) at the University of the Witwatersrand (Johannesburg, South Africa). Throughout my years there, I benefited enormously from continual exchanges with my colleagues Sarah Nuttall, Keith Breckenridge, Pamila Gupta, Sara Duff, Jonathan Klaaren, Cath Burns, and, more recently, Hlonipa Mokoena and Shireen Hassim. Adam Habib, Tawana Kupe, Zeblon Vilakazi, Ruksana Osman, and Isabel Hofmeyr never ceased to bestow all manner of encouragement on me. The postdoctoral seminar that I ran with my colleague Sue van Zyl at WISER, and to which Charne Lavery, Claudia Gastrow, Joshua Walker, Sarah Duff, Kirk Side, and Timothy Wright regularly contributed, proved an invaluable space of inquiry and creativity.

Paul Gilroy, David Theo Goldberg, Jean Comaroff, John Comaroff, Françoise Vergès, Éric Fassin, Laurent Dubois, Srinivas Aravamudan, Charles Piot, Elsa Dorlin, Grégoire Chamayou, Charles Piot, Ackbar Abbas, Dilip Gaonkar, Beth Povinelli, my late friend T. K. Biaya, Nadia Yala Kisukidi, Eyal Weizman, Judith Butler, Ghassan Hage, Ato Quayson, Souleymane Bachir Diagne, Adi Ophir, Célestin Monga, Siba Grovogui, Susan van Zyl, Henry Louis Gates, and Felwine Sarr have all been fertile sources of inspiration and, often unbeknownst to them, absolutely first-rate interlocutors.

I thank my colleagues from the (now decommissioned) Johannesburg Workshop in Theory and Criticism, Leigh-Ann Naidoo, Zen Marie, and Kelly Gillespie, as well as Najibha Deshmukh and Adila Deshmukh for their profound friendship.

My publisher Hugues Jallon and his team, Pascale Iltis, Thomas Deltombe, and Delphine Ribouchon, have all, as usual, been unfailing in their support. This essay is dedicated to a man beyond names, Fabien Éboussi Boulaga, and to two steadfast friends, Jean-François Bayart and Peter L. Geschiere.

INTRODUCTION
THE ORDEAL
OF THE WORLD

If you want to make use of a book, simply picking it up will not suffice. My original aim was to write a book that not a hint of mystery shrouded. In the end, I found myself with a short essay of sketched hachures, of parallel chapters, of more or less discontinuous lines, of raw and rapid gestures, and even slight movements of withdrawal followed by abrupt reversals.

It is true that the roughness of the topic did not afford a violin note. It was enough to suggest the presence of bone, a skull, or a skeleton inside the element. This bone, this skull, and this skeleton all have names: repopulation of the Earth, exit from democracy, society of enmity, relation without desire, voice of blood, and terror and counterterror as our time's medication and poison (chapters 1 and 2). The best way to access these different skeletons was to produce a form, not a spineless one but a tense and energy-charged one. In any case, this text is one on whose surface the reader can glide freely, without control points or visas, sojourning as long as desired, moving about at will, returning and leaving at any moment and through any door. The reader may set off in any direction and maintain—in relation to each of its words and to each of its affirmations—an equal critical distance and, if need be, a hint of skepticism.

Every gesture of writing is intended to engage a force, or even a *différend*—what I here call an element. In the present case, we are dealing with a raw element and a dense force. This is a force of separation rather than one that is bond-intensifying—a force of scission and real isolation that is exclusively turned upon itself and that, while pretending to ensure the world's government, seeks exemption from it. What follows is a reflection on today's planetary-scale renewal of the relation of enmity and its multiple reconfigurations. Its pivotal point is the Platonic concept of *phar-makon*—the idea of a medication that acts at once as remedy and as poison. Frantz Fanon's political and psychiatric work forms part of the basis for my showing how, in the wake of decolonization, war (in the figure of conquest and occupation, of terror and counterinsurgency) has become the sacra-ment of our times, at this, the turn of the twenty-first century.

This transformation has liberated movements of passion that are in-creasingly pushing liberal democracies to don the garb of the exception, to perform unconditioned acts in faraway places, and to seek to exercise dic-tatorship over themselves and against their enemies. Among other things, I ponder the consequences of this inversion and the novel terms within which the question of the relations between violence and law, norm and exception, the state of war, the state of security, and the state of freedom are now posed. Backdropped by the world's narrowing and the Earth's re-population, as well as new cycles of population movements, this essay en-deavors not merely to open new paths for a critique of atavistic national-isms. Indirectly it also reflects on the possible foundations of a mutually shared genealogy and thus of a politics of the living beyond humanism.

This book indeed deals with the sort of arrangement with the world—or even of its use—that, at this beginning of the century, consists in count-ing whatever is not oneself for nothing. This process has a genealogy and a name—the race for separation and *de-linking*, a race being run against the backdrop of a simple anxiety of annihilation. Nowadays a good many individuals are beset with dread, afraid of having been invaded and being on the verge of disappearing. Entire peoples labor under the apprehension that the resources for continuing to assume their identities are spent. They maintain that an outside no longer exists such that to protect themselves against threats and danger the enclosures must be multiplied. Wanting not to remember anything any longer, least of all their own crimes and mis-deeds, they dream up bad objects that return to haunt them and that they then seek violently to rid themselves of.

Constantly contriving the evil genies by which they are possessed and that, in a spectacular turnaround, now surround them, they have begun to raise questions. These questions are similar to those that non-Western societies were asking only recently, caught as they were in the snare of the far more destructive forces of colonization and imperialism.[1] Questions such as: Can the Other, in light of all that is happening, still be regarded as my fellow creature? When the extremes are broached, as is the case for us here and now, precisely what does my and the other's humanity consist in? The Other's burden having become too overwhelming, would it not be better for my life to stop being linked to its presence, as much as its to mine? Why must I, despite all opposition, nonetheless look after the other, stand as close as possible to his life if, in return, his only aim is my ruin? If, ultimately, humanity exists only through being in and of the world, can we found a relation with others based on the reciprocal recognition of our common vulnerability and finitude?

Today, manifestly little interest is shown in making the circle more inclusive. Rather, the idea is to make borders as the primitive form of keeping at bay enemies, intruders, and strangers—all those who are not one of us. In a world characterized more than ever by an unequal redistribution of capacities for mobility, and in which the only chance of survival, for many, is to move and to keep on moving, the brutality of borders is now a fundamental given of our time. Borders are no longer sites to be crossed but lines that separate. Within these more or less miniaturized and militarized spaces, everything is supposed to remain still. Many are those who, encountering them, now meet their ends or, when not simple victims of shipwrecks or electrocution, are deported.

Today we see the principle of equality being undone by the laws of autochthony and common origin, as well as by divisions within citizenship, which is to say the latter's declension into "pure" citizenship (that of the native born) and borrowed citizenship (one that, less secure from the start, is now not safe from forfeiture). Confronted with the perilous situations so characteristic of the age, the question, at least in appearance, is no longer to know how to reconcile the exercise of life and freedom with the knowledge of truth and solicitude for those different from oneself. From now on, it is to know how, in a sort of primitive outpouring, to actualize the will to power by means that are half-cruel, half-virtuous.

Consequently, war is determined as end and necessity not only in democracy but also in politics and in culture. War has become both remedy and poison—our pharmakon. Its transformation into the pharmakon of our time has, in turn, let loose gruesome passions that are increasingly pushing our societies to exit democracy and, as was the case under colonization, to transform into societies of enmity. Under contemporary conditions, the societies of the North are not left unscathed by this planetary renewal of colonial relations and their multiple reconfigurations, all of which is only amplified through the war on terror and the global-scale creation of a "state of exception."

Now who today could really discuss war as the pharmakon of our time without calling on Frantz Fanon, in whose shadow this essay has been written? Colonial war—since this is essentially what Fanon speaks about—is ultimately, if not the matrix of the *nomos* of the Earth in the last instance, then at least a privileged means of its institutionalization. As wars of conquest and occupation, and, in many aspects, of extermination, colonial wars were simultaneously wars of siege as much as foreign wars and racial wars. But how can we forget all the aspects they also shared in common with civil wars, wars of defense, and did not even wars of liberation demand so-called counterinsurgency wars? In truth, this interlocking of wars, as causes and consequences of one another, is why they give rise to so much terror and atrocity. It is also why, among those who have suffered them or participated in them, they sometimes provoke a belief in an illusory all-powerfulness, or sometimes even a terror and the vanishing, pure and simple, of the feeling of existing.

Similar to the majority of contemporary wars—including the war on terror and diverse forms of occupation—colonial wars were wars of extraction and predation. On the sides of the winners and the losers alike, they invariably led to the ruin of something unfigurable, almost nameless, entirely difficult to pronounce—how can one recognize in the enemy's face that one seeks to blow away, but whose wounds one could equally treat, another face that renders them in their full humanity, and thus as similar to oneself (chapter 3)? The forces of passion these wars released have increased tenfold humans' faculty to divide themselves. They compelled some people to confess more openly than in the past their most repressed desires and to communicate more directly than before with their most obscure myths. In others, they opened the chance to exit their abyssal sleep and experience—perhaps for the first and only time—the power of being of surrounding worlds and, incidentally, the chance to suffer their own vulnerability and incompleteness. In others still, they afforded the experience of being touched and affected by this brutal exposure to the unknown suffering of others as well as a chance to abruptly exit the circle of indifference in which they had once walled themselves off and to answer the call of these innumerable bodies of pain.

Confronted with colonial power and war, Fanon understood that the only subject is a living one (chapter 3). As living, the subject is immediately open onto the world. Fanon grasped his own life only by understanding the life of other living and nonliving beings, for only then did he himself exist as a living form, and only then could he rectify the asymmetry of relations and introduce into them a dimension of reciprocity and care for humanity. On the other hand, Fanon regarded the gesture of care as a practice of re-symbolization, the stake of which is the possibility of reciprocity and mu-tuality (an authentic encounter with others). His advice to colonized per-sons who refused castration was to turn their backs on Europe; in other words, he suggested that one begin with oneself and stand tall outside the categories that brought one to bow and scrape. The difficulty involved not only one's being assigned a race but one's internalizing of the terms of this assignation, that is, one's coming to the point of desiring and becoming the accomplice of castration. For everything, or nearly everything, encouraged colonized peoples to inhabit as their skin and their truth the fiction that the Other had produced in their regard.

To oppressed individuals who sought to rid themselves of race's burden, Fanon thus proposed a long course of therapy. This therapy began in and through language and perception, via the knowledge of the fundamental reality according to which becoming a human being in the world means accepting one's being exposed to the other. It continued with a colossal working on oneself, with new experiences of the body, of movement, of being-together—and even of communion, as the shared commonality that is most alive and vulnerable in humanity—and, possibly also, new experi-ences of the practice of violence. This violence was to be directed against the colonial system. This system's particularity lay in its manufacturing a panoply of suffering that, in response, solicited neither the accepting of re-sponsibility nor solicitude nor sympathy and, often, not even pity. To the contrary, it did everything to deaden people's capacity to suffer because the natives were suffering, everything to dull their ability to be affected by this suffering. Further still, colonial violence worked to capture the force of desire of the subjugated and channel it into unproductive investments. By claiming to be acting on behalf of the interests of the natives, and thus in their stead, the colonial machinery sought not merely to block their desire to live. It aimed to affect and diminish their capacities to consider them-selves moral agents.

Fanon's clinical and political practice stood resolutely opposed to this colonial order. Better than others, he put his finger on one of the great contradictions inherited from the modern era, one that his time struggled to resolve. The vast movement of repopulation of the world inaugurated at the edge of modern times ended in a massive "taking of lands" (colonization) on a scale and using technologies never before seen in the history of humanity. Far from leading to democracy's spread across the planet, the race for new lands opened onto a new law (*nomos*) of the Earth, the main characteristic of which was to establish war and race as history's two privileged sacraments. The sacramentalization of war and race in the blast furnace of colonialism made it at once modernity's antidote and poison, its twofold pharmakon.

In these conditions, thought Fanon, decolonization as a *constituting* political event could hardly forgo the use of violence. In any case, as a primitive active force, violence preexisted the advent of decolonization, which consisted in setting in motion an animated body able to completely and unreservedly deal with that which, being anterior and external to it, prevented it from arriving at its concept. But pure and unlimited violence, however creative it was set on being, could never be safeguarded from potential blindness. If caught in a sterile repetition, it could degenerate at any moment and its energy be placed in the service of destruction for destruction's sake.

For its part, the primary function of the medical gesture was not the absolute eradication of illness or the suppression of death and the advent of immortality. The ill human was the human with no family, no love, no human relations, and no communion with a community. It was the person deprived of the possibility of an authentic encounter with other humans, others with whom there were a priori no shared bonds of descent or of origin (chapter 3). This *world of people without bonds* (or of people who aspire only to take their leave of others) is still with us, albeit in ever shifting configurations. It inhabits the twists and turns of renewed Judeophobia and its mimetic counterpart, Islamophobia. It inhabits the desire for apartheid and endogamy that harry our epoch and engulf us in the hallucinatory dream of a "community without strangers."

Almost everywhere the law of blood, the law of the talion, and the duty to one's race—the two supplements of atavistic nationalism—are resurfacing. The hitherto more or less hidden violence of democracies is rising to the surface, producing a lethal circle that grips the imagination and is increasingly difficult to escape. Nearly everywhere the political order is re-constituting itself as a form of organization for death. Little by little, a terror that is molecular in essence and allegedly defensive is seeking legitimation by blurring the relations between violence, murder, and the law, faith, com-mandment, and obedience, the norm and the exception, and even free-dom, tracking, and security. No longer is the concern to eliminate, via the law and justice, murder from the books of life in common. Every occasion is now one in which the supreme stake is to be risked. Neither the *human-of-terror* nor the terrorized human—both of them new substitutes for the citizen—foreswear murder. On the contrary, when they do not purely and simply believe in death (given or received), they take it as the ultimate guarantee of a history tempered in iron and steel—the history of Being.

Fanon's concerns from start to finish, in his thinking as well as in his practice, bore on the irreducibility of the human link, the inseparability of humans and other living creatures, as well as the vulnerability of human-kind and especially of the ill-human-of-war, and further, the care required to write the living into time. The chapters that follow deal with these in-terrogations, diagonally and through altering figures. As Fanon evinced a particular solicitude toward Africa and permanently linked his fate to the continent's own, the African world has naturally come to occupy the fore-front of the reflection herein (chapters 5 and 6).

There are most certainly names that refer little to things but instead pass above or alongside them. Their function is one of disfiguration and distor-tion. This is why *the* thing, in its truth, tends to resist both the name and all translation. This is not because the thing sports a mask but because its force of proliferation renders every qualifier superfluous forthwith. For Fanon, such was the case for Africa and its mask, the Negro. Did the thing "Africa" simply operate as a catchall entity, woolly and devoid of historical weight or depth, on the subject of which anyone could say almost anything with-out its leading to any consequence? Or did it have its own force, and thus constitute a project able, by virtue of its own reserves of life, to reach its own concept and write itself into this new planetary age?

Fanon attended closely to people's experience of surfaces and depths, of lights and reflections, and of shadows. He endeavored to report on the worlds of living beings, without foundering in repetition. As regard final meanings, he knew that they were to be sought in the structural as much as in the obscure side of life. Whence the extraordinary attention that he gave to language, speech, music, theater, dance, ceremonials, settings, and all sorts of technical objects and psychic structures. That said, this essay is not at all about singing back the dead but rather aims to evoke in fragmentary fashion a great thinker of *transfiguration*.

In so doing, I found nothing more appropriate than a figural style of writing that oscillates between the vertiginous, dissolution, and dispersal. This style is one composed of crisscrossed loops, the edges and lines of which meet back up with their vanishing point each time. The reader will have understood—language's function in such writing is to return to life what had been abandoned to the powers of death. It is to reopen access to the deposits of the future, beginning with the future of those in whom, not so long ago, it was hard to say which part pertained to the human and which to the animal, object, thing, or commodity (chapter 6).

ONE
EXIT FROM
DEMOCRACY

This book aims to contribute—from Africa, where I live and work (but also from the rest of the world, which I have not stopped surveying)—to a critique of our time. This time is one of the repopulation and the planetarization of the world under the aegis of militarism and capital and, in ultimate consequence, a time of exit from democracy (or of its inversion). To carry this project through, I take a transversal approach, attentive to the three motifs of opening, crossing, and circulation. This sort of approach is fruitful only if it makes room for a *reverse reading* of our present.

The approach sets out from the presupposition according to which a genuine deconstruction of the world of our time begins with the full recognition of the perforce provincial status of our discourses and the necessarily regional character of our concepts—and therefore with a critique of every form of abstract universalism. This doing, it endeavors to break with the spirit of the times, which, we know, is about closure and demarcations of all sorts, and in which borders between here and there, the near and the distant, the inside and the outside, serve as a Maginot Line for a major part of what passes as "global thinking" today. Now, global thinking can only ever be that which, turning its back on theoretical segregation, rests on the archives of what Édouard Glissant called the "All-world" (*Tout-monde*).

Reversal, Inversion, and Acceleration

For the needs of the reflection that I sketch herein, there are four characteristic features of our times worth emphasizing. The first is the narrowing of the world and the repopulation of the Earth in view of the demographic transition now under way thanks to the worlds of the South. Our coming to modernity involved decisive events such as the geographical and cultural uprooting of entire populations, as well as their voluntary relocation or forced settlement, across the vast territories once inhabited by indigenous peoples.[1] On the Atlantic side of the planet, two significant moments, both tied to the expansion of industrial capitalism, gave rhythm to this process of the redistribution of populations across the planet.

These are the moments of colonization (from its inception in the early sixteenth century with the conquest of the Americas) and the Negro slave trade. The slave trade and colonization alike broadly coincided with the formation of mercantilist thought in the West, if they were not purely and simply at its origins.[2] The slave trade thrived on its hemorrhaging and draining of the most useful arms and most vital energies of the slave-providing societies.

In the Americas, slave labor of African origin was put to work as part of a vast project to subordinate the environment in view of its rational and profitable development. In several respects, the plantation regime was essentially about cutting down, burning, and routinely razing forests and trees; about replacing the natural vegetation with cotton and sugar cane; about remodeling ancient landscapes; about destroying the existing vegetal formations; and about replacing an ecosystem with an agrosystem.[3] However, the plantation was not merely an economic measure. For the slaves transplanted into the New World, it was also the scene on which another beginning played out. Here, life came to be shaped according to an essentially racial principle. But, thus understood, race, far from being a simple biological signifier, referred to a worldless and soilless body, a body of combustible energy, a sort of double of nature that could, through work, be transformed into an available reserve or stock.[4]

As for colonization, it thrived by excreting those who were, in several regards, deemed superfluous, a surfeit within the colonizing nations. This was the case, in particular, of the poor viewed as scrounging off society and the vagabonds and delinquents seen as harmful to the nation. Colonization was a technology for regulating migratory movements. At the time many people considered that this form of migration would ultimately be of advantage to the country of departure. "Not only will a large number of men who live in idleness here, and represent a weight, a burden and do not relate to this kingdom, thus be put to work, but also their children between twelve and fourteen years or less will be removed from idleness, tasked with doing thousands of futile things, and perhaps producing good merchandise for this country," wrote, for example, Antoine de Montchrestien in his *Traité d'économie politique* at the start of the seventeenth century. And further still he added, "Our idle women . . . will be employed to pull out, dye and separate feathers, to pull, beat and work hemp, and to gather cotton, and diverse things for dyeing." The men will be able, for their part, "to be given employment working in the mines and ploughing, and even hunting whale . . . as well as fishing for cod, salmon, herring, and felling trees," he concluded.[5]

From the sixteenth to nineteenth centuries, these two modalities of re-populating the planet through human predation, natural wealth extraction, and setting subaltern groups to work constituted the major economic, political, and, in many respects, philosophical stakes of the period.[6] Economic theory and the theory of democracy alike were built partly on the defense or critique of one or other of these two forms of spatial redistribution of populations.[7] These two forms were, in turn, at the origin of numerous conflicts and wars of partition or monopolization. Resulting from this planetary-scale movement, a new partition of the Earth emerged with, at its center, Western powers and, in the margins, the peripheries, that is, domains of excessive struggle that were destined for occupation and pillage.

It is also necessary to consider the generally conventional distinction between commercial colonialism — or even trading-post colonialism — and settler colonialism properly speaking. Certainly, in both cases, the colony's — every colony's — enrichment made sense only if it contributed to enriching the metropole. The difference between them, however, resides in the fact that settler colonies were conceived as an extension of the nation, whereas trading-post or exploitation colonies were only a way to grow the metropole's wealth by means of asymmetrical, inequitable trade relations, almost entirely lacking in heavy local investment.

In addition, the stranglehold exerted over trading-post colonies was in principle preordained to end, so the settling of Europeans in these places was entirely provisional. In the case of settler colonies, however, migration policy aimed to maintain in the nation's bosom people who would have been lost to it had they stayed. The colony served as a pressure relief valve for all the undesirables, for the categories of the population "whose crimes and debaucheries" could have been "rapidly destructive" or whose needs would have driven them toward prison or forced them to beg, while rendering them useless for the country. This scission of humanity into "useful" and "useless"—"excess" and "superfluidity"—has remained the rule, with utility being essentially measured against the capacity to deploy a labor force.

The repeopling of the Earth at the beginning of the modern era did not only pass through colonization. Religious factors also go toward explaining the migrations and mobilities. Upon the revocation of the Edict of Nantes, from 1685 to 1730 between 170,000 and 180,000 Huguenots fled France. Religious emigration affected many other communities. International movements of different types were intertwined with one another, such as the Portuguese Jews whose trade networks wove together around the great European ports of Hamburg, Amsterdam, London, and Bordeaux; the Italians who invested in the world of finance, in trade, or in highly specialized professions in glass and luxury goods; or even soldiers, mercenaries, and engineers who, due to the manifold conflicts of the time, passed blithely from one market of violence to another.[8]

At the dawn of the twenty-first century, the Earth's repeopling is no longer carried out through slave trafficking and the colonization of remote regions of the globe. Work, in its traditional sense, is no longer perforce the privileged means of value creation. The moment is nevertheless about shake-ups, large and small dislocations and transfers, in short, new figures of exodus.[9] The new circulatory dynamics and creation of diasporas pass in large part via trade and commerce, wars, ecological disasters and environmental catastrophes, including cultural transfers of all sorts.

From this viewpoint, the accelerated aging of human groupings in the world's wealthy nations represents an event of considerable impact. It is the opposite of the aforementioned demographic surpluses typical of the nineteenth century. Geographical distance as such no longer represents an obstacle to mobility. The major migration pathways are diversifying, and increasingly sophisticated measures for bypassing borders are being put in place. As a result, if, being centripetal, migratory flows are moving in several directions simultaneously, Europe and the United States nonetheless remain the major points of fixation for the multitudes in movement—in particular those from the planet's centers of poverty. Here new agglomerations are rising up and new polynational cities are, in spite of everything, being built. The ordeal of these new international movements is yielding—

little by little and across the entire planet—diverse assemblages of mosaic territories.

This new swarming—which adds to the previous waves of migration from the South—blurs criteria of national belonging. To belong to the nation is no longer merely an affair of origin but also of choice. An ever-growing mass of people henceforth participates in several types of nationalities (nationality of origin, of residence, of choice) and of identity attachments. In some cases, they are summoned to decide, to merge with the population by ending double loyalties, or, if they commit an offense that endangers "the existence of the nation," they run the risk of being stripped of the host nationality.[10]

Further still, humans are not the only ones to be found at the heart of the Earth's repeopling. Being human no longer determines the limits of those occupying the world. More than ever, these occupants include a number of artifacts and all living, organic, and vegetal species. Even geological, geomorphological, and climatological forces complement the panoply of the Earth's new inhabitants.[11] Certainly, it is not a matter of beings or groups or families of beings as such. At the limit, it is a matter neither of the environment nor of nature. It is one of agents and milieus of life—water, air, dust, microbes, termites, bees, insects—that is, authors of specific relations. We have therefore passed from the *human condition* to the *terrestrial condition*.

The second characteristic trait of our times is the ongoing redefinition of the human in the framework of a general ecology and a henceforth broadened geography, one that is spherical and irreversibly planetary. In fact, the world is no longer considered an artifact that humans make. Leaving behind the ages of stone and silver, of iron and gold, the human for its part is tending to become plastic. The advent of the plastic human and its corollary, the digital subject, goes flush against a number of convictions that until recently were held to be immutable truths.

So it is with the belief that humans possess an alleged "specificity," a "genericity" separating them from the animal or the vegetal world, or again that the Earth that humans inhabit and exploit is a mere passive object of humankind's interventions. So it is also with the idea according to which, of all living species, "humans" are the only ones to have in part freed themselves from their animality. Having broken the chain of biological necessity, humanity had allegedly almost raised itself to the level of the divine. Yet, contrary to these articles of faith and many others, it is now admitted that humankind is only part of a greater set of the universe's living subjects, which also include animals, vegetanimals, plants, and other species.

Going no further than biology and genetic engineering, there can be said, properly speaking, to be no "essence of man" to safeguard, no "human nature" to protect. This being the case, the potential to modify the biological and genetic structure of humanity is almost limitless. At bottom, by opening up to genetic and germinal manipulations, it is thought to be possible not only to "enhance" the human being but also, in a spectacular act of self-creation, to produce the living through technomedicine.

The third constitutive feature of the era is the generalized introduction of tools and calculating or computational machines into all aspects of social life. Aided by the power and ubiquity of the digital phenomenon, no impenetrable separation exists between the screen and life. Life now transpires on the screen, and the screen is now the plastic and simulated form of living that, in addition, can be grasped by a code. Moreover, "it's no longer through the face-to-face encounter with the portrait, or the figure of the mirroring-presenting double, that the subject is tested, but through the construction of a form of presence of the subject closer to tracing and projected shadow."[12]

As a result, the work of subjectivation and individuation by which, until only recently, every human being became a person endowed with a more or less indexable identity, is partly foreclosed. Whether one wants it or not, the era is thus one of plasticity, pollination, and grafts of all sorts — plasticity of the brain, pollination of the artificial and the organic, genetic manipulations and informational grafts, ever finer adjustments (*appareillage*) between the human and the machine. All these mutations do not only give free rein to the dream of a truly limitless life. They henceforth make *power over the living* — or again, the capacity to voluntarily alter the human species — the absolute form of power.

The articulation between the capacity to voluntarily alter the human species — and even other living species and apparently inert materials — and the power of capital constitute the fourth striking feature of the world of our times. The power of capital — at once a living and creative force (when it comes to extending markets and accumulating profits) and a bloody process of devouring (when it comes to destroying, without return, the life of beings and species) — increased tenfold when the stock markets opted to employ artificial intelligences to optimize the movement of liquidity. As most of these high-frequency operators use cutting-edge algorithms to deal with the mass of information exchanged on the stock markets, they operate at microtemporal scales inaccessible to humans. Today, the transfer time of information passing between the stock exchange and the operator is calculated in milliseconds. Coupled with other factors, this extraordinary compression of time has led to a paradox: we see, on the one hand, a spectacular increase in the fragility and the instability of the markets and, on the other, their almost unlimited power of destruction.

The question that thus arises is to know whether the modes of exploiting the planet might still be averted from tipping over into absolute destruction. This question is an especially topical one, as never before has the symmetry between the market and war been as evident as it is today. The preceding centuries had war as their matrix of technological development. Today all sorts of military machines continue to play this role, that is, on top of the capitalist market, which, in turn, functions more than ever according to the model of war—but a war that henceforth pits species against one another, and nature against human beings.[13] This tight imbrication of capital, digital technologies, nature, and war, and the new constellations of power that it makes possible is, without a doubt, what most directly threatens the idea of the political that had hitherto served as the bedrock for that form of government that is democracy.

The Nocturnal Body of Democracy

This idea of the political is relatively simple: it states that, as a matter of principle, the community of humans has no ground (or immutable basis) not subject to debate. The community is political insofar as, cognizant of the contingency of its foundations and their latent violence, it is continually disposed to put its origins at stake. It is democratic insofar as, having guaranteed this permanent opening onto the sea, the life of the state acquires a public character; its powers are placed under citizens' control; and these citizens are free to seek and assert, constantly and whenever necessary, the truth, reason, justice, and the common good. The notions of equality, the state of right, and publicness had hitherto stood opposed to the ideal of force, to states of fact (political arbitrariness), and to the taste for secrecy. But in fact, these myths of origins are no longer sufficient to legitimate the democratic order in contemporary societies.

Moreover, if modern democracies always derived their strength from their capacity for self-reinvention and the constant invention not only of their form but also of their idea or concept, the price for it often involved dissimulating or occulting the violence of their origins. The history of this simultaneous enterprise of invention and reinvention, of dissimulation and occultation, could not be more paradoxical, or indeed chaotic. It shows, in any case, the point to which the democratic order is, in the diversity of its trajectories, notoriously equivocal.

According to the official story, democratic societies are pacified societies. This feature is held to be what distinguishes them from warrior societies. Democratic societies have thus if not banished brutality and physical violence, then at least brought them under control. Owing to the state's monopoly of force and individuals' internalization of constraints, the hand-to-hand struggle through which physical violence was expressed in medieval society until the Renaissance has supposedly given way to self-pressuring, self-control, and civility. This new form of the government of bodies, conducts, and affects is alleged to have led to the pacification of social spaces.

Allegedly, then, the force of forms has replaced the violence of bodies. Regulating behaviors, governing conducts, preventing disorder and violence—all this is now achieved, as it were, by means of fully recognized rituals.[14] By imposing a distance between individuals, forms and rituals are to have contributed to a civilization of mores through mores. As a result, democratic societies do not, it is thought, rest on the principle of obedience to a strong man, in contrast with tyrannical or monarchical regimes, in which a society's self-disciplining requires it to have such a man. The strength of democratic societies, so the argument goes, largely resides in the strength of their forms.[15]

The idea according to which life in a democracy is fundamentally peaceful, policed, and violence-free (including in the form of war and devastation) does not stand up to the slightest scrutiny. The emergence and consolidation of democracies did, it is true, go hand in hand with manifold attempts to control individual violence, to regulate it, reduce it, and even abolish its most spectacular and most abject manifestations by way of moral reprobation or legal sanctions.

But the brutality of democracies has simply been swept under the carpet. From their origins, modern democracies have always evinced their tolerance for a certain political violence, including illegal forms of it. They have integrated forms of brutality into their culture, forms borne by a range of private institutions acting on top of the state, whether irregular forces, militias, or other paramilitary or corporatist formations.

The United States was long both a state and a *pro-slavery democracy*. In his *Black Reconstruction*, W. E. B. Du Bois recalls the paradox at the heart of this nation, which proclaimed the equality of all men from its birth, whose government was supposed to draw its power from the consent of the governed, but that, through the practice of slavery, accommodated an absolute moral disjunction.[16] The United States had close to two million Negroes (Nègres) on the cusp of the 1830s, and they came to constitute 11.6 percent of the population by 1900. Their fate and the whites' own are closely linked. However, by no means could the respective conditions of blacks and whites, to say nothing of their futures, be confounded. As many historians have remarked, both groups have as much difficulty separating completely from one another as they do uniting. Concerning the law, slaves occupied the position of the foreigner within a society of fellow humans. Being either born in the United States or of mixed descent (the case of 90 percent and 13 percent of slaves, respectively, at this time), changed nothing as to the state of baseness to which they were reduced nor the ignominy with which they were struck and that passed down from generation to generation as a poisoned heritage.

A pro-slavery democracy is therefore characterized by its bifurcation. Two orders coexist within it—a *community of fellow creatures* governed, at least in principle, by the law of equality, and a *category of nonfellows*, or even of those without part, that is also established by law. A priori, those without part have no right to have rights. They are governed by the law of inequality. This inequality and the law establishing it, and that is its base, is founded on the prejudice of race. The prejudice itself, as much as the law founding it, enabled a practically unbridgeable distance to be upheld between the community of fellow creatures and its others. Pro-slavery democracy, supposing it to be a community, could only be a *community of separation*.

Thus, notes Alexis de Tocqueville in 1848:

> In nearly all the states where slavery is abolished, the Negro has been given electoral rights; but if he presents himself to vote, he risks his life. Oppressed, he can make a complaint, but he finds only whites among

his judges. The law opens the juror's seat to him, but prejudice pushes him away from it. His son is excluded from the school where the descendant of the European goes to be instructed. In the theaters he cannot, even at the price of gold, buy the right to sit next to the one who was his master; in the hospitals he lies apart. The Black is allowed to beseech the same God as the whites, but not to pray to him at the same altar. He has his priests and his churches. The gates of heaven are not closed to him: but inequality scarcely stops at the edge of the other world. When the Negro is no more, his bones are thrown aside, and the difference in conditions is found again even in the equality of death.[17]

In a pro-slavery democracy, the nonfellows cannot claim "possession of a single piece of land."[18] Moreover, the obsessive fear of pro-slavery democracies does not merely concern how to keep these slaves carefully out of the way. It is above all about knowing how to toss them out, by getting them to leave the country willingly or, when need be, by deporting them en masse.[19] And if, from time to time, they get the nod to move on our level, and are even allowed to associate with us, it is precisely only so that they can be "thrown back into the dust" — that natural state of debased races.[20] For the slave is not a subject of right but instead a commodity like any other. The most dramatic scene of this throwing back into the dust is lynching, which is the arresting, grotesque, and exhibitionist form of racist cruelty. It does not take place behind the outer walls of a prison but in public space.[21] Through the publicness of executions, racist democracy stages an unbearable brutality, kindling the emotions of the scaffold. As a technology of racist power, the aim of the ritual of execution is to sow terror in the minds of its victims and revive the lethal passions underpinning white supremacy.[22]

A large slave owner, Thomas Jefferson was keenly aware of the dilemma posed by the plantation regime and by the status of servility in a so-called free society. He was constantly moved to pity by the "unhappy influence on the manners of our people produced by the existence of slavery among us." Indeed, in his eyes the practice of slavery boiled down to absolute licentiousness. It led to the continual exercise of the most uncontrollable passions. As the accursed part of American democracy, slavery was the manifestation of a corrupted and impenitent despotism, one that rested on the abject degradation of those whom one had enslaved.[23] The plantation is indeed a "third place" in which the most spectacular forms of cruelty have free rein, whether it comes to injuring bodies, torture, or summary executions.

In eighteenth-century England, plantation owners in the West Indies amassed the money to enable the financing of a nascent culture of taste, art galleries, and cafés—places par excellence of learning civility. Colonial barons like William Beckford, plantocrats such as Joseph Addison, Richard Steele, and Christopher Carrington, all assured the patronage of cultural institutions. They handed out commissions to artists, architects, and composers. Civility and the consumption of luxury items went hand in hand, as coffee, sugar, and spices became lifetime necessities for the civilized human being. In the meantime, colonial barons and Indian nabobs recycled ill-gotten fortunes with the aim of re-creating an aristocratic identity for themselves.[24]

Last, the "civilization of mores" was also made possible thanks to the new forms of wealth accumulation and consumption inaugurated by the colonial adventure. Indeed, from the seventeenth century on, foreign trade was considered the best way to shore up the wealth of state. While control over international trade flows henceforth presumed mastery of the seas, the capacity to create unequal exchange relations became a decisive element of power. If the gold and silver found abroad were coveted by all states and the various princely courts of Europe, such was also the case for pepper, cinnamon, cloves, nutmeg, and other spices. But it was also the case for cotton, silk, indigo, coffee, tobacco, sugar, balms, liqueurs of all sorts, resins, and the medicinal plants that one bought at piddling prices far away and sold at exorbitant prices on European markets.

To pacify mores, you must help yourself to a few colonies, set up concessionary companies, and consume ever more products from far-flung parts of the world. Civil peace in the West thus depends in large part on inflicting violence far away, on lighting up centers of atrocities, and on the fiefdom wars and other massacres that accompany the establishment of strongholds and trading posts around the four corners of the planet. It depends on the supply of canvas, masts, timber, pitch, flax, and rope for sailing ships, but also luxury goods such as raw silk, glazed and printed calico, salt to preserve fish, potash and dyes for the textile industry, to say nothing of sugar.[25] In other terms, envy, the love of luxury, and other passions were no longer subject to vexing condemnation. Rather, the fulfillment of these new desires depended on institutionalizing a regime of inequality at the planetary scale. Colonization was the main wheel of this regime.[26] In this respect, the historian Romain Bertrand suggests that the colonial state "remained a state on a war footing."[27] That said, he refers not merely to the exactions committed during wars of conquest, nor even to the exercise of a cruel private justice or to the ferocious repression of nationalist movements. He has in mind what must be called "the colonial policy of terror," that is to say, the deliberate crossing of a threshold by exacting violence and cruelty on people who, in the lead-up, have been deprived of all rights. The desire to tear them to pieces is expressed by the generalization of practices such as torching villages and rice-growing fields, executing simple villagers to set an example, pillaging collective food reserves and granaries, rounding up civilians with extreme brutality, or systematic torture.

The colonial system and the slave system thus represent democracy's bitter sediment, that which, precisely, as an intuition by Jefferson has it, corrupts the body of freedom, driving it ineluctably toward decomposition. Relaying one another, all three orders—the order of the plantation, of the colony, and of democracy—do not ever separate, just as George Washington and his slave and companion William Lee never did, or again as Thomas Jefferson and his slave Jupiter. Each order lends its aura to the others, in a strict relation of apparent distance and repressed proximity and intimacy.

Mythologies

The critique of the violence of democracies is not new. It can be directly read in the counterdiscourses and practices of struggle that accompany both its emergence and then its triumph in the nineteenth century. Take, for example, the diverse variants of socialism, that other new idea of the nineteenth century, or again the anarchism of the late nineteenth century and the traditions of revolutionary unionism in France before the First World War and in the wake of the 1929 crisis.

One of the fundamental questions that arose around that time was to know whether politics could be something other than a state-related activity, one in which the state is utilized to guarantee the privileges of a minority. The other was to know under which conditions the radical forces aiming to precipitate the advent of the future society could invoke a right to use violence to ensure the realization of their utopias. On the philosophical level, the question was one of how humanity could develop, and without any recourse to transcendence, its capacities and increase its power of acting, as the only way for human history to produce itself.

Toward the end of the nineteenth century, the notion of direct action made its appearance. Direct action was conceived as a violent action performed independently of state mediation. Its aim was to get free of the constraints that prevent humans from communicating with their own reserves of energy and, doing so, to self-engender. The consummate example here is revolution. A way of violently eliminating every objective counterforce that stands opposed to changing society's foundations, revolution aims at the abolition of class antagonisms and the advent of an egalitarian society.

Another example is the expropriating general strike, the aim of which is to establish another mode of production. This sort of mediation-free conflict proscribes, by definition, all compromise. In addition, it refuses all reconciliation. Revolution is thought of as a violent event. This violence is planned. On the occasion of revolutionary events, this violence may target persons who embody the order about to be overturned. Although inevitable, it must be checked by turning against structures and institutions. Revolutionary violence indeed has something irreducible about it. It aims at the destruction and elimination of an established order—an elimination that cannot occur peacefully. It assails the order of things rather than that of persons.[28]

Anarchism, under its different figures, presents itself as a surpassing, notably, of parliamentary democracy.[29] The main anarchist currents strove to think through the political beyond bourgeois domination. Their project was to be done with all political domination—parliamentary democracy being one of its modalities. For Mikhail Bakunin, for example, surpassing bourgeois democracy happens by surpassing the state, that institution whose specificity is to aim at its own preservation as well as that of the classes that, having monopolized the state, proceed to colonize it. Surpassing the state inaugurates the advent of the "commune," which, more than a simple economic or political entity, is the figure par excellence of self-management of the social.

The other criticism of the brutality of democracies is the work of revolutionary trade unionists, for whom at issue is not so much to weigh upon the existing system as to destroy it through violence. Violence differentiates itself from force. "The object of force," writes Georges Sorel, "is to impose a certain social order in which the minority governs." It seeks to "bring about an automatic obedience." Violence, by contrast, "tends to the destruction of that order" and to "smashing that authority."[30] From 1919 to the start of the 1930s in France, manifold worker demonstrations aimed expressly at this goal. Most of them ended in deaths, street occupations, and the building of barricades. The cycle of provocation-repression-mobilization contributed to the asserting of class identity along with lengthy strike movements and recurrent clashes with the forces of order. The idea here was that proletarian violence maintained a moral superiority over the reactionary violence of the state apparatus. Nearly two decades after the Commune's repression and the First International's dissolution in 1876, anarchism spread quickly in France. Its declared objectives were to destroy property and expropriate owners, and the terror borne by the oppressed was one of its weapons. In the 1890s, this terror was about performing feats of daring as part of an economy of sacrifice — sacrifice for the proletarian cause.[31]

These critiques of democracy — articulated from the viewpoint of the social classes that originally endured democracy's brutality in the West itself — are relatively well known. What has not been emphasized enough, however, are its multiple genealogies and their entanglement. The history of modern democracies gets painted as though it reduces to a history internal to Western societies, as if, closed in on themselves and closed to the world, these societies confined themselves to the narrow limits of their immediate environment. Well, never has this been the case. The triumph of modern democracy in the West coincides with the period of its history during which this region of the world was engaged in a twofold movement of internal consolidation and expansion across the seas. The history of modern democracy is, at bottom, a history with two faces, and even two bodies — the solar body, on the one hand, and *the nocturnal body*, on the other. The major emblems of this nocturnal body are the colonial empire and the pro-slavery state — and more precisely the plantation and the penal colony.

The penal colony, in particular, is a place where sentences of exclusion are served. These sentences aimed to remove and eliminate those subjected to them. At the origin of the penal colony, these sentences were given to political opponents, common law convicts subject to forced labor, and even recidivist delinquents.[32] In France, the Law of August 26, 1792, de facto instituted political deportation. Between 1852 and 1854, colonial penal colonies underwent rapid expansion. Mass deportations took place throughout the nineteenth century, notably in Guyana, where sometimes light prison sentences were transformed into lifelong sentences.[33] In several regards, the colonial penal colony prefigures the mass imprisonment typical of the contemporary era—that of extreme and generalized coercion and solitary confinement.[34] The violent treatment of prisoners and the forms of privation imposed on them mix two rationales, one of neutralization and one of exile.[35]

To dissimulate the contingency of its foundations and the violence constituting its hidden aspects, modern democracy needed at its inception to envelop itself in a quasi-mythological structure. As we have just seen, the orders of democracy, the plantation, and colonialism have long maintained relations of twinship (*rapports de gémellité*). These relations were far from being accidental. Democracy, the plantation, and the colonial empire are objectively all part of the same historical matrix. This originary and structuring fact lies at the heart of every historical understanding of the violence of the contemporary global order.

For a proper understanding of the nature of the relations between, on the one hand, the democratic order and, on the other, the colonial-imperial order, and the way in which this relation determines the violence of democracies, several factors must be considered, factors of a political, technological, demographic, epidemiological, and even botanical nature.[36] The most decisive of all the technological tools that contributed to shaping colonial empires from the eighteenth century were probably weapons technologies, medicine, and means of locomotion. However, more was needed than to acquire empires, occasionally at bargain-basement prices, as we see in the paltry loans and troop numbers committed to the conquests. The new lands also had to be populated and effectively exploited. Such is what, making the most of the declines of the Moghul Empire, the Javanese Kingdom, and the Ottoman beyliks, by way of example, Great Britain, the Netherlands, and France all did in India, in Indonesia, and in Algeria, respectively, sometimes with the use of pre-industrial technologies.[37]

Quinine's impact on the monopolizing of the world by the West can never be emphasized enough. The widespread use of cinchona bark, its cultivation in plantations in India and in Java, and its harvesting in the Andes provided a leap forward for the white man's capacities to acclimatize to the tropics. Similarly, neither can enough emphasis be placed on the outlaw character of the colonial wars that democracies conducted outside Europe. For Africa in particular, the colonial upsurge coincided with one of the first military revolutions of the industrial era. From the 1850s on, weapons technology and projectile speed began to transform military confrontation into a "truly inhuman process."[38] Added to the canons, harquebuses, fortifications, and battle fleets of the preceding periods were, pell-mell, indirect-fire artillery and long-range, rapid-fire weapons to support infantry like machine guns, and even automobiles and planes.

Also during this time, democracies strove as hard as they could to transfer the industrial principles of mass production onto the art of warfare and into the service of mass destruction. Thanks to the new industrial weapons, some of which were tried out during the American War of Secession (1861–65) and during the Russo-Japanese conflict of 1904–5, the idea was to increase the firepower tenfold against the backdrop of a more or less fatalist acceptance of death and submission to technology. From this viewpoint, colonial conquests constituted a privileged field of experimentation. They gave rise to a thinking about power and technology that, taken to its ultimate consequences, paved the way for concentration camps and modern genocidal ideologies.[39]

Colonial conquests witnessed an acceleration of the confrontation between human and machine, itself the premise for "industrial war" and the butcheries emblematized by the 1914–18 war. Also on the occasion of colonial conquests, a habituation was cultivated to higher human losses, notably among enemy troops. Moreover, the wars of conquest were asymmetrical wars from start to finish.[40] Throughout one and a half centuries of colonial warfare, colonial armies lost few men. Historians estimate the losses at between 280,000 and 300,000 — relatively low figures if we consider that close to 250,000 died during the Crimean War alone. During the three main "dirty wars" of decolonization (Indochina, Algeria, Angola and Mozambique), 75,000 deaths were recorded on the colonial side and 850,000 on the indigenous side.[41] The tradition of "dirty wars" originates in these colonial conflicts. They generally end in a massive wiping out of the native populations and in deep mutations of the pathological ecology of the thus devastated regions.

Led by regimes that appeal to rights, most colonial wars, notably at the moment of conquest properly speaking, are not wars of self-defense. They are not undertaken with the aim of recuperating one's goods or bringing justice wherever it is flouted. To begin with, no offense has been committed whose seriousness can be objectively gauged. These wars give rise to a violence that obeys no rule of proportionality. Practically no formal limit exists to the devastation that strikes entities declared to be enemies. Many innocent people are killed, not because of errors they had committed but instead for yet-to-be-committed errors. The war of conquest is thus not about upholding the law. If it criminalizes the enemy, the aim is not to apply justice. Whether or not he bears arms, the enemy to be punished is an intrinsic enemy, *an enemy by nature*. In short, colonial conquest paves the way to a sphere of unregulated war, to *war outside-the-law* led by some democracy, which, in so doing, externalizes violence to a third place ruled by nonnormative conventions and customs.

Paradoxically, this sphere of war outside the law flourished just as many efforts to transform both *jus in bello* (right in the conduct of war) and *jus ad bellum* (the right to wage war) took place in the West. Begun in the seventeenth century, these latter bear, among other things, on the nature of the antagonism (what type of war is being waged?); the qualification of the enemy (what type of enemy are we dealing with, against whom are we fighting and how?); the manner of conducting war; and the general rules to be observed depending on whether one is a combatant, a noncombatant, or some other person exposed to its violence and devastation. At the end of the nineteenth century the foundations of an international humanitarian law emerged. Among other things, this law aimed at "humanizing" war. It emerged just as the "war of brutalization" in Africa was in full swing. The modern laws of war were first formulated during the Conventions in Brussels in 1874, and then at The Hague in 1899 and 1907. But the development of international principles on the subject of war did not necessarily change the conduct of European powers on the ground. Such was the case yesterday; such is the case today.

The violence of democracies was forthwith exteriorized onto the colonies and took the form of brute acts of oppression. As, indeed, no extant legitimacy authorizes power in the colony, power seeks to impose itself in the manner of a destiny. In imagination and in practice, the life of conquered and subjugated natives is represented as a succession of predestined events. This life, it is said, is condemned to be this way. Each time, then, the violence performed by the state pertains to a measure that is not only necessary but also innocent. This is because colonial power is in no way structured by the opposition between the legal and the illegal. Colonial law is unconditionally subject to political imperatives. This conception of the law as an absolute instrumentality worked to free power holders of any meaningful constraint, whether in the exercise of war, in criminalizing resistance, or in the government of the everyday. Its constitutive moment is one of empty force, because as force it is unreserved.

Colonial war, being almost always haunted by the desire for extermination (eliminationism), is, by definition, a borderless war, *outside of law*.[42] Once the occupation is assured, the subjugated population is never entirely shielded from a massacre.[43] In addition, it is not surprising that the main colonial genocides took place in settler colonies. What prevails in them is well and truly a zero-sum game. European occupation, to be legitimated, required that one engage in disavowing and effacing all traces of prior native presence. Together with major episodes of bloodshed, a molecular violence raged and was rarely checked — an active and primitive force, of a quasi-sedimentary and miniaturized nature, one that saturated the entirety of the social field.[44] The law applied to natives was never the same as the law applied to settlers. The crimes committed by natives were punished in a normative framework in which these latter scarcely figured as fully entitled legal subjects. Conversely, for every settler accused of committing a crime against a native (murder included), escaping conviction was as simple as invoking a legitimate defense or evoking the possibility of reprisals.[45]

Many historians have remarked that colonial empires were anything but systems endowed with an absolute coherence. Improvisation, ad hoc reactions in the face of unforeseen situations, and, very often, informality and weak institutionalization were the rule.[46] But far from attenuating the brutality and atrocities of colonial empires, this porosity and this segmentarity only made them more pernicious. Wherever the thick veil of secrecy worked to shroud acts of misprision, the zones of immunity could be extended beyond all reason by invoking the imperative of security, zones whose impenetrability made them into quasi-natural machines of inertia.[47] Little did it matter that the world depicted in these representations did not exactly align with the phenomenal world. Forgoing evidence, one needed only to invoke secrecy and security. The colonial world, as an offspring of democracy, was not the antithesis of the democratic order. It has always been its double or, again, its nocturnal face. No democracy exists without its double, without its colony — little matter the name and the structure. The colony is not external to democracy and is not necessarily located outside its walls. Democracy bears the colony within it, just as colonialism bears democracy, often in the guise of a mask.

As Frantz Fanon indicated, this nocturnal face in effect hides a primordial and founding void — the law that originates in nonlaw and that is instituted as law outside the law. Added to this founding void is a second void — this time one of preservation. These two voids are closely imbricated in one another. Paradoxically, the metropolitan democratic order needs this twofold void, first, to give credence to the existence of an irreducible contrast between it and its apparent opposite; second, to nourish its mythological resources and better hide its underneath on the inside as well as on the outside. In other terms, the cost of the mythological logics required for modern democracies to function and survive is the exteriorization of their originary violence to third places, to nonplaces, of which the plantation, the colony, or, today, the camp and the prison, are emblematic figures.

The exteriorized violence in the colonies remained latent in the metropole. Part of the work of democracies is to deaden any awareness of this latency; it is to remove any real chance of interrogating its foundations, its underneath, and the mythologies without which the order that ensures the reproduction of state democracy suddenly falters. The great fear of democracies is that this violence, latent on the interior and exteriorized in the colonies and other third places, suddenly resurfaces, and then threatens the idea that the political order was created out of itself (instituted all at once and once and for all) and had more or less managed to pass itself off as common sense.

Consuming the Divine

The era's paranoid dispositions crystallize around the grand narratives of the (re)commencement and of the end — Apocalypse. Very few things seem to distinguish the time of (re)commencement and that of the end, since enabling both are destruction, catastrophe, and devastation. From this point of view, domination is exerted by modulating the thresholds of catastrophe. If specific forms of control pass via confinement and strangulation, others proceed via indifference and abandonment, pure and simple. Whatever the case, in the Judeo-Greek heritage of philosophy that has so stamped the European humanities, a structural relation appears to exist between, on the one hand, the future of the world and the destiny of Being and, on the other, catastrophe as a category at once political and theological.

So it goes that, to reach its apogee, Being must pass through a phase of purification by fire. This singular event prefigures the last act, that during which, in Heidegger's terms, the Earth will blow itself up. This self-blowing-up represents, in his eyes, the "supreme accomplishment" of technology, a term that, for the German philosopher, refers as much to science as to capital. He considers that the Earth will blow itself up and "actual humanity" will disappear along with it. Now, for a part of the Judeo-Christian tradition, the disappearance of "actual humanity" in no way represents an irremediable loss that opens onto the void. It merely signals the end of the first beginning and, potentially, the start of "another beginning" and "another history," of another history of another humanity and a different world.

It is not certain, however, that the history of Being is granted this relation with the theology of catastrophe for all humanity. In ancient African traditions, for example, the point of departure for the questioning of human existence is not the question of being but that of relation, of mutual implication, that is to say of the discovery and the recognition of a different flesh from mine. It is the question of knowing how to transport myself to faraway places that are at once different from mine and implicated in it. From this perspective, identity is a matter not of substance but of plasticity. It is a matter of co-composition, of opening onto the over-there of another flesh, of reciprocity between multiple fleshes and their multiple names and places.

From this point of view, history's creation consists in untying and retying the knots and potentials of situations. History is a succession of paradoxical situations of transformation without rupture, of transformation in continuity, of the reciprocal assimilation of multiple segments of that which lives. Whence the importance attached to the work of relating contraries, of phagocytosis, and of assembling singularities. Little importance is granted in these traditions to the idea of an end of the world or that of another humanity. When all is said and done, this obsession may well be specific to Western metaphysics. For many human cultures, the world, simply, does not end; the idea of a recapitulation of time corresponds to nothing at all precise. This does not mean that all is eternal, that all is repetition, or that all is cyclical. It simply means that the world, by definition, is opening, and that time arises only in and through the unexpected, the unforeseen. As a result, the event is precisely that which nobody can foresee, measure, or calculate with accuracy. This being so, "humankind's specificity" is to be in a constant state of wakefulness, disposed to welcoming the unknown and to embracing the unexpected, since surprise lies at the origin of the procedures of enchantment without which the world is not a world.

At another level, and for a large share of humanity, the end of the world has already occurred. The question is no longer to know how to live life while awaiting it; instead it is to know how living will be possible the day after the end, that is to say, how to live with loss, with separation. How can the world be re-created in the wake of the world's destruction? For this share of humanity, a loss of world obliges the undoing of that which, hitherto, had constituted the essential aspect of material, psychic, and symbolic investments, to develop an ethics of renunciation in relation to what was there yesterday, has disappeared today, and must now be forgotten since, in any case, a life is always there after the end. The end does not amount to the ultimate limit of life. Something in the principle of life defies all ideas of the end. By contrast, loss and its corollary, separation, represent a decisive crossing. But though all separation is, somewhere, a loss, not all loss necessarily amounts to an end of the world. There are liberating losses that open onto other registers of life and relation. There are losses that participate in necessity, because they guarantee survival. There are objects and investments from which one must separate precisely so as to ensure their continued existence. Similarly, an attachment to certain objects and investments can only, in the end, result in the destruction of the ego and the objects in question.

That said, the era is decidedly one of a double movement: on the one hand, it involves an enthusiasm for origins and recommencement; on the other, an exit from the world, an end of times, bringing the existing to an end, and the coming of another world. Both forms of enthusiasm naturally adopt specific figures depending on the place. In the postcolony, wherein a particular form of power rages, wherein the dominant and the subjugated are specifically linked in one and the same bundle of desire, enthusiasm for the end is often expressed in the language of the religious. One reason why is that the postcolony is a relatively specific form of capture and emasculation of the desire for revolt and the will to struggle. Society's energies are reinvested not necessarily in work, profit-seeking, or the recapitulation of the world and its renewal, but in a sort of unmediated, immediate enjoyment, which is simultaneously empty of enjoyment and a libidinal sort of predation—all things that explain both the absence of revolutionary transformation and the established regimes' lack of hegemony.

The enthusiasm for origins thrives by provoking an affect of fear of encountering the other—an encounter that is not always material but is certainly always phantasmatic, and in general traumatic. Indeed, many are concerned that they have preferred others over themselves for a long time. They deem that the matter can no longer be to prefer such others to ourselves. Everything is now about preferring ourselves to others, who, in any case, are scarcely worthy of us, and last, it is about making our object choices settle on those who are like us. The era is therefore one of strong narcissistic bonds. In this context the functions that an imaginary fixation on the stranger, the Muslim, the veiled woman, the refugee, the Jew, or the Negro play are defensive ones. There is a refusal to recognize that, in truth, our ego has always been constituted through opposition to some Other that we have internalized—a Negro, a Jew, an Arab, a foreigner—but in a regressive way; that, at bottom, we are made up of diverse borrowings from foreign subjects and that, consequently, we have always been *beings of the border*—such is precisely what many refuse to admit today.

In addition, a generalizing and democratizing of the affect of fear are taking place, backdropped by deep mutations, for starters in our regimes of belief, and consequently also in the stories that people tell themselves. These stories need not be grounded in truth. Henceforth, what is true is not what has effectively happened or taken place but what is believed. Stories of threat. Of serpent-headed men, half-cows and half-bulls. Of enemies who have it in for us and who seek to kill us gratuitously, by surprise. Of humans-of-terror, whose force resides in the fact that they have overcome the life instinct in themselves and can thus die, preferably by killing others. In fact, a new kind of war, utterly planetary, has apparently already been launched and is unfolding on all fronts, being imposed upon us entirely from the outside. We are in no way responsible either for its causes or for its progress, or for the situations of extremity that it engenders far away from our homes. Its cost in finances, blood, and bodies is said to be incalculable. Short of being able to stop it or destroy our enemies, it will, it is argued, ineluctably lead to the death of the ideas that we, not so long ago, held to be sacrosanct. Because we are in the precise position of being a victim to an external attack, it is within our rights to retaliate, especially as such retaliation is simply, when all is said and done, an honorable form of legitimate defense. If, during this retaliation, our enemies or the peoples and states that offer them sanctuary or protect them are laid waste, this is nothing other than a fair return. Are they not, ultimately, the bearers of their own destruction?

These stories all share a common thread: the norm is now to *live* by the sword. Including in democracies, political struggle increasingly consists in a struggle to know who can develop the most repressive measures faced with the enemy threat. Not only has contemporary war changed its face. During the special operations conducted by formally constituted armed forces, supposed enemies are coldly dispatched, at point-blank range, without warning, with no way out, and without any risk that the said enemies might retaliate. Assassination does not only provide the occasion for a passing salvo. It marks the return to an archaic mode of functioning, in which the distinction no longer exists between the libidinal drives properly speaking and the death drives as such. For the Id's encounter with mortality to be able to take place without reply, the other must really be out of my life for good.[48] Is the act of killing innocent civilians with a drone, or through — albeit precision — air strikes, blinder, more moral, or more clinical than slitting someone's throat or his decapitation? Does the human-of-terror kill his enemies for what they are and for that alone? Does he deny them the right to live for what they think? Does he really want to know what they say and what they do, or does he need only *their being there,* armed or not, Muslim or impious, locals or not, at the wrong place and time?

The general atmosphere of fear also feeds on the idea that the end of humanity — and thus of the world — is near. Now, the end of humanity does not necessarily imply that of the world. The history of the world and the history of humanity, although entangled, will not necessarily have a simultaneous end. The end of humans will not necessarily lead to the world's end. By contrast, the material world's end will undoubtedly entail that of humans. Humanity's end will open up another life sequence, perhaps a "life without history," inasmuch as the concept of history has been inseparable from that of humanity, to the point that it was once thought that the only history is that of humanity. Such is clearly no longer the case today. And it may well be that humanity's end will only pave the way for a history of the world without humans; a history without humans, but with other living beings, with all the traces that humanity will have left behind it; in any case, it will resolutely be *a history in humanity's absence*.

Strictly speaking, humanity will perhaps end up in a state of universal inanition, but the end of humanity will not mean the end of all imaginable ends. The age of humankind does not coincide perfectly with that of the world. The world is older than humanity, and the two can hardly be confounded. There will be no humanity without the world. But it may well be that a certain figure of the world survives humanity — the world without humans. Whether this world without humans will be inaugurated by a cloud-cloaked angel descending in full force from heaven, with a rainbow on its head, a face like the sun, and feet like pillars of fire, nobody can say. Will it stand with its right foot placed on the sea, its left foot on the Earth? No one knows. Standing tall on the sea and on the Earth, will it raise its hand toward heaven and swear by the One who inhabits the century of centuries? Many people believe so. They really believe that there will no longer be any time, but upon the day of the seventh angel's trumpet, God's mystery will be consummated.

They glimpse an end that spells a final interruption of time, or again an entry into a new regime of historicity characterized by the consumption of the divine. God will have ceased to be a mystery. It will now be possible to accede to his unmediated truth in the most absolute of transparencies. After having long been separated, completion, finitude, and revelation will finally be reunited. A time, whose nature is to come to an end, will do so, in order that another time, an unending one, may come. Passing over to the other side will be possible at last. It will be possible at last to leave behind, from this side here, the time of finitude and mortality. At the heart of the technotheologically connoted political violence of our times is thus the idea that a basically liberating power exists that will explode almost out of nothingness once the end is truly accomplished.[49]

Relation without Desire

Terrorism is not—regardless of what is included under this name—a fiction. Nor are the wars of occupation, or the counterterror and counterinsurgency campaigns that supposedly aim to deal with this terrorism. Terror and counterterror are in fact two faces of one and the same reality, *a relation without desire*. Terrorist activism and antiterrorist mobilization have more than one thing in common. Both strike the law and rights at their very roots.

On the one hand, the terrorist project aims to effect the collapse of a society of rights, whose deepest foundations it objectively threatens; on the other, antiterrorist mobilization relies on the idea that extraordinary measures alone will enable enemies to be overcome and that state violence ought to be able to bear down on these enemies unreservedly. In this context, the suspension of rights and lifting of the guarantees that protect individuals are presented as the condition of survival of these same rights. In other terms, the law cannot be protected by the law—only nonlaw can protect it. To protect the state of law against terror, it is deemed, violence must be done to the law, or we must constitutionalize what only yesterday was seen as an exception or as outright lawlessness. At the risk of the means becoming an end in itself, every undertaking to defend the state of law and our mode of existence is seen to imply an absolute use of sovereignty.

But at what point does "legitimate defense" (or even retaliation) transform, in its principle as well as in its functioning, into a vulgar reduplication of the terrorist institution and mechanics? Are we not in the presence of an entirely different political regime whenever the suspension of law and freedoms is no longer an exception, even if, in addition, nor is it the rule? Where does justice stop and where does vengeance begin when laws, decrees, searches, checks, special tribunals, and other emergency measures aim above all to generate a category of *a priori suspects*, yielding a state of suspicion that (in the case of Islam) is only intensified by the injunction to abjure? How can one demand that ordinary and innocent Muslims answer in the name of those who, at any rate, are scarcely concerned with their lives and, in a pinch, want them dead? In this era of great brutality, while everybody is killing with chain saws, is it necessary to continue to stigmatize those who flee death because they seek refuge in our countries instead of stoically consenting to dying in the same place they were born?

No credible answer to these questions is possible that does not take as its point of departure the apparent generalizing of forms of power and modes of sovereignty, a key characteristic of which is to produce death on a large scale. This production is carried out on the basis of a purely instrumental calculation of life and of the political. We have, it is true, always lived in a world deeply marked by diverse forms of terror, that is to say, of squandering human life. There is nothing new about having to live under terror, and therefore under a regime of squanderers. Historically, one of the strategies of the dominant states has always consisted in spatializing and discharging that terror by confining its most extreme manifestations in some racially stigmatized third place — the plantation under slavery, the colony, the camp, the compound under apartheid, the ghetto or, as in the present-day United States, the prison. Private authorities were occasionally able to exercise these forms of confinement and occupation, along with this power of segmentation and destruction, often unchecked. This led to the emergence of modes of *domination without responsibility*, as capital confiscated for itself the right of life and death over those it subjugated. Such was the case, for example, at the start of the colonial period during the times of concessionary companies.

In many regions of the postcolonial world, the turning point was to be the generalizing of belligerent relations, often as the ultimate consequence of the authoritarian course that many political regimes took to deal with intense protests. In Africa in particular, terror itself donned several forms. The first was state terror, notably when it came to containing the eruption of protest movements, when needed via a repression that was sometimes deceitful and sometimes expeditious, brutal, and unrestrained (imprisonment, shootings, establishing of emergency measures, diverse forms of economic coercion). To facilitate the repression, the regimes sought to depoliticize social protest. Sometimes they sought to give the confrontation ethnic contours. In certain cases, entire regions were placed under a twofold civil and military administration. Wherever established regimes felt most threatened, they took the logic of radicalization to the utmost limit, by creating or supporting the emergence of gangs or militias controlled either by abettors (*affidés*) and other entrepreneurs of violence operating in the shadows, or by political or military heads with positions of power in official state structures. Some militias progressively increased in autonomy, becoming genuine armed formations with command structures paralleling the regular armies. In others, the official military structures served to conceal outlawed activities, the increase in trafficking going hand in hand with political repression properly speaking.

A second form of terror set in wherever there was a dividing of the monopoly of power, subsequent to which there occurred an inequitable redistribution of the means of terror within society. In such contexts, the dynamic of deinstitutionalization and informalization accelerated. A new social division has arisen separating those who are protected (because armed) from those who are not. Last, more than in the past, political struggles tend to be settled by force, with the spread of weapons throughout society now a key factor of division and a central element in the dynamics of insecurity, protection of life, and access to property. The state's progressive loss of the monopoly of violence has ended in a gradual devolution of this monopoly to a multiplicity of bodies operating either outside the state or else within it but in relative autonomy. The breakup of this monopoly also sanctions the outbreak of private operators, some of whom have little by little acquired capacities for capturing and remobilizing the resources of violence for economic ends, and even capacities to engage in by-the-book warfare.

On another level, the forms of violent resource appropriation increased in complexity, with links appearing between the armed forces, the police, the administering of justice, and criminal milieus. Wherever repression and trafficking of all sorts feed off one another, a politicocultural configuration has appeared that grants a large place to the possibility that anyone whomever can be killed by anyone whomever at whatever moment, using any pretext at all. By establishing a relative relation of equality upon the capacity to kill and its corollary (the possibility of being killed) — a relative equality suspended only by the possession or nonpossession of weapons — this configuration accentuates the functional character of terror and makes possible the destruction of all social links other than the link of enmity. This link of enmity justifies the active relation of dissociation of which war is a violent expression. This link also makes it possible to institute and normalize the idea that power can be acquired and exercised only at the price of another's life.

In government by terror, at issue is no longer so much to repress and discipline as it is to kill either en masse or in small doses. War no longer necessarily opposes armies to others, or sovereign states to others. The actors of war are, pell-mell, properly constituted states, armed formations acting or not behind the mask of the state, armies without states but that control quite distinct territories, states without armies, corporations or concessionary companies tasked with extracting natural resources but that, moreover, have arrogated to themselves the right to wage war. Regulating the population is done by means of wars that consist, for their part, in processes of appropriating economic resources. In such contexts, the imbrication of war, terror, and the economy is such that no longer is it merely a matter of a war economy. By creating new military markets, war and terror have transformed into modes of production, period.

Terror and atrocities are justified by the desire to eradicate the corruption of which still existing tyrannies are allegedly guilty. In appearance, terror and atrocities thus form part of an immense therapeutic liturgy, mixing in with which is the desire for sacrifice, messianic eschatologies, the debris of knowledge forms linked either to native imaginations of the occult or to modern discourses of utilitarianism, materialism, and consumerism. Whatever their discursive foundations, they are politically expressed through attritional wars during which thousands, indeed hundreds of thousands of victims are massacred, and hundreds of thousands of survivors are either displaced, confined, or interned in camps. In these conditions, power is infinitely more brutal than under the authoritarian period. It is more physical, more bodily, and more burdensome. No longer does it aim at taming populations as such. While it remains steadfast in its strict surveillance of bodies (or in its agglomerating them within the perimeters it controls), this is done not so much to discipline them as to extract a maximum of utility from them and, sometimes, forms of enjoyment (notably with sexual slavery).

The ways of killing are themselves varied. When it comes to massacres in particular, bodies stripped of being are quickly returned to the state of simple skeletons, simple residues of an unburied pain; emptied and insignificant corporeities; strange deposits plunged into a cruel stupor.[50] Oftentimes, the most striking thing is the tension between the petrification of bones and their strange coldness, on the one hand, and their obstinacy in wanting to signify something at all costs, on the other. In other circumstances, no serenity seems to inhabit these bits of bone marked by impassibility, nothing but the illusory refusal of a death already come. In other cases, in which physical amputation replaces direct death, removing a limb or two paves the way for the use of techniques of incision, ablation, and excision that also take bones as their favored target. This demiurgic surgery leaves traces that persist long after the event and that take the form of human beings who are assuredly living but whose bodily totality has been replaced by pieces, fragments, folds, and even immense wounds and scars that are continually held up before the victim's eyes, and the eyes of those he rubs shoulders with, to display the morbid spectacle of his severing.

Further, without falling into any geographical or climatic naturalism, the forms donned by terror in the age of the Anthropocene may be said to depend necessarily on climatic contexts and on the kinds of life specific to various ecological milieus. A particular point in case is the Sahelian-Saharan space in Africa, where the dynamics of violence tend to marry those of spatial mobility and circulation typical of desert, or semidesert, nomadic worlds. Here, where the strategies of states since colonial times have been founded on the mastery of territories, the various formations of violence (including terrorist) rest on mastering movement as well as social and market networks. One of the desert's characteristics is its fluctuation. If the desert fluctuates, then so, too, do its borders, with the variation of climatic events.

Also typical of Saharan desert spaces is the importance of markets and routes linking the forests of the South to the towns of the Maghreb. Terrorism here is a terrorism of strata, located at the interface between the caravan, nomadic, and sedentary regimes. This is because space and populations are constantly moving. Space is not only crossed by movement. It is itself in movement. According to Denis Retaillé and Olivier Walther, "this capacity of movement of places is made possible by the fact that these places are not first and foremost determined by the existence of rigid infrastructures." What counts most, they add, is "a more subtle form of organization than the zonal model founded on a division of space into several bioclimatic domains."[51] The capacity to move across considerable distances, to entertain shifting alliances, to privilege flows to the detriment of territories, and to negotiate uncertainty is necessary to influence the regional markets of terror.

In these more or less mobile and segmentary forms of administration of terror, sovereignty consists in the power to manufacture an entire crowd of people who specifically live at the edge of life, or even on its outer edge — people for whom living means continually standing up to death, and doing so under conditions in which death itself increasingly tends to become spectral, thanks both to the way in which it is lived and to the manner in which it is given. This life is a superfluous one, therefore, whose price is so meager that it has no equivalence, whether market or—even less—human; this is a species of life whose value is extra-economic, the only equivalent of which is the sort of death able to be inflicted upon it.

As a rule, such death is something to which nobody feels any obligation to respond. Nobody even bears the slightest feelings of responsibility or justice toward this sort of life or, rather, death. Necropolitical power proceeds by a sort of inversion between life and death, as if life was merely death's medium. It ever seeks to abolish the distinction between means and ends. Hence its indifference to objective signs of cruelty. In its eyes, crime constitutes a fundamental part of revelation, and the death of its enemies is, in principle, deprived of all symbolism. Such death has nothing tragic about it. This is why necropolitical power can multiply it infinitely, either by small doses (the cellular and molecular modes) or by spasmodic surges—the strategy of "small massacres" inflicted one day at a time, using an implacable logic of separation, strangulation, and vivisection, as we see in all the contemporary theaters of terror and counterterror.[52]

To a large extent, racism is the driver of the necropolitical principle insofar as it stands for organized destruction, for a sacrificial economy, the functioning of which requires, on the one hand, a generalized cheapening of the price of life and, on the other, a habituation to loss. This principle is at work in the present-day process by which the permanent simulation of the state of exception justifies "the war against terror"—a war of eradication, indefinite, absolute, that claims the right to cruelty, torture, and indefinite detention—and so a war that draws its weapons from the "evil" that it pretends to be eradicating, in a context in which the law and justice are applied in the form of endless reprisals, vengeance, and revenge.

Perhaps more than about difference, the era is thus about the fantasy of separation, and even extermination. It is about that which does not fit together, about that which does not unify, about that which one is not disposed to share. Gradually replacing the proposition of universal equality, which, not so long ago, made it possible to contest substantial injustices, is the oftentimes violent separation of a "world without." This is the "world of undesirables": of Muslims encumbering the city; of Negroes and other strangers that one owes it to oneself to deport; of (supposed) terrorists that one tortures by oneself or by proxy; of Jews, so many of whom one regrets managed to escape the gas chambers; of migrants who flow in from everywhere; of refugees and all the shipwrecked, all the human wrecks whose bodies resemble piles of garbage that are hard to tell apart, and of the mass treatment of this human carrion, in its moldiness, its stench, and its rot.

Further still, the classic distinction between executioner and victim—which previously served as the basis for the most elementary justice—has largely attenuated. Today victim, tomorrow executioner, then victim once again—the hateful cycle does not stop growing, twisting and spreading its coils everywhere. Few misfortunes are deemed unjust from this point on. There is neither guilt nor remorse nor reparation. Nor are there injustices that we ought to put right or tragedies that we can avoid. In order to get together, it is necessary to divide, and each time that we say "we," we must exclude someone at any price, strip him of something, undertake some sort of confiscation.

Through a strange transmutation, victims are now summoned to bear, in addition to the prejudice suffered, the guilt that their executioners ought to feel. Instead of their tormentors, who are dispensed of all remorse and relieved of the necessity to make right the ravages they have inflicted, it is the victims who must expiate. In return, former victims—survivors of all sorts—have no misgivings about transforming themselves into executioners and projecting on those weaker than they are the terror they once suffered, thus reproducing on occasion, and excessively so, the logics that presided over their own extermination.

At any rate, the temptation of the exception and its corollary, immunity, hover everywhere. How were we able to inflect democracy itself, and even take our leave of it? How was it possible to harness and confiscate, when needed, this unbounded social, economic, and symbolic violence, institutionalize it and direct it against a "great enemy"—anyone at all, little matter whom—that we must annihilate at any price? Where the merging of capitalism and animism is no longer subject to doubt, intertwining the tragic and the political tends to become the norm. This is the question that our era—that of *democracy's inversion*—does not stop posing.[53]

Practically everywhere discourse is therefore at the point of suspension, restriction, or pure and simple abolition—of the constitution, the law, rights, public freedoms, nationality, all sorts of protections and guarantees that, until recently, were taken for granted. The majority of contemporary wars, not to mention the associated forms of terror, aim not only at recognition but at the constitution of a *world outside relation*. Whether or not given as provisional, the process of *exiting from democracy* and the movement of suspension of rights, constitutions, and freedoms are paradoxically justified by the necessity to protect these same laws, freedoms, and constitutions. And with exit and suspension comes enclosure—that is, all sorts of walls, barbed-wire fences, camps and tunnels, in-camera hearings, as if, in truth, one had finished and for good with a certain order of things, a certain order of life, a certain imaginary of the in-common in the city of the future.

In several regards, the question that we raised yesterday is exactly the same one that we must raise anew today. This is the question of knowing if it was ever possible, if it is possible, and if it will ever be possible, for us to encounter the other differently than as a given object, one that is simply there, at arm's length. Can there be anything that links us to others with whom we can declare that we are together? What forms might this solicitude take? Is another politics of the world possible, a politics that no longer necessarily rests upon difference or alterity but instead on a certain idea of the kindred and the in-common? Are we not condemned to live in our exposure to one another, sometimes in the same space?

Owing to this structural proximity, there is no longer any "outside" that might be opposed to an "inside," no "elsewhere" that might be opposed to a "here," no "closeness" that might be opposed to a "remoteness." One cannot "sanctuarize" *one's own home* by fomenting chaos and death far away, *in the homes of others*. Sooner or later, one will reap at home what one has sown abroad. Sanctuarization can only ever be mutual. To achieve this, we are going to have to think through democracy beyond the juxtaposition of singularities as much as beyond the simplistic ideology of integration. In addition, a democracy-to-come will rely on a clear-cut distinction between the "universal" and the "in-common." The universal implies inclusion in some already constituted thing or entity, where the in-common presupposes a relation of co-belonging and sharing—the idea of a world that is the only one we have and that, to be sustainable, must be shared by all those with rights to it, all species taken together. For this sharing to become possible and for a planetary democracy to come to pass, the democracy of species, the demand for justice and reparation is inescapable.[54]

These large-scale mutations, we must understand, deeply affect the relationship between democracy, memory, and the idea of a future that humanity as a whole might share. Now concerning "humanity as a whole," it must also be admitted that, in its dispersion, this humanity is today like a mortuary mask—something, a remainder, anything but a perfectly recognizable figure, face, or body—in this era of swarming, proliferation, and the grafting of everything onto nearly everything else. Indeed, no longer can there be said to be some *thing*. But has this half-carrion and half-recumbent "something" ever really been there, before us, except in the form of an extravagant carcass—at best, an at once elementary, originary, and unreserved struggle to escape the dust?[55] The time is far from being one of reason, and nothing assures us it ever will be again, at least not in the short term. Helped along by the need for mysteries and the return of a spirit of crusade, ours is rather a time of paranoid dispositions, hysterical violence, and procedures to annihilate all those that democracy will have constituted as enemies of state.[56]

TWO
THE SOCIETY
OF ENMITY

Perhaps it has always been this way.[1] Perhaps democracies have always been communities of fellow beings, and therefore—as I maintained in the previous chapter—societies of separation. They may well have always had slaves, a set of people who, in one way or another, are regarded as pertaining to the foreigner, members of a surplus population, undesirables of whom one hopes to be rid, and who, in this way, must be left "completely or partially without rights."[2] This is possible.

It is equally possible that no "universal democracy of humanity" has ever existed "anywhere on earth," and that, with the Earth being divided into states, it is within such states that one seeks to realize democracy, that is, in the last instance, a state politics that, by clearly distinguishing its own citizens—those fellow beings—from other people, keeps at arm's length all those non–fellow beings.[3] For the moment, it suffices to repeat the following: the contemporary era is, undeniably, one of separation, hate movements, hostility, and, above all, struggle against an enemy. Consequently, liberal democracies—already considerably leached by the forces of capital, technology, and militarism—are now being sucked into a colossal process of inversion.[4]

The Terrifying Object

Now whoever speaks about "movement" necessarily suggests the setting into motion of a drive, which, even if impure, is composed of a fundamental energy. This energy is enlisted, whether consciously or not, in the pursuit of a desire, ideally a master-desire. This master-desire—at once comprising a field of immanence and a force composed of multiplicities—invariably has one or several objects as its fixation point. Yesterday, "Negro" and "Jew" were the favored names for such objects. Today, Negroes and Jews are known by other names: Islam, the Muslim, the Arab, the foreigner, the immigrant, the refugee, the intruder, to mention only a few.

Desire (master or otherwise) is also that movement through which the subject—enveloped on all sides by a specific fantasy (whether of omnipotence, ablation, destruction, or persecution, it matters little)—sometimes seeks to turn back on itself in the hope of protecting itself from external danger, and sometimes goes outside of itself to confront the windmills of its imagination that henceforth assail it. In fact, once uprooted from its structure, desire sets out to conquer this terrifying object. But since this object has never actually existed—does not and never will exist—desire must continually invent it. Dreaming it up, however, still does not work to make it a reality, except as a sort of empty yet bewitching space, a hallucinatory zone, at once enchanted and evil, that it inhabits as a sort of fate.

The desire for an enemy, the desire for apartheid (for separation and enclaving), the fantasy of extermination—all today occupy the space of this enchanted circle. In a number of cases, a wall is enough to express such desire.[5] Several sorts of wall exist, and not all fulfill the same functions.[6] A separation wall is supposed to resolve a problem of excess of presence, the very presence that some see as the origin of situations of unbearable suffering. To regain the feeling of existing henceforth depends on breaking with that excess presence, whose absence (or indeed disappearance pure and simple) will by no means be felt as a loss. This also means accepting that there is nothing common to be shared between us and them. The anxiety of annihilation thus goes to the core of contemporary projects of separation.

Everywhere, the building of concrete walls and wire fences and other "security barriers" is in full swing. Alongside the walls, other security structures are emerging: checkpoints, enclosures, watchtowers, trenches, all manner of demarcations that in many cases have no other function than to intensify the enclaving of entire communities, without ever fully succeeding in keeping away those considered a threat. This is the case with all those Palestinian towns that are literally surrounded by areas under Israeli control.[7]

As it happens, the Israeli occupation of Palestinian territories serves as a laboratory for a number of techniques of control, surveillance, and separation that are today proliferating in other places on the planet. These techniques range from the regular sealing off of entire areas to restricting the number of Palestinians allowed to enter Israel and the occupied territories, from the repeated imposition of curfews within Palestinian enclaves and controls on movement to the objective imprisonment of entire towns.[8]

Permanent or random checkpoints, cement blocks and mounds of earth designed to block roads, the control of air and marine space, of the import and export of all sorts of products, frequent military incursions, demolitions of houses, the desecration of cemeteries, uprooting whole olive groves, obliterating and turning infrastructure to dust, high- and medium-altitude bombings, targeted assassinations, urban counterinsurgency techniques, the profiling of minds and bodies, constant harassment, the ever smaller subdivision of land, cellular and molecular violence, the generalization of the camp form — every feasible means is put to work to impose a regime of separation whose functioning paradoxically depends on a proximate intimacy with those who have been separated.[9]

Such practices variously recall the reviled model of apartheid, with its Bantustans, vast reservoirs of cheap labor, its white zones, its multiple jurisdictions and wanton violence. However, the metaphor of apartheid does not fully account for the specific character of the Israeli separation project. First, this project rests on a rather singular metaphysical and existential base. The apocalyptic and catastrophist resources underwriting it are far more complex, and derive from a longer historical horizon, than those that made South African Calvinism possible.[10]

Second, with its "high-tech" character, the effects of the Israeli project on the Palestinian body are far more formidable than the relatively primitive operations undertaken by the apartheid regime in South Africa between 1948 and the early 1980s. This also goes for the miniaturization of violence — its cellularization and molecularization — as well as its various techniques of material and symbolic effacement.[11] It is also evidenced in the procedures and techniques of demolition of almost everything — infrastructures, houses, roads, the countryside — and the dynamic of frenzied destruction whose essence lies in transforming the lives of Palestinians into a heap of ruins or a pile of garbage destined for cleansing.[12] In South Africa, the mounds of ruins never did reach such a scale.

If every form of inclusion is necessarily disjunctive, separation can conversely only ever be partial. In South Africa wholesale separation would have undermined the very survival of the oppressor. Short of exterminating entire native populations from the outset, it was impossible for the white minority to undertake a systematic ethnic and racial cleansing on the model of other settler colonies. Mass expulsions and deportations were hardly an option. Once the entwining of different racial segments had become the rule, the dialectic of proximity, distance, and control could never have reached the paroxysmal levels seen in Palestine.

In the Occupied Territories, proximity is attested notably by Israel's ongoing control of the population register and its monopoly over the issuing of Palestinian identity cards. Similarly with nearly all the other aspects of daily life in the occupied territories, such as daily trips, obtaining various permits, and tax control. Peculiar to this model of separation is not only that it can be tailored to the demands of occupation (or abandonment, if need be).[13] Further, at any moment, it can be transformed into an instrument of strangulation. Occupation is in every respect hand-to-hand combat in a tunnel.

The desire for apartheid and the fantasy of extermination are hardly new phenomena, however. They have continued to metamorphose over the course of history, particularly within the old settler colonies. Chinese, Mongols, Africans, and Arabs — in some cases long before Europeans — were behind the conquest of vast territorialities. They established complex long-distance trade networks across seas and oceans. But it was Europe that, perhaps for the first time in modern history, inaugurated a new epoch of global resettlement.[14] This repeopling of the world, which occurred between the sixteenth and nineteenth centuries, presents a twofold characteristic: it was at once a process of social excretion (for the migrants who left Europe to found overseas colonies) and a historic tipping point. For the colonized, it came at the cost of new forms of enslavement.

Over the course of this long period, the repopulation of the world often took the shape of innumerable atrocities and massacres, unprecedented instances of "ethnic cleansing," expulsions, transfers, and the assembling of entire populations in camps, and indeed of genocides.[15] The colonial enterprise was driven by a mixture of sadism and masochism, applied gropingly and in response to largely unexpected events. It was inclined to smash all forces standing in the way of its drives, to inhibit their course toward all sorts of perverse pleasures. The limits to what it considered "normal" were constantly shifting, and few desires were subject to straightforward repression, let alone embarrassment or disgust. The colonial world's capacity to cope with the destruction of its objects — natives included — was astonishing. If any object came to be lost, another could easily replace it, or so it was thought.

Further still, the principle of separation lay at the root of the colonial undertaking. Colonizing broadly consisted in a permanent work of separation: on one side, my living body; on the other, all those "body-things" surrounding it; on one side, my human flesh, through which all those other "flesh-things" and "flesh-meats" exist for me. On one side, therefore, is me — fabric par excellence and zero point of worldly orientation — and, on the other, others with whom I can never completely blend; the Others that I can bring to myself but with whom I can ever genuinely entertain relations of reciprocity or mutual implication.

In the colonial context, this permanent work of separation (and thus differentiation) was partly a consequence of the annihilation anxiety felt by the settlers themselves. Numerically inferior but endowed with powerful means of destruction, the settlers lived in fear of being surrounded on all sides by "bad objects" that threatened their very survival and were ever liable to take away their existence: natives, wild beasts, reptiles, microbes, mosquitoes, nature, the climate, illnesses, even sorcerers.

The apartheid system in South Africa and the destruction of Jews in Europe — the latter in an extreme fashion and within a distinct context — constitute two emblematic manifestations of this fantasy of separation. Apartheid in particular openly challenged the possibility of a single body comprehending more than one individual. It presupposed the existence of originary and distinct (already constituted) subjects, each made of a "flesh-of-race," of a "blood-of-race" able to develop according to their own precise rhythms. It was deemed enough to assign them to specific territorial spaces in order to renaturalize their foreignness with respect to one another. These originary, distinct subjects were called upon to act as if their past had never been one of "prostitution," of paradoxical dependencies, and all manner of intrigues, that is, to act out a fantasy of purity.[16] Historical apartheid's failure to secure, once and for all, impenetrable frontiers between a plurality of different fleshes demonstrates a posteriori the limits of the colonial project of separation. Short of its total extermination, the Other is no longer external to us. It is within us, in the double figure of the alter ego and the altered ego (*l'autre Moi et du Moi autre*), each mortally exposed to the other and to itself.

The colonial undertaking drew a great deal of its substance and surplus energy from its ties with all sorts of drives, with more or less openly avowed desires, in the main located below the conscious I of the agents concerned. To exercise a lasting hold over the native people they had subjugated, and from whom they wanted to differentiate themselves at all costs, the settlers had somehow to constitute them as *physical objects* of various sorts. In this sense, the whole game of representations under colonialism consisted indeed in turning the natives into a variety of type-images.

These images largely corresponded to the debris of these natives' real biographies, their primary status before the encounter. Thanks to the imaged material thus produced, an entirely artificial secondary status of psychic objects came to be grafted onto their primary status as authentic human persons. For the natives, the dilemma thus became to know how, in everyday practice, to discern what pertained to the psychic object they had been asked to interiorize — and often forced to assume as their selves — and what to the human person that they had been, that they were despite everything, but that, in colonial conditions, they were forced to forget.

Once invented, these psychic motifs became constitutive of the colonial self. Their position of exteriority with respect to the colonial self was thus always rather relative. The continued psychic functioning of the colonial order rested on investment in these objects. Without such objects and motifs, affective, emotional, and psychic life in the colonies would have lost its substance and coherence. It gravitated around these motifs. It depended for its vitality on permanent contact with them, and indeed showed itself to be particularly vulnerable to being separated from them. In colonial or paracolonial situations, the bad object (that which has survived an initial destruction) can never be thought of as completely external to myself. It is divided from the outset, at once subject and object. Since I bear it at the same time as it bears me, sheer persecution and obstinacy are not enough to simply be rid of it. In the end, try as I might to destroy everything I abhor, this can never release me from my link to this destroyed third party, or the third party from which I have separated myself. This is because *the bad object and I are never entirely separable. At the same time, we are never entirely together.*

The Enemy, the Other That I Am

Irrepressible, the desire for an enemy, for apartheid, the fantasy of extermination, all constitute the line of fire, indeed the decisive trial, at the beginning of this century. As the fundamental vectors of contemporary brainwashing, they push democratic regimes everywhere into a kind of vicious stupor and, inebriated and reeking, to engage in drunken behavior. As both diffuse psychic structures and generic passionate forces, they stamp the dominant affective tonality of our times and stir many contemporary struggles and mobilizations. These struggles and mobilizations thrive on a vision of the world that is threatening and anxiogenic, one that grants primacy to logics of suspicion, and indeed to all that which is secret, or pertains to conspiracy and the occult.[17] Pushed to their ultimate consequences, they lead almost inexorably to a desire to destroy — spilt blood, blood made law, in an express continuity with the Old Testament's *lex talionis* (law of the talion).

In this depressive period in the psychic life of nations, the need, or even the drive, for an enemy is thus no longer purely a social need. It amounts to a quasi-anal need for ontology. In the context of the mimetic rivalry exacerbated by the "war on terror," having an enemy at one's disposal (preferably in a spectacular fashion) has become an obligatory stage in the constitution of the subject and its entry into the symbolic order of our times. For that matter, everything transpires as if being denied an enemy were lived, within oneself, as a deep narcissistic wound. To be deprived of an enemy — or to not have lived through a terrorist attack or any other bloody acts fomented by those who hate us and our way of life — means being deprived of the kind of relation of hatred that authorizes the giving of a free rein to all sorts of otherwise forbidden desires. It means being deprived of that demon without which all is not permitted, whereas the time seems to be urgently calling for absolute license, unbridling, and generalized disinhibition. It equally means being frustrated in one's compulsion to be afraid, in one's capacity to demonize, in the kind of pleasure and satisfaction felt when a presumed enemy is shot down by special forces, or else when, captured alive, he is subjected to endless interrogations, rendered and tortured in one of the many black sites that stain the surface of our planet.[18]

This era is thus eminently political, since "the specificity of the political," at least if we follow Carl Schmitt, is the "discrimination between friend and enemy."[19] In Schmitt's world, which has become our own, the concept of enemy is to be understood in its concrete and existential meaning, and not at all as a metaphor or as an empty and lifeless abstraction. The enemy Schmitt describes is neither a simple competitor nor an adversary nor a private rival whom one might feel hate or antipathy toward. The enemy refers to a supreme antagonism. In both body and flesh, the enemy is that individual whose physical death is warranted by his existential denial of our own being.

Distinguishing between friends and enemies is one thing; identifying the enemy with accuracy is quite another. A disconcerting figure of ubiquity, the enemy is henceforth more dangerous by being everywhere: without face, name, or place. If the enemy has a face, it is only a *veiled face, the simulacrum of a face.* And if the enemy has a name, this might be only a borrowed name, a false name whose primary function is dissimulation. Such an enemy advances, at times masked, at other times openly, among us, around us, and even within us, ready to emerge in the middle of the day or in the heart of night, each time his apparition threatening the annihilation of our way of life, our very existence.

Yesterday as today, the political as conceived by Schmitt owes its volcanic charge to the fact that it is closely connected to an existential will to power. As such, it necessarily and by definition opens up the extreme possibility of an infinite deployment of pure means without ends, as embodied in the execution of murder. Underwritten by the law of the sword, the political is the antagonism "whereby men could be required to sacrifice [their] life" (*to die for others*), and under the aegis of the state, that in the name of which such men could be authorized to shed blood, and kill other human beings" (*to kill others*) on the basis of their actual or supposed belonging to an enemy camp.[20] The political is, from this point of view, a particular form of grouping together in preparation for a fight that is at once decisive and profoundly obscure. But it is not merely the business of the state, and hence an exercise in delegated death, since it also concerns not only the possibility of sacrifice or of self-sacrifice — the giving of one's life — but also, and very literally, the possibility of suicide.

For, in the end, suicide brutally interrupts every dynamic of subjection and all possibility of recognition. To willingly take leave of one's own existence by committing suicide is not necessarily to make oneself disappear. Rather, it is willingly to abandon the risk of being touched by the Other and by the world—a gesture of disinvestment that forces the enemy to confront his own void. The person who commits suicide no longer wishes to communicate, either by word or by violent gesture, except perhaps when, by putting an end to his own life, he also ends the life of his targets. The killer kills himself while killing others or after having killed. In any case, he no longer seeks to participate in the world as it is. He gets rid of himself and, in the process, of some enemies. Doing so, he takes his leave of what he once was and of the responsibilities that, as a living being, were once his to attend to.[21]

The person who commits suicide—killing his enemies in an act in which he also kills himself—shows how, as far as the political is concerned, the true contemporary fracture opposes those who cling onto their bodies, who take their bodies as the basis of life itself, to those for whom the body can pave the way to a happy life only when expunged. The martyr-to-be is engaged in a quest for a joyous life. This life, he believes, rests only in God himself. It is born of a will to truth that is likened to a will to purity. And only through conversion can an authentic relationship to God arise, through that act whereby one becomes other than oneself, and, in so doing, escapes from the facticity of life—that is, impure life. By committing to martyrdom, a vow is taken to destroy such impure corporeal life. Indeed, often nothing of the fundamentalist's body is left but debris scattered among other objects: bloody traces that appear more vivid against other traces, prints, enigmatic fragments such as bullets, guns, phones, sometimes scratches or marks. Today, however, would-be suicides are rarely without their technical devices, placing them at the intersection between ballistics and electronics—chips to unsolder, memory chips to test. In the strict sense of the term, to bring an end to one's life, to *abolish oneself*, is thus to undertake the dissolution of that seemingly simple entity that is one's body.

That hatred of the enemy, the need to neutralize him, and the desire to avoid the danger and contagion he is seen to bring are the last word on the political in the contemporary mind can all be explained. On the one hand, and by dint of being persuaded that they now face a permanent threat, contemporary societies have become more or less constrained to live out their daily lives as repeating "small traumas"—an attack here, a hostage taken there, first a gun battle, then a permanent state of alert, and so on. The use of new technologies has made it possible to gain access to individuals' private lives. Insidious techniques of mass surveillance, secret and sometimes improper, target people's thoughts, opinions, movements, and privacy. Aided by the heightened reproduction of the affect of fear, liberal democracies have not stopped manufacturing bogeymen apt to scare themselves—today the young veiled woman, tomorrow the terrorist novice returning from the battlefields of the Near and Middle East, and, more generally, lone wolves and sleeper cells that, dormant in the crevices of society, lie in wait looking for the right moment to strike.

What are we to say about the "Muslim," the foreigner, or the immigrant, those about whom one has continued, beyond all reasonable bounds, to weave images that, little by little, speak to each other by association? That such images do not tally with reality matters little. Primary fantasies know neither doubt nor uncertainty. As Freud argued, the mass is only "excited by immoderate stimuli. Anyone seeking to move it needs no logical calibration in his arguments, but must paint with the most powerful images, exaggerate, and say the same thing over and over again."[22]

The current epoch is marked by the triumph of mass morality.[23] Contemporary psychic regimes have brought to a maximum level of exacerbation the exaltation of affectivity and, paradoxically, in this technetronic and digital age, the desire for mythology, and even a thirst for mysteries. The increasing expansion of algorithmic reason—which, as we know, serves as the crucial basis for the financialization of the economy—goes hand in hand with the rise of mythoreligious-type reasoning.[24] Zealous belief is no longer considered antithetical to rational knowledge. On the contrary, the one serves as support for the other, and both are put in the service of visceral experiences, one of whose summits is a "communion of martyrs."

Convictions and private certainties acquired at the end of a long "spiritual" path, one punctuated by revolt and conversion, pertain neither to feeble fanaticisms nor to barbaric madness or delusions but rather to an "inner experience" that can be shared only by those who, professing the same faith, obey the same law, the same authorities, and the same commandments. Essentially, they belong to the same community. This community is made up of communicants, the "damned of the faith," who are doomed to testify, by word and deed, to the "hardline" character of divine truth itself, if necessary to the bitter end.

In the mythoreligious logic specific to our times, the divine (just like the market, capital, or the political) is almost always perceived as an immanent and immediate force: vital, visceral, and energetic. The paths of faith are believed to lead to states or acts considered scandalous from the stand-point of simple human reason, or even to risks, apparently absurd ruptures, and bloody die-hard approaches—terror and catastrophe in the name of God. One of the effects of faith and zeal is to arouse great enthusiasm, of the kind that opens the door to a *great decision*.

Indeed, many people today live purely in anticipation of such an event. Martyrdom is one of the means used by the damned of the faith to bring an end to this wait. Humans of faith and humans of enthusiasm seek to make history through a great decision, that is to say, the commission of vertiginous acts of an immediate and sacrificial nature. By means of such acts, the damned of the faith confront, and with open eyes, a dimension of expenditure and loss. Animated by a will to totality, they seek to become singular subjects by diving into disjunctive sources, daemons of the sacred. Embracing an accepted loss—that which destroys language as much as the subject of discourse—makes it possible to inscribe the divine into the flesh of a world become gift and grace. The matter is no longer one of agony but of annihilation: a crossing from the self to God. The ultimate aim of these sacrificial acts is to master the life not of the outside but of the inside, to produce a new morality and, at the end of a decisive (and if need be bloody, and at any rate definitive) battle, one day to experience exultation and an ecstatic and sovereign affirmation.

The Damned of the Faith

Mythoreligious reasoning is not the exclusive privilege of terrorist forma-tions. In their effort to suppress terrorism and complete their transforma-tion into security states, liberal democracies no longer hesitate to turn to grand mythological schemas. In fact, barely any of them today do not ap-peal to bellicose enthusiasm, often with the aim of patching back together their old nationalist fabrics. For every attack that results in casualties, a kind of bespoke mourning is automatically produced. The nation is summoned to shed its tears of rancor in public and rise up against the enemy. And on each occasion the path from tears to weapons is paved anew. Clothed in the rags of international law, human rights, democracy, or, simply, "civili-zation," militarism no longer needs a mask to advance.[25] Breathing life back into hatred, yesterday's and today's accomplices are suddenly transformed into the "enemies of humanity in general," whereby might becomes right.

For, just as they needed, only relatively recently, to divide humanity into masters and slaves, liberal democracies today still depend for their survival on defining a sphere of common belonging against a sphere of others, or in other words, of friends and "allies" and of enemies of civilization. Without enemies they struggle to keep themselves going alone. Whether such enemies really exist matters little. It suffices to create them, find them, unmask them, and bring them out into the open.

Now this endeavor became increasingly onerous with the conviction that the fiercest and most intrepid enemies had lodged themselves in the deepest pores of the nation, forming a kind of cyst that destroys the nation's most fertile promises from within. How, then, are we to separate the nation from that which gnaws at it without harming its very body — civil war? Searches, raids, various forms of control, house arrests, the recording of charges under emergency laws, increases in practices of exception, extended powers for police and intelligence services, and, if required, loss of nationality: everything is put into effect so that in return ever-harder blows can be dealt those who have struck us, blows that do not necessarily need to land on the authors of these evils, but in passing, merely on those who resemble them. What else is being done here but the perpetuating of the very thing one claims to oppose? By demanding the death of all those who are not unconditionally on our side, is the risk not that we forever reproduce all the tragedy of a humanity gripped by hatred and unable to get free?

Just as in the past, this war against existential enemies is once again understood in metaphysical terms. As a great ordeal, it engages the whole of being, its truth. These enemies, with whom no agreement is either possible or desirable, generally appear as caricatures, clichés, and stereotypes. Caricatures, clichés, and stereotypes grant them a figural sort of presence, a presence that, in turn, serves only to confirm the type of (ontological) threat that they bring to bear on us. Spectral figure and figural presence, therefore, in an age of blood-and-soil reenchantment, as much as of growing abstraction, whereas cultural and biological elements relay one another and now form a single bundle.

With their imaginations whipped up by hatred, liberal democracies do not stop to feed on all sorts of obsessions about the real identity of the enemy. But who is this enemy really? Is it a nation, a religion, a civilization, a culture, or an idea?

State of Insecurity

Taken together, hate movements, groups invested in an economy of hostility, of enmity, and multiform struggles against the enemy, have all contributed, upon this exit from the twentieth century, to a significant raising in the acceptable levels and forms of violence that one can (or should) inflict on the weak, on enemies and intruders (anyone considered not to be one of us). They have also contributed to a widespread instrumentalization of social relations, as well as to profound mutations within contemporary regimes of collective desire and affects. Further still, they have fostered the emergence and consolidation of a state form often referred to as the surveillance or security state.

The security state thrives on a *state of insecurity*, which it participates in fomenting and to which it claims to be the solution. If the security state is a structure, the state of insecurity is a kind of passion, or rather an affect, a condition, or even a force of desire. In other words, the state of insecurity is the condition upon which the functioning of the security state relies insofar as the latter is ultimately a structure charged with the task of investing, organizing, and diverting the constitutive drives of contemporary human life. As for war, which is tasked with conquering fear, it is neither local, national, nor regional. Its surface is global and its privileged theater of action is everyday life itself. Because the security state presupposes that a "cessation of hostilities" between ourselves and those who threaten our way of life is impossible — and thus also the existence of an irreducible enemy that ceaselessly metamorphoses — this war is henceforth permanent. Responding to threats — whether internal or coming from the outside and then relayed into the domestic sphere — today requires that a set of extramilitary operations as well as enormous psychic resources be mobilized. Last, the security state — being explicitly animated by a mythology of freedom that at bottom stems from a metaphysics of force — is, in short, less concerned with the distributions of places and remuneration than by the project to control human life in general, whether it is a case of its subjects or of those designated as enemies.

This release of psychogenetic energy manifests through a surfeit of attachment to what was once called illusion. In its classic conception, illusion stood opposed to reality. Mistaking effects for causes, illusion enshrines the triumph of images and the world of appearances, reflections, and simulacra. It participates in a world of fiction, in contrast with the real world that arises from the inmost fabric of things and of life. The *demand of an originary surplus*, necessary for everyday life, has not only accelerated — it has become irrepressible. This imaginary surplus is not perceived as the complement to an existence that would be more "real" because supposedly more in keeping with Being and its essence. For many, it is instead experienced as the motor of the real, the very condition of its plenitude and splendor. Once administered by religions of salvation, the production of this surplus is today increasingly delegated to capital and to all kinds of objects and technologies.

The domain of objects and machines, as much as capital itself, is increasingly presented in the guise of an animistic religion. Everything is put into question up to and including the status of truth. Certainties and convictions are held to be the truth. Reason needs not to be employed. Simply believing and surrendering oneself is enough. As a result, public deliberation, which is one of democracy's essential features, no longer consists in discussing and seeking collectively, before the eyes of all citizens, the truth and, ultimately, justice. The great opposition no longer being that between truth and falsity, the worst thing is henceforth doubt. For, in the concrete struggle opposing us to our enemies, doubt hinders the total freeing of the voluntarist, emotional, and vital energies necessary for the use of violence and, if necessary, for shedding blood.

The reserves of credulity have similarly accrued. Paradoxically, this accrual has gone hand in hand with an exponential acceleration of technological development and industrial innovation, the unremitting digitalization of facts and things, and the relative generalizing of what might be called *electronic life and its double* or *robotically adjusted life*.[26] A new and unprecedented phase in the history of humanity has effectively begun, in which it will become increasingly difficult, if not impossible, to distinguish human organisms from electronic flows, the life of humans from that of processors. This phase is made possible by accumulated know-how concerning the storage of enormous data flows, by the extreme power and speed of their processing, and by advances in algorithmic computation. The terminal point of this digital-cognitive turn could well be a widespread infiltration of microchips into biological tissues. Already under way, this humanomachinic coupling has not only led to the genesis of new mythologies of the technical object. It has also had the immediate consequence of calling into question the very status of the modern subject stemming from the humanist tradition.

The other decisive factor in this process of release is a lifting of drive inhibitions (a return of the excluded part, of the structures embracing the repressed element) and a multiplication of enhanced pleasures resulting from this lifting and from the fact that moral consciousness is ousted, when it is not simply decommissioned. What sorts of pleasure gains might be possible today for those lacking in inhibition and whose moral consciences are decommissioned? What might explain the contemporary attraction exerted on the multitude by the idea of absolute and irresponsible power? What of the mood for the most extreme actions, the receptiveness to the simplest and most flawed arguments? And what of the swiftness with which many fall into line with others, and with which world powers engage in all sorts of infamy owing simply to a consciousness of their own strength?

Answering these questions demands that we say something about the fundamental mechanisms of the life of passions under present conditions.[27] Almost complete interconnectedness, by means of new technologies, has not only given rise to new strategies in the formation of masses. Today, creating a mass is nearly the same as creating a horde. In truth, this era is not one of masses but one of virtual hordes. Insofar as the mass survives, however, it is still only "excited by immoderate stimuli."[28] As Freud argues, the mass "respects strength and is only moderately influenced by the good, which it sees simply as a kind of weakness. What it expects in its heroes is brawn, even a tendency to violence. It wants to be dominated and suppressed and to fear its master."[29]

Almost everywhere, then, the traditional field of antagonisms has exploded. Inside national borders, new forms of association and social struggles have emerged. These are driven less by class belonging than by kinship—and thus blood—relations. Superposing itself on the old friend and enemy distinction is now the conflict between kin and nonkin, namely between those linked through blood or origin and those considered to belong to a different blood, culture, or religion. Having come from elsewhere, these different people, with whom we can have almost nothing in common, could never be considered our fellow citizens.

While they live among us, they are not genuinely one of us, and so must be rejected, put back in their place, or simply deported, under the aegis of a new security state that has come to dominate our lives. Domestic pacification, what might be termed a molecular or "silent" civil war, mass incarcerations, the decoupling of nationality from citizenship, extrajudicial executions sanctioned by new legal and criminal powers — all these factors contribute to blurring the old distinction between internal and external security, against an intensification of racist affects.

Nanoracism

At first sight, the cause, it might be said, is understood. Our epoch seems finally to have discovered its truth. All it lacked was the courage to declare it.[30] Having reconciled itself to its true face, it can finally allow itself to wander naked, free of all inhibition, rid of all the old masks and obligatory disguises that had once served as its fig leaves. The great repression (in supposing that it never really took place) is therefore followed by a great release. But at what price, for whom, and for how long?

Indeed, in the salt marshes of this beginning of this century, there is strictly nothing left to hide. The barrel now scraped, all taboos have been broken, after an attempt to kill off secrecy and the forbidden as such, all is brought to its transparency and therefore also called to its ultimate realization. The tank is almost full and twilight cannot be delayed. Whether or not this denouement takes place in a deluge of fire, we really will find out soon enough.

In the meantime, the tide does not stop rising. Racism — in Europe, South Africa, Brazil, the United States, the Caribbean, and the rest of the world — will remain with us for the foreseeable future.[31] It will continue to proliferate not only as a part of mass culture but also (we would do well not to forget it) within polite society; not only in the old settler colonies but also in other areas of the globe, long deserted by Jews, and where neither Negroes nor Arabs have ever been seen.

In any case, one had better get used to it: yesterday we entertained ourselves with games, circuses, plots, conspiracies, and gossip. As Europe (and also elsewhere) begins to turn into a sort of boring ice floe, we will now entertain ourselves with nanoracism, that sort of narcotherapy that somewhat resembles an owlet, diminished but with a powerful beak that is hooked and pointed — the bromide par excellence of times of numbness and flaccid paralysis; when all has lost its elasticity, it now appears as if to suddenly contract. Contracture and tetany—that is what we really ought to be talking about, with their lot of cramps, spasms, and narrowing of the spirit—are that out of which nanoracism has come.

Yet, in the end, what is nanoracism, if not that narcotic brand of prejudice based on skin color that gets expressed in seemingly anodyne everyday gestures, often apropos of nothing, apparently unconscious remarks, a little banter, some allusion or insinuation, a slip of the tongue, a joke, an innuendo, but also, it must be added, consciously spiteful remarks, like a malicious intention, a deliberate stamping underfoot or tackle, a dark desire to stigmatize and, in particular, to inflict violence, to injure and humiliate, to sully those not considered to be one of us?

Of course, even in an era of shameless nanoracism—when everything comes down to "us versus them," whether expressed in upper or lower case doesn't matter—no one wants to hear about it anymore. They should stay home, we hear it said. Or if *they* really persist in wanting to live next to *us*, in *our* home, they should have their pants down, rears out in the open. Nanoracism defines an era of scullion racism, a sort of pocketknife racism, a spectacle of pigs wallowing in the mud pit.

Its function is to turn each of us into billy-goat leather mercenaries. It consists in placing the greatest number of those that we regard as undesirable in intolerable conditions, to surround them daily, to inflict upon them, repeatedly, an incalculable number of racist jabs and injuries, to strip them of all their acquired rights, to smoke them out of their hives and dishonor them until they are left with no choice but to self-deport. And, speaking of racist injuries, it should be remembered that these lesions and cuts are endured by human subjects who have suffered one blow or many blows of a specific character: they are painful and hard to forget because they attack the body and its materiality, but also, above all, they attack the intangible (dignity, self-esteem). Their traces are mostly invisible and their scars difficult to heal.

Speaking also of lesions (*lésions*) and cuts, it is now clear that on this European ice floe of a continent—as well as in America, South Africa, Brazil, the Caribbean, and elsewhere—those who suffer daily racist injuries must today be counted in the hundreds of thousands. They constantly run the risk of letting themselves be cut to the quick by someone, by an institution, a voice, or a public or private authority, that asks them to justify who they are, why they are here, where they have come from, where they are going, why they do not go back to where they came from, that is, a voice or authority that deliberately seeks to occasion in them a large or small jolt, to irritate them, to upset them, to insult them, to get them to lose their cool precisely so as to have a pretext to violate them, to unceremoniously undermine that which is most private, most intimate, and vulnerable in them.

With regard to this serial violation, it should be added that nanoracism is not the prerogative of small-minded "whites," that subaltern group of individuals tormented with resentment and rancor, who deeply hate their own condition but who would nonetheless never commit suicide, and whose ultimate nightmare is to wake up one day in the garb of a Negro or with the swarthy skin of an Arab, and not as before, far away in some colony, but—to cap it all—right here at home in their own country.

Nanoracism has become the obligatory complement to hydraulic racism—that of juridicobureaucratic and institutional micro- and macro-measures, of the state machine, one that recklessly shuffles clandestine workers and illegals around, that continues to camp the rabble at the urban outskirts like a jumble of odd objects, that multiplies the number of un-documented workers by the shovelful, that presides over their removal from the territory and electrocution at the borders, when it does not simply turn to account shipwrecks on the high seas; a state that carries out racial profiling in buses, airport terminals, underground trains, streets, that *unveils* Muslim women and strives to keep its own women on file, that multi-plies its immigration and other detention centers, that invests extrava-gantly in deportation techniques; a state that discriminates and performs segregation in broad daylight while swearing to the neutrality and impar-tiality of the secular republican state—"indifferent to difference"—and still talks nonsense about that open-air putrefaction that no longer stiffens its phallus but that, against all good sense, one persists in calling "the rights of man and the citizen."

Nanoracism, in its banality and capacity to infiltrate into the pores and veins of society, is racism turned culture and into the air one breathes, at a time of the generalized idiotizing, machinic decerebration and bewitch-ment of the masses. The great visceral fear is of a Saturnalia of sorts, of the moment when today's *jinns*, which could easily be mistaken for those of the past, that scattering of satyr droppings, namely Negroes, Arabs, Mus-lims—and, because they are never far away, Jews—take the place of their masters and transform the nation into an immense dump, Muhammad's dump.

Now the distance that separates the phobia of the dump from the camp has always been very short. Refugee camps, camps for the displaced, migrant camps, camps for foreigners, waiting areas for people pending status, transit zones, administrative detention centers, identification or expulsion centers, border crossings, temporary welcome centers, ones for asylum seekers, refugee towns, migrant integration towns, ghettos, jungles, hostels, migrant homes—the list goes on ever further, as Michel Agier observed in a recent study. This endless list does not stop referring to an ever-present reality, though often largely invisible, not to say all-too-familiar and in the end banal. The camp, it ought to be said, has not only become a structural feature of our globalized condition. It has ceased to scandalize. Better still, the camp is not just our present. It is our future: our solution for "keeping away what disturbs, for containing or rejecting all excess, whether it is human, organic matter or industrial waste."[32] In short, it is a form of government of the world.

Now, unable to face the basic fact that what once pertained to the exception is now the norm (that liberal democracies are also capable of exuding criminality within their system), we find ourselves thrown into an interminable traffic of words and gestures, symbols and language, kicks and bucks delivered with increasing brutality. Of mimetological blows, too: secularism and its inverted mirror image, fundamentalism, the whole in perfect cynicism, for precisely all the surnames have lost their first names, as it were, and there are no more names to name the scandal, no language left in which to speak of that which is heinous, for practically nothing holds good any longer, bar the purulent and viscous snot that flows from the nostrils as the need to sneeze leaves us. All over, we hear the appeal to good sense, to the good old republic with its rounded and decrepit back, the appeal to good old smart-ass humanism, to a certain rotten feminism—calls for which equality henceforth rhymes with the duty-to-make-the-veiled-Muslim-girl-wear-a-thong-and-shave-the-bearded-man.[33]

Just as in the colonial era, the disparaging interpretation of how Negroes and Muslim Arabs treat "their women" engages in a mix of voyeurism and envy—envy of the harem. The manipulation of questions of gender for racist ends, by way of illustrating the Other's masculine domination, is almost always aimed at concealing the reality of phallocracy at home. The overinvestment in virility as a symbolic and political resource is not specific to the "new barbarians." It is the northern divide of all forms of power; it is that which gives it its speed, including in our democracies. In some sense, power is everywhere and always a mode of confrontation with the statue (*la statue*), while investment in femininity and maternity serves to channel sexual enjoyment into a politics of rapture, whether secular or not. For that matter, to be taken even remotely seriously, it is important at some point to show that "one has balls." In this hedonist culture the father is still granted the role of first planter. Haunted as this culture is by the figure of the incestuous father who is possessed by a desire to have sex with his own virgin daughter or son, the annexing of the woman's body to one's own as a complement to man's defective statue has become utterly banal. All these scorched and atrophied mythologies must thus be forgotten, and we must certainly move on to something else, but to what exactly?

Despite all the horrors of the Negro slave trade, colonialism, fascism, Nazism, the Holocaust, and other massacres and genocides, Western nations especially—their bowels bloated with all sorts of gases—continue to mobilize racism in aid of all manner of more or less harebrained and murderous histories. Histories about foreigners and about hordes of migrants in whose faces our doors must be slammed shut; about the barbed wire that we must hastily erect lest we get swamped by a tide of savages; about the borders that must be reestablished as if they had never disappeared; about nationals, including those from very old colonies, who still need to be labeled as immigrants; about intruders that must be driven out; about enemies that must be eradicated; about terrorists who have it in for us because of our way of life and who must be targeted from high altitude by drones; about human shields transformed into the collateral damage of our bombardments; histories about blood, throat-slitting, soil, fatherland, traditions, identity, pseudo-civilizations besieged by barbarous hordes, about national security, and all kinds of epithet-dissonant histories; histories to induce fear in oneself and to turn everything as black as soot, endless histories that are continuously recycled in the hope of pulling the wool over the eyes of the most gullible.

It is true that, having fomented misery and death far away—far from the gaze of their own citizens—Western nations now dread the return of the law of the sword, its arrival in one of those pious acts of vengeance demanded by the law of the talion. In order to protect themselves from these vengeful drives, they employ racism like a hooked blade, the poisonous addition to a beggar's nationalism, that is, one reduced to its last rags in an hour when the real centers of decision-making are denationalized, wealth is offshored, powers and mass debt are enclaved, and whole territories are zoned, while entire populations suddenly become superfluous.

But if racism has become so insidious, it is also because it has now become a part of the constitutive drives and economic subjectivity of our times. It has not only become a product to be consumed just like other goods, objects, and commodities. In this era of salaciousness, without this resource the "society of the spectacle" described by Guy Debord simply no longer exists. In many cases it has acquired an almost sumptuary status. One allows oneself some racism not because it is something unusual but by way of reply to neoliberalism's general call to lubricity. *Out* with the general strike. *In* with brutality and sex. In this era, which is so dominated by a passion for profit, this mix of lubricity, brutality, and sexuality fosters the "society of the spectacle's" assimilating of racism and its molecularizing through structures of contemporary consumption.

Racism is practiced without one's being conscious of it. Then one expresses one's amazement when someone else draws attention to it or takes one to task. It feeds our hunger for entertainment and allows us to escape the ambient boredom and monotony. We pretend to profess that the acts are harmless and do not have the meaning attributed to them. We take offence when the police of another order deprives us of our right to laugh, of the right to humor, one that is never directed against ourselves (self-derision) or against the powerful (satire in particular) but always against those weaker than ourselves—the right to laugh at the expense of those we are out to stigmatize. A kind of merry and frenzied nanoracism that is utterly moronic, that takes pleasure in wallowing in ignorance and that claims a right to stupidity and to the violence that it institutes—herein lies the spirit of our times.

We should fear that the switchover may have already happened. That it is not already too late. And that, at bottom, the dream of a decent society is no longer simply a mirage. We should fear a violent return to an era in which racism was not yet relegated to the "shameful parts" of our societies, parts that, short of eradicating, one strove to conceal. A strapping and bold brand of racism will from now on be sported, and, owing to this, hitherto muted rebellion against society will become increasingly open and vehement, at least on the part of the recluse.

The question of belonging remains unanswered. Who is from here and who is not? Those who should not be here: what are they doing in our home? How do we get rid of them? But what do "here" and "there" mean in a time in which worlds are intertwining (being networked) but also re-Balkanizing? If the desire for apartheid is indeed one of the characteristics of our times, then actual Europe, for its part, will never again be as before—that is, monocolored. In other words, never again will there be (if it was ever the case) a unique center of the world. From now on, the world will be conjugated in the plural. It will be lived in the plural, and absolutely nothing can be done to reverse this new condition, which is as irreversible as it is irrevocable. One of the consequences of this new condition is the reactivation, among many, of the fantasy of annihilation.

This fantasy is present in every context in which social forces tend to conceive the political as a struggle to the death against unconditional enemies. Such struggle is then qualified as existential. It is a struggle with no possibility of mutual recognition, and even less of reconciliation. It opposes distinct essences to one another, each possessing a quasi-impenetrable substance, or one that only those who—under the combined laws of blood and soil—are said to belong to the same species. Now political history as well as the history of thought and metaphysics in the West are saturated with this problematic. The Jews, as we know, paid the price for it at the very heart of Europe. Before that, Negroes and indigenous peoples, especially in the New World, were the first ones to embark on this bloody Way of Sorrows.

This conception of the political is the almost natural outcome of Western metaphysics' long-standing obsession with, on the one hand, the question of Being and its supposed truth and, on the other, the ontology of life. According to this myth, history is the unfolding of the essence of being. In Heideggerian terminology, "being" is opposed to "beings." Moreover, the West is held to be the decisive site of being because it alone is deemed to have developed the capacity consisting in the experience of a recommencement. All else is only beings. Only the West could have developed this capacity for recommencement, since it is allegedly the decisive site of being. That is what makes it universal, its meanings being valid unconditionally, beyond all topographical specificity, that is to say, in all places, in all times, independently of all language, all history, indeed of any condition whatsoever. Concerning the history of being and the politics of being, it can thus be argued that the West has never properly thought through its own finitude. It has always posited its own horizon of action as something inevitable and absolute, and this horizon has always wished to be, by definition, planetary and universal. The conception of the universal at issue here is not necessarily the equivalent of that which is valid for all humans as humans. Neither is it synonymous with a broadening of my own horizons or a care for the conditions of my own finitude. The universal here is the name given to the violence of the victors of wars that are, of course, conflicts of predation. These predatory conflicts are also and above all ontohistorical conflicts, since in them a history — in truth, a destiny — is played out.

Pushed to its logical conclusion, the fantasy of annihilation or destruction envisions not only the blowing up of the planet but also the disappearance of humans, their outright extinction. This is not an Apocalypse as such, if only because the Apocalypse presupposes the existence of a survivor, somewhere, of a witness whose task it is to recount what he has seen. At issue is a form of annihilation conceived not as a catastrophe to be feared but rather as purification by fire. However, purification is the same thing as the annihilation of current humanity. This annihilation is supposed to open the way to another beginning, the beginning of another history without today's humanity. It is, then, a fantasy of ablation.

In these anxiogenic times, the signs of a return to the themes of ontological difference are all there. Owing to the "war on terror" and in line with aerial bombardments, extrajudicial executions (preferably with the help of drones), massacres, attacks, and other forms of carnage that set the overall tone, the idea according to which the West as the only province of the world able to understand and institute the universal is reemerging. Humanity's division into native and foreign peoples is far advanced. If, with Schmitt or Heidegger, yesterday's fundamental demand was to find the enemy and bring him out in the open, today it suffices to create him so as to rise up against him, to confront him with the prospect of total annihilation and destruction. For, indeed, these are enemies with whom no communication is either possible or desirable. No understanding is possible with those who lie beyond the confines of humanity.

Can one truly come to presence in the world, inhabit the world, or cross it, on the basis of this impossibility of sharing it with others, of this unsurpassable distance? Is it enough to shoot down enemies and expel foreigners to be truly rid of them, to doom them to the eternity of that which is to be forgotten? This attitude demands that such acts of death and banishment succeed in erasing—during the enemy's life, his death, and his relegation—what, in his face, belonged to his humanity. The undertaking of disfigurement and erasure is almost a precondition for execution within the contemporary logic of hatred. Within societies that continue to multiply the measures of separation and discrimination, the relation of care toward the Other has been replaced by a relation without desire. Explaining and understanding, knowledge and recognition, are no longer essential. Never have hospitality and hostility been so directly opposed. Whence the interest in returning to those figures for whom the adversity of humans and the suffering of enemies were never mere "silent residues of policy."[34] Instead, they were always combined with a demand for recognition, notably in contexts where the experience of being unrecognized, humiliated, alienated, and mistreated was the norm.

THREE
NECROPOLITICS

The ultimate expression of sovereignty largely resides in the power and capacity to dictate who is able to live and who must die.[1] To kill or to let live thus constitutes sovereignty's limits, its principal attributes. To be sovereign is to exert one's control over mortality and to define life as the deployment and manifestation of power.

This sums up what Michel Foucault meant by *biopower*: that domain of life over which power has asserted its control.[2] But under what practical conditions is the power to kill, to let live, or to expose to death exercised? Who is the subject of this right? What does the implementation of such a right tell us about the one who is thus put to death and about the relation of enmity that sets such a person against his murderer? Can the notion of biopower account for the contemporary ways in which the political takes as its primary and absolute objective the enemy's murder, doing so under the guise of war, resistance, or the war on terror? War is, after all, a means of achieving sovereignty as much as a way of exercising the right to kill. When politics is considered a form of war, the question needs to be asked about the place that is given to life, death, and the human body (in particular when it is wounded or slain). How are these aspects inscribed in the order of power?

The Work of Death

To answer these questions, this essay draws on the concept of biopower and explores this concept's relation to the notions of sovereignty (*imperium*) and the state of exception.[3] I would like to examine briefly a number of empirical and philosophical questions that arise in this context. As is well known, the concept of the state of exception has been often discussed in relation to Nazism, totalitarianism, and the concentration/extermination camps. Various interpretations of the death camps in particular have taken them as the central metaphor for sovereign and destructive violence and as the ultimate sign of the absolute power of the negative. As Hannah Arendt puts it, "There are no parallels to the life in the concentration camps. Its horror can never be fully embraced by the imagination for the very reason that it stands outside of life and death."[4] Because its inhabitants have been divested of political status and reduced to bare life, the camp is, for Giorgio Agamben, "the place in which the most absolute *conditio inhumana* ever to appear on Earth was realized."[5] He adds that, in the political-juridical structure of the camp the state of exception ceases to be a temporal suspension of the state of law, acquiring a permanent spatial arrangement that remains continually outside the law's normal state.

This essay does not aim to debate the singularity of the extermination of the Jews or to hold it up by way of example.[6] I set out from the idea that modernity is at the origin of multiple concepts of sovereignty, and thus also of the biopolitical. Disregarding this multiplicity, late modern political criticism has unfortunately privileged normative theories of democracy and made the concept of reason into one of the most important elements of both the project of modernity and the topos of sovereignty.[7] From this perspective, the ultimate expression of sovereignty is the production of general norms by a body (the demos) comprising free and equal individuals. These individuals are posited as full subjects capable of self-understanding, self-consciousness, and self-representation. Politics, therefore, is doubly defined as a project of autonomy and as the reaching of agreement within a collective through communication and recognition. This, we are told, is what differentiates it from war.[8]

In other words, on the basis of a distinction between reason and unreason (passion, fantasy), late modern criticism has been able to articulate a certain idea of the political, the community, the subject — or, more fundamentally, of the good life, how to achieve it, and how to become, in the process, a fully moral agent. Within this paradigm, reason is the truth of the subject, and politics is the exercise of reason in the public sphere. The exercise of reason amounts to the exercise of freedom, a key element for individual autonomy. The romance of sovereignty, in this case, rests on the belief that the subject is both master and controlling author of his own meaning. Sovereignty is therefore defined as a twofold process of *self-institution* and *self-limitation* (fixing one's own limits for oneself). Exercising sovereignty, in turn, is about society's capacity for self-creation with recourse to institutions inspired by specific social and imaginary significations.[9]

Several critiques have already been addressed to this strongly normative reading of the politics of sovereignty, so I will not rehearse them here.[10] My concern is those figures of sovereignty whose central project is not the struggle for autonomy but *the generalized instrumentalization of human existence and the material destruction of human bodies and populations*. Such figures of sovereignty are far from a piece of prodigious insanity or the expression of a rupture between the impulses and interests of the body and those of the mind. Indeed, like the death camps, these figures constitute the *nomos* of the political space in which we continue to live. Furthermore, contemporary experiences of human destruction suggest that a reading of politics, sovereignty, and the subject may be developed that differs from the one bequeathed us by the philosophical discourse on modernity. Instead of considering reason as the subject's truth, we can look to other foundational categories that are less abstract and more tangible, such as life and death.

Hegel's discussion of the relation between death and "becoming subject" is significant here. His account of death centers on a twofold concept of negativity. First, the human negates nature (a negation that is exteriorized in the human's effort to reduce nature to human needs); second, the negated element is transformed through work and struggle. By transforming nature, the human being creates a world, but in the process, this human being is also exposed to his own negativity. In the Hegelian paradigm, human death is essentially voluntary. It is the result of the subject's consciously assuming risks. According to Hegel, through these risks the "animal" that constitutes the human subject's natural being is defeated.

In other words, the human being thus truly *becomes a subject*—that is, separated from the animal—in the struggle and work through which death (understood as the violence of negativity) is confronted. Through this confrontation with death, the human being is cast into the incessant movement of history. Becoming a subject therefore supposes upholding the work of death. To uphold the work of death, such is precisely how Hegel defines the life of Spirit. The life of Spirit, he says, is not the life that is frightened of death and spares itself destruction, but the life that assumes death and lives with it. Spirit attains its truth only by finding itself in absolute dismemberment.[11] Politics is therefore a death that lives a human life. Such, too, is the definition of absolute knowledge and sovereignty: risking one's life as a whole.

Georges Bataille also offers critical insights into how death structures the concepts of sovereignty, the political, and the subject. Bataille displaces Hegel's conception of the linkages between death, sovereignty, and the subject in at least three ways. First, he interprets death and sovereignty as the paroxysm of exchange and superabundance—or, to use his own terminology: *excess*. For Bataille, life is defective only when death has taken it hostage. Life itself exists only in bursts and in exchange with death.[12] He argues that death is the putrefaction of life, the stench that is at once life's source and repulsive condition. So, although it destroys what was to be, obliterates what was supposed to continue being, and reduces to nothing the individual who takes it, death does not amount to the pure annihilation of being. Rather, it is essentially self-consciousness; moreover, it is the most luxurious form of life, that is, of effusion and exuberance: a power of proliferation. Even more radically, Bataille subtracts death from the horizon of meaning. In Hegel, by contrast, nothing is definitively lost in death; indeed, death for him holds great signification as a means to truth.

Second, Bataille firmly anchors death in the realm of *absolute expenditure* (the other characteristic of sovereignty), whereas Hegel tries to keep death within the economy of absolute knowledge and meaning. Life beyond utility, Bataille says, is the domain of sovereignty. This being the case, death is therefore the point at which destruction, suppression, and sacrifice constitute so irreversible and radical an expenditure—an expenditure without reserve—that they can no longer be determined as negativity. Death is therefore the very principle of excess—an *anti-economy*. Hence the metaphor of luxury and *the luxurious character of death*.

Third, Bataille establishes a correlation among death, sovereignty, and sexuality. Sexuality, for him, is inextricably linked to violence and to the dissolution of the body's and the Self's boundaries by way of orgiastic and excremental impulses. As such, sexuality concerns two major forms of polarized human impulses—excretion and appropriation—as well as the regime of the taboos surrounding them.[13] The truth of sex, and its deadly attributes, resides in the experience of loss of the boundaries separating reality, events, and fantasized objects.

For Bataille, then, sovereignty takes many forms. But it ultimately takes that of a refusal to accept the limits that the fear of death would have the subject respect. The sovereign world, Bataille argues, "is the world in which the limit of death is done away with. Death is present in it, its presence defines that world of violence, but while death is present it is always there only to be negated, never for anything but that. The sovereign," he concludes, "is he who is, as if death were not. . . . He has no more regard for the limits of identity than he does for limits of death, or rather these limits are the same; he is the transgression of all such limits." Since the natural domain of prohibitions includes death, among others (e.g., sexuality, filth, and excrement), sovereignty requires "the strength to violate the prohibition against killing, although it's true this will be under the conditions that customs define." And contrary to the subordination ever rooted in necessity and the alleged need to avoid death, sovereignty definitely calls for the risk of death.[14]

By conceiving sovereignty as a violating of prohibitions, Bataille reopens the question of the limits of the political. The political, in this case, is not the forward dialectical movement of reason. It can be traced only as a spiral transgression, as that difference that disorients the very idea of the limit. More specifically, it is the difference put into play by the violation of a taboo.[15]

The Relation of Enmity

After this presentation of politics as the work of death, I now turn to sovereignty, defined as the right to kill. For the purposes of my demonstration, I relate Foucault's notion of biopower to two other concepts: the state of exception and the state of siege.[16] I examine the trajectories by which the state of exception and the relation of enmity have become the normative basis of the right to kill. In such instances, power (which is not necessarily state power) continuously refers and appeals to the exception, emergency, and a fictionalized notion of the enemy. It also labors to produce these same exceptions, emergencies, and fictionalized enemies. Thus the question becomes: What is the relationship between politics and death in those systems that operate only through a state of emergency?

Biopower, in Foucault's work, appears to function by dividing people into those who must live and those who must die. As it proceeds on the basis of a split between the living and the dead, such power defines itself in relation to the biological field — of which it takes control and in which it invests itself. This control presupposes a distribution of human species into groups, a subdivision of the population into subgroups, and the establishment of a biological caesura between these subgroups. Foucault refers to this using the seemingly familiar term "racism."[17]

That *race* (or indeed *racism*) figures so prominently in the calculus of biopower is easy to understand. After all, racial thinking more than class thinking (where class is an operator defining history as an economic struggle between classes) has been the ever-present shadow hovering over Western political thought and practice, especially when the point was to contrive the inhumanity of foreign peoples and the sort of domination to be exercised over them. Referring to both this ever-presence and the phantom-like world of race in general, Arendt locates their roots in the shattering experience of otherness. She suggests that the politics of race is ultimately linked to a politics of death.[18] Indeed, in Foucault's terms, racism is above all a technology aimed at permitting the exercise of bio-power, "that old sovereign right to kill." In the economy of biopower, the function of racism is to regulate the distribution of death and to make possible the state's murderous functions. It is, he says, "the condition for the acceptability of putting to death."[19]

Foucault clearly posits that the sovereign right of the sword and the mechanisms of biopower are part of the functioning of all modern states;[20] indeed, they can be seen as constitutive elements of state power in modernity. According to him, the Nazi state was the most complete example of a state exercising the right to kill. This state, he claims, made the management, protection, and cultivation of life coextensive with the sovereign right to kill. He argues that, through a biological extrapolation of the theme of the political enemy, the Nazi state's organizing of war against its adversaries and simultaneous exposing of its own citizens to war opened the way for a formidable consolidation of the right to kill, culminating in the project of the "final solution." In doing so, it became the archetype of a formation of power combining the characteristics of the racist state, the murderous state, and the suicidal state.

It has been argued that the Nazi state is unique in its conflation of war and politics (and racism, homicide, and suicide), to the point of rendering them indistinguishable from one another. The perception of the existence of the Other as an attempt on my life, as a mortal threat or absolute danger whose biophysical elimination would strengthen my life potential and security—this is, I maintain, one of the many imaginary dimensions characteristic of sovereignty in both early and late modernity. Recognition of this perception to a large extent underpins most traditional critiques of modernity, whether they are dealing with nihilism and its proclamation of the will for power as the essence of the being, with reification understood as the *becoming-object* of the human being, or the subordination of everything to impersonal logic and to the reign of calculability and instrumental rationality.[21] Indeed, from an anthropological perspective, what these critiques implicitly contest is a definition of politics as the warlike relation par excellence. They also challenge the idea that the calculus of life perforce passes through the death of the Other, or that sovereignty consists of the will and the capacity to kill so as to live.

Taking a historical perspective, many analysts have argued that, on the one hand, the material premises of the Nazi extermination are also found in colonial imperialism and, on the other, in the serialization of technical mechanisms for putting people to death—mechanisms developed between the Industrial Revolution and the First World War. According to Enzo Traverso, the gas chambers and ovens were the culmination of a long process of dehumanizing and industrializing death, one of the original features of which was to integrate instrumental rationality with the productive and administrative rationality of the modern Western world (the factory, the bureaucracy, the prison, the army). After mechanization, serialized execution was transformed into a purely technical, impersonal, silent, and rapid procedure. In part, this development was aided by racist stereotypes and the flourishing of a class-based racism that, by translating the social conflicts of the industrial world in racial terms, ended up comparing the working classes and "stateless people" of the industrial world to the "savages" of the colonial world.[22]

In reality, the links between modernity and terror spring from multiple sources. Some are to be found in the political practices of the ancien régime. From this perspective, the tension between the public's passion for blood and notions of justice and revenge is critical. In *Discipline and Punish*, Foucault describes how, much to the crowd's satisfaction, the execution of the would-be regicide Damiens lasted for hours.[23] The long procession of the condemned through the streets prior to execution, the parade of body parts — a ritual that became a standard feature of popular violence — and the display of a severed head mounted on a pike. In France, the advent of the guillotine marks a new phase in the "democratization" of the means of disposing of the enemies of state. Indeed, this form of execution that had once been the prerogative of the nobility is extended to all citizens. In a context in which decapitation is viewed as less demeaning than hanging, innovations in the technologies of murder aimed not only at "civilizing" the ways of killing. They also aimed at disposing of a large number of victims in a relatively short span of time. At the same time, a new cultural sensibility emerges in which killing the enemy of the state is an extension of play. More intimate, lurid, and leisurely forms of cruelty begin to take shape.

But nowhere is the conflation of reason and terror so manifest as during the French Revolution.[24] During the French Revolution, terror is construed as an almost necessary part of politics. An absolute transparency is claimed to exist between the state and the people. As a political category, "the people" is gradually displaced from concrete reality to rhetorical figure. As David Bates has shown, the theorists of terror believed it possible to distinguish between authentic expressions of sovereignty and the actions of the enemy. They also believed it possible to distinguish, in the political sphere, between the citizen's "error" and the counterrevolutionary's "crime." Terror thus became a way of marking aberration in the body politic, and politics came to be read both as the mobile force of reason and as an errant attempt to create a space where "error" would only be reduced and the truth enhanced and the enemy dispatched.[25]

Finally, terror is not linked solely to the utopian belief in the unfettered power of human reason. It is also clearly related to various narratives of mastery and emancipation, most of which are underpinned by Enlightenment understandings of truth and error, the "real" and the symbolic. Marx, for example, conflates labor (the endless cycle of production and consumption required to maintain human life) with work (the creation of lasting artifacts that add to the world of things). Labor is viewed as the vehicle for humankind's historical self-creation.

The historical self-creation is itself a life-and-death conflict over what paths might lead to the truth of history: overcoming capitalism and the commodity form, and the contradictions associated with each of them. According to Marx, with the advent of communism and the abolition of exchange relations, things will appear as they really are; the "real" will present itself as it actually is, and the distinction between subject and object, or being and consciousness, will be transcended.[26] But by making human emancipation dependent upon the abolition of commodity production, Marx blurs the all-important divisions between the human-made realm of freedom, the nature-determined realm of necessity, and the contingent in history.

The commitment to the abolition of commodity production and the dream of direct and unmediated access to the "real" make these processes—the fulfillment of the so-called logic of history and the fabrication of humankind—almost necessarily violent processes. As Stephen Louw has shown, the central tenets of classical Marxism leave no choice but to "try to introduce communism by administrative fiat, which, in practice, means that social relations must be decommodified forcefully."[27] Historically, these attempts have taken such forms as labor militarization, the collapse of the distinction between state and society, and revolutionary terror.[28] It may be argued that they have aimed at eradicating the basic human condition of plurality. Indeed, the overcoming of class divisions, the withering away of the state, the flowering of a truly general will—all presuppose a view of human plurality as the chief obstacle to the eventual realization of a predetermined telos of history. In other words, the subject of Marxian modernity is, fundamentally, a subject who is intent on proving his or her sovereignty by staging a fight to the death. Similar to Hegel, the narrative of mastery and emancipation here is clearly linked to a narrative of truth and death. Terror and killing become the means of realizing the already known telos of history.

Any historical account of the rise of modern terror needs to address slavery, which could be considered one of the first instances of biopolitical experimentation. In many respects, the very structure of the plantation system and its consequences express the emblematic and paradoxical figure of the state of exception.[29] This figure is paradoxical here for two reasons. First, in the context of the plantation, the slave's humanity appears as the perfect figure of a shadow. Indeed, the slave condition results from a triple loss: loss of a "home," loss of rights over one's body, and loss of political status. This triple loss is identical with absolute domination, natal alienation, and social death (expulsion from humanity altogether). To be sure, as a political-juridical structure, the plantation is a space where the slave belongs to a master. It is not a community if only because a community, by definition, implies the exercise of the power of speech and thought. As Paul Gilroy says, "The extreme patterns of communication defined by the institution of plantation slavery dictate that we recognize the anti-discursive and extralinguistic ramifications of power at work in shaping communicative acts. There may, after all, be no reciprocity on the plantation outside of the possibilities of rebellion and suicide, flight and silent mourning, and there is certainly no grammatical unity of speech to mediate communicative reason. In many respects, the plantation inhabitants live non-synchronously."[30] As an instrument of labor, the slave has a price. As a property, the slave has a value. The slave's labor is needed and used, so he is therefore kept alive, but in a *state of injury*, in a phantom-like world of horrors and intense cruelty and profanity. The violent tenor of the slave's life is manifested through the overseer's disposition to behave in a cruel and intemperate manner, as well as in the spectacle of pain inflicted on the slave's body.[31] Violence, here, becomes an element in manners, like whipping, or taking the slave's life itself: an act of caprice and pure destruction aimed at instilling terror.[32] Slave life, in many ways, is a form of death-in-life. As Susan Buck-Morss has suggested, the slave condition produces a contradiction between the freedom of property and freedom of the person. An unequal relationship is established along with the inequality of the power over life. This power over the life of another takes the form of commerce: a person's humanity is dissolved to the point that the slave's life can be said to be possessed by the master.[33] Because the slave's life is like a "thing," possessed by another person, slave existence appears as the perfect figure of a shadow.

In spite of this terror and symbolic sealing off, the slave maintains alternative perspectives toward time, work, and self. This is the second paradoxical element of the plantation world as a manifestation of the state of exception. The slave, treated as no longer existing except as a mere tool and instrument of production, is nevertheless able to introduce almost any object, instrument, language, or gesture into a performance, and then stylize it. Breaking with uprootedness and the pure world of things of which he is a mere fragment, the slave is able to demonstrate the protean capabilities of the human bond through music and the body itself that was supposedly possessed by another.[34]

If, in the plantation system, the relations between life and death, the politics of cruelty and the symbolism of profanity, get blurred, what comes into being in the colony and under apartheid is a peculiar formation of terror, to which I now turn.[35] The most original feature of this terror formation is its concatenation of biopower, the state of exception, and the state of siege. Race is, once again, crucial to this concatenation.[36] In most instances, racial selection, prohibiting mixed marriages, forced sterilization, and indeed exterminating vanquished peoples found their first testing ground in the colonial world. The first syntheses arise here between massacre and bureaucracy—that incarnation of Western rationality.[37] Arendt develops the thesis that there is a link between national socialism and traditional imperialism. According to her, the colonial conquest revealed a hitherto unseen potential for violence. World War II shapes up as an extension of methods previously reserved for the "savages" to the "civilized" peoples of Europe.

That the technologies which produced Nazism originated in the plantation or in the colony, or that—Foucault's thesis—Nazism and Stalinism actually only amplified a series of already extant mechanisms of Western European social and political formations (subjugation of the body, health regulations, social Darwinism, eugenics, medicolegal theories on heredity, degeneration, and race) is, in the end, irrelevant. Yet one fact remains: in modern philosophical thought and in the imaginary and practice of European politics, the colony represents a site in which sovereignty fundamentally consists in exercising a power outside the law (*ab legibus solutus*) and in which "peace" is more likely to assume the face of "endless war."

Indeed, this view is in keeping with the definition of sovereignty that Carl Schmitt forged at the beginning of the twentieth century, one that sees it as the power to decide on the state of exception. To assess properly the colony's efficacy as a formation of terror, we need to take a detour through the European imaginary itself as it relates to the critical issue of the domestication of war and the creation of a European juridical order (*Jus publicum Europaeum*). Two key principles lay at the basis of this order. The first postulates the juridical equality of all states, an equality that was notably applied to *the right to wage war* (the taking of life). The right to wage war meant two things. On the one hand, that killing or concluding peace was recognized as one of the preeminent functions of any state. This function went hand in hand with the recognition that no state could make claims to rule outside of its borders. But conversely, the state could recognize no authority above it within its own borders. On the other hand, the state, for its part, undertook to "civilize" the ways of killing and to attribute rational objectives to the very act of killing.

The second principle was related to the territorialization of the sovereign state, that is, the determination of its borders in the context of a newly imposed global order. In this order Jus publicum rapidly assumed the form of a distinction between, on the one hand, those parts of the globe available for colonial appropriation and, on the other, Europe (where the Jus publicum was to hold sway).[38] This distinction, as we will see, is crucial in terms of assessing the colony's efficacy as a structure of terror. Under Jus publicum, a legitimate war is largely a war conducted by one state against another or, more precisely, a war between "civilized" states. The state's centrality in the calculus of war derives from the state's being the model of political unity, a principle of rational organization, the embodiment of the idea of the universal, and a moral sign.

In the same context, colonies are similar to frontiers. Inhabited by "savages," colonies are not organized as a state form and do not create a human world. Their armies do not form a distinct entity, and their wars are not wars between regular armies. They do not imply the mobilization of sovereign subjects (citizens) who respect each other as enemies. They do not establish a distinction between combatants and noncombatants, or again between an "enemy" and a "criminal."[39] Concluding peace with them is thus impossible. In sum, colonies are zones in which war and disorder, internal and external figures of the political, stand side by side or alternate with each other. The colony is thus the site par excellence where controls and guarantees of judicial order can be suspended—the zone where the violence of the state of exception is deemed to operate in the service of "civilization."

That colonies could be ruled in absolute lawlessness was due to the racial denial of any common bond between the conqueror and the native. In the conqueror's eyes, *savage life* is just another form of *animal life*, a horrifying experience, something alien beyond imagination or comprehension. In fact, according to Arendt, what makes savages different from other human beings is less the color of their skin than the fear that they behave like a part of nature, that they treat nature as their undisputed master. For nature thereby remains, in all its majesty, an overwhelming reality compared to which they appear to be phantoms, unreal, and ghostlike. Savages are, as it were, "natural" human beings who lack a specifically human character, a specifically human reality, "so that when European men massacred them they somehow were not aware that they had committed murder."[40]

For all of the above reasons, the sovereign right to kill is not subject to any rule in the colonies. In the colonies, the sovereign might kill at any time or in any manner. Colonial warfare is not subject to legal and institutional rules. It is not a legally codified activity. Instead, colonial terror constantly intertwines with colonially generated fantasies of wilderness, and death and fictions, workings to create an effect of the real.[41] Peace is not necessarily the natural outcome of a colonial war. In fact, the distinction between war and peace does not hold. Colonial wars are conceived as the expression of an absolute hostility setting the conqueror against an absolute enemy.[42] All the manifestations of war and hostility that a European legal imaginary relegated to the margins find a place to reemerge in the colonies. Here, the fiction of a distinction between war's "ends" and its "means" collapses, as does the fiction according to which war is a rule-governed contest, as opposed to pure slaughter without risk or instrumental justification. It becomes futile, therefore, to attempt to resolve one of the intractable paradoxes of war that Alexandre Kojève captured so well in his reinterpretation of Hegel's *Phenomenology of the Spirit*: its simultaneous idealism and apparent inhumanity.[43]

Necropower and Occupation in Late Modernity

The ideas developed above, it might be thought, relate to a distant past. In the past, indeed, imperial wars had the objective of destroying local powers, installing troops, and instituting new models of military control over civil populations. A group of local auxiliaries could assist in the management of conquered territories annexed to the empire. Within the empire, the status given to the defeated populations enshrined their despoilment. In these configurations, violence constituted the original form of the right, and exception provided the structure of sovereignty. Each stage of imperialism also involves certain key technologies (the gunboat, quinine, steamship lines, submarine telegraph cables, colonial railroads).[44]

Colonial occupation itself consisted in seizing, delimiting, and asserting control over a geographical area—of writing a new set of social and spatial relations on the ground. The writing of new spatial relations (territorialization) ultimately amounted to the production of boundaries and hierarchies, zones and enclaves; the subversion of existing property arrangements; the differential classification of people; resource extraction; and, finally, the manufacturing of a large reservoir of cultural imaginaries. These imaginaries gave meaning to the establishing of different rights for different categories of people, rights with different goals but existing within the same space—in short, the exercise of sovereignty. Space was thus the raw material of sovereignty and of the violence it bears within it. Sovereignty meant occupation, and occupation meant relegating the colonized to a third zone between subjecthood and objecthood.

Such was the case of the apartheid regime in South Africa. Here, the *township* was the structural form and the *homelands* became the reserves (rural bases) whereby the flow of migrant labor could be regulated and African urbanization held in check.[45] As Belinda Bozzoli has shown, the township in particular was a place where "severe oppression and poverty were experienced on a racial and class basis."[46] As a sociopolitical, cultural, and economic structure, the township was a peculiar spatial institution scientifically planned for the purposes of control.[47] The functioning of the homelands and townships entailed severe restrictions for blacks on producing for markets in white areas, the terminating of landownership by blacks except in reserved areas, the illegalization of black residence on white farms (except as servants in the employ of whites), the control of urban influx, and, later, the denial of citizenship to Africans.[48]

Frantz Fanon describes the spatialization of colonial occupation in vivid terms. First and foremost, he argues, colonial occupation entails a division of space into compartments. It involves the setting of boundaries and internal frontiers epitomized by barracks and police stations; it is regulated by the language of pure force, immediate presence, and frequent and direct action; and it is premised on the principle of reciprocal exclusivity.[49] But more important, this is how necropower operates: "The town belonging to the colonized people . . . is a place of ill fame, peopled by men of evil repute. They are born there, it matters little where or how; they die there, it matters not where, nor how. It is a world without spaciousness; men live there on top of each other. The native town is a hungry town, starved of bread, of meat, of shoes, of coal, of light. The native town is a crouching village, a town on its knees."[50] In this case, sovereignty means the capacity to define who matters and who does not, who is *disposable* and who is not.

Late modern colonial occupation differs in many ways from early modern occupation, particularly in its combining of the disciplinary, the biopolitical, and the necropolitical. The most accomplished form of necropower is the contemporary colonial occupation of Palestine. Here, the colonial state derives its fundamental claim of sovereignty and legitimacy from the authority of its own particular narrative of history and identity. This narrative is itself underpinned by the idea that the state has a divine right to exist, a narrative that competes with another for the same sacred space. Because the two narratives are incompatible and the two populations are inextricably intertwined, a demarcation of the territory on the basis of pure identity is quasi-impossible. Violence and sovereignty, in this case, claim a divine foundation: peoplehood itself is forged by the worship of one deity, and national identity is imagined as an identity against an Other, against other deities.[51] History, geography, cartography, and archaeology are supposed to back these claims, thereby closely binding identity and topography. As a consequence, colonial violence and occupation are profoundly underwritten by the sacred terror of truth and exclusivity (mass expulsions, resettlement of "stateless" people in refugee camps, settlement of new colonies). Underneath the terror of the sacred there are missing bones, which are constantly being unearthed; the permanent remembrance of torn bodies, hewn in a thousand pieces and never self-same; the limits, or better, the impossibility of representing for oneself an "original crime," an unspeakable death: the terror of the Holocaust.[52]

To return to Fanon's spatial reading of colonial occupation, the late modern colonial occupation in Gaza and the West Bank presents three major characteristics concerning the working of the specific structure of terror that I have called necropower. The first involves the dynamics of territorial fragmentation—the sealing off and expansion of settlements. This process has a twofold objective: to render all movement impossible and to implement forms of separation on the model of an apartheid state. The occupied territories have thus been divided into a web of intricate internal borders and various isolated cells. According to Eyal Weizman, by departing from a planar division of territory and embracing a principle of creation of three-dimensional boundaries within a territory, dispersal and segmentation clearly redefine the relationship between sovereignty and space.[53]

These actions, for Weizman, constitute "the politics of verticality." The resultant form of sovereignty might be qualified as "vertical sovereignty." Under a regime of vertical sovereignty, colonial occupation operates through schemes of over- and underpasses, a separation of airspace from the ground. The ground itself is divided between its crust and the subsoil. Colonial occupation is also dictated by the very nature of the terrain and its topographical variations (hilltops and valleys, mountains, and bodies of water). Thus, high ground offers strategic advantages not found in the valleys (better vision and self-protection, a panoptic fortification enabling the gaze to be directed in multiple directions). As Weizman puts it, "Settlements could be seen as urban optical devices for surveillance and the exercise of power." Under the conditions of late modern colonial occupation, surveillance is oriented both inwardly and outwardly, the eye acting as weapon, and vice versa. Instead of the conclusive division between two nations across a boundary line, Weizman claims, "the organization of the West Bank's particular terrain has created multiple separations, provisional boundaries, which relate to each other through surveillance and control." Under these circumstances, colonial occupation not only amounts to control, surveillance, and separation but is also synonymous with isolation. It is a *splintering occupation* in keeping with the splintering urbanism characteristic of late modernity (suburban enclaves or gated communities).[54]

From an infrastructural point of view, a splintering form of colonial occupation is characterized by a network of fast bypass roads, bridges, and tunnels that weave over and under one another in an attempt to maintain the Fanonian "principle of reciprocal exclusivity." According to Weizman, "the bypass roads attempt to separate Israeli traffic networks from Palestinian ones, preferably without allowing them ever to cross. They therefore emphasize the overlapping of two separate geographies that inhabit the same landscape. Where the networks do cross, a makeshift separation is created. Most often, small dust roads are dug out to allow Palestinians to cross under the fast, wide highways on which Israeli vans and military vehicles rush between settlements."[55]

Under these conditions of vertical sovereignty and splintering colonial occupation, communities get separated along a y-axis. The sites of violence duly proliferate. Battlegrounds are not located solely at the Earth's surface. Underground and airspace are transformed into conflict zones as well. No continuity exists between the ground and the sky. Even the airspace boundaries are divided between lower and upper layers. Everywhere, the symbolics of the *top* (of who is on top) is reiterated. Occupation of the skies therefore acquires a critical importance, since most of the policing is done from the air. Various other technologies are mobilized to this effect: sensors aboard unmanned air vehicles, aerial reconnaissance jets, early warning Hawkeye planes, assault helicopters, an Earth-observation satellite, techniques of "hologrammatization." Killing becomes precision-targeted.

Such precision is combined with the tactics of medieval siege warfare adapted to the networked sprawl of urban refugee camps. An orchestrated and systematic sabotage of the enemy's societal and urban infrastructure network complements the appropriation of land, water, and airspace resources. Critical to these techniques of disabling the enemy is *bulldozing*: demolishing houses and cities, uprooting olive trees, riddling water tanks with bullets, bombing and jamming electronic communications, digging up roads, destroying electricity transformers, tearing up airport runways, disabling television and radio transmitters, smashing computers, ransacking cultural and politicobureaucratic symbols of the proto-Palestinian state, and looting medical equipment—in other words, *infrastructural warfare*.[56] While Apache helicopter gunships are used to police the air and kill from overhead, armored bulldozers (the Caterpillar D-9) are used on the ground as weapons of war and intimidation. In contrast to early modern colonial occupation, both weapons establish the superiority of the high-tech tools of late modern terror.[57]

As the Palestinian case illustrates, late modern colonial occupation is a concatenation of multiple powers: disciplinary, biopolitical, and necropolitical. The combination of the three grants the colonial power absolute domination over the inhabitants of the occupied territory. The *state of siege* is itself a military institution. It allows for a modality of killing that does not distinguish between the external and the internal enemy. Entire populations are the target of the sovereign. Besieged villages and towns are sealed off and isolated from the world. Daily life is militarized. Local military commanders have the discretionary freedom to decide whom to shoot and when. Movement between the territorial cells requires formal permits. Local civil institutions are systematically destroyed. The besieged population is deprived of their means of income. Invisible killing is added to outright executions.

War Machines and Heteronomy

After having examined the workings of necropower under the conditions of late modern colonial occupation, I would like now to turn to contemporary wars. Contemporary warfare belongs to a new moment and can hardly be understood through earlier theories of "contractual violence" or typologies of "just" and "unjust" wars, or even Carl von Clausewitz's instrumentalism.[58] According to Zygmunt Bauman, the wars of the globalization era do not include the conquest, acquisition, and takeover of a territory among their objectives. They are, ideally, hit-and-run affairs.

The growing gap between high-tech and low-tech means of war was never as evident as it was in the Gulf War and in the Kosovo campaign. In each case, the doctrine of "overwhelming or decisive force" was implemented to full effect, thanks to a military-technological revolution that has intensified the capacity for destruction in unprecedented ways.[59] Aerial warfare as it relates to altitude, ordnance, visibility, and intelligence is a case in point. During the Gulf War, the combined use of smart bombs and bombs coated with depleted uranium, high-tech standoff weapons, electronic sensors, laser-guided missiles, cluster and asphyxiation bombs, stealth capabilities, unmanned aerial vehicles, and cyber intelligence quickly crippled the capabilities of the enemy.

In Kosovo, the "degrading" of Serbian capabilities took the form of an infrastructural war that targeted and destroyed bridges, railroads, highways, communications networks, oil storage depots, heating plants, power stations, and water treatment facilities. As can be surmised, the execution of such a military strategy, especially when combined with the imposition of sanctions, results in shutting down the enemy's life-support system. The enduring damage to civilian life is particularly telling. For example, during the Kosovo campaign, the destruction of the Pancevo petrochemical complex on Belgrade's outskirts "left the vicinity so toxic with vinyl chloride, ammonia, mercury, naphtha and dioxin that pregnant women were directed to seek abortions, and all local women were advised to avoid pregnancy for two years."[60]

Globalization-era warfare therefore aims to force the enemy into submission regardless of the military actions' immediate consequences, side effects, or "collateral damage." In this sense, contemporary wars recall more the warfare strategy of the nomad than that of sedentary nations, or of modernity's "conquer-and-annex" wars for territory. In Bauman's words, "They rest their superiority over the settled population on the speed of their own movement; their own ability to descend from nowhere without notice and vanish again without warning, their ability to travel light and not to bother with the kind of belongings which confine the mobility and the maneuvering potential of the sedentary people."[61]

This new moment is one of global mobility. An important feature of the age of global mobility is that states no longer have the monopoly on military operations and exercising the right to kill and that the "regular army" is no longer the sole means of carrying out these functions. The claim to ultimate or final authority in a particular political space is not easily made. Instead, a patchwork of overlapping and incomplete rights to rule emerges, rights that are inextricably superimposed and entangled, wherein different de facto juridical instances are geographically interwoven and plural allegiances, asymmetrical suzerainties, and enclaves abound.[62] In this heteronymous organization of territorial rights and claims, there can be little sense in insisting on clearly demarcated boundaries between "internal" and "external" political realms.

Take Africa, where the political economy of statehood dramatically changed over the last quarter of the twentieth century. Many African states can no longer claim to hold a monopoly on violence or on the means of coercion within their territory. Nor can they claim a monopoly on territorial boundaries. Coercion itself has become a market commodity. Military manpower is bought and sold on a market in which the identity of suppliers and purchasers means almost nothing. Urban militias, private armies, armies of regional lords, private security firms, and state armies all claim the right to exercise violence or to kill. Neighboring states or rebel movements lease armies to poor states. Nonstate deployers of violence supply two critical, coercive resources: labor and minerals. Increasingly, the vast majority of armies are composed of citizen soldiers, child soldiers, mercenaries, and privateers.[63]

What are thus emerging alongside armies we might, following Deleuze and Guattari, refer to as *war machines*.[64] War machines are made up of segments of armed men that split up or merge with one another, depending on the tasks to be carried out and the circumstances involved. Polymorphous and diffuse organizations, war machines are characterized by their capacity for metamorphosis. Their relation to space is mobile. They sometimes enjoy complex links with state forms (from autonomy to incorporation). The state may, of its own doing, transform itself into a war machine. It may, moreover, appropriate for itself an existing war machine or help to create one. War machines function by borrowing from regular armies while incorporating new elements adapted to the principle of segmentation and deterritorialization. Regular armies, in turn, may readily appropriate some of the characteristics of war machines.

A war machine combines a plurality of functions. It has the features of a political organization and a mercantile company. It operates through capture and depredations and can even coin its own money. To fuel the extraction and export of natural resources located in the territories they control, war machines forge direct connections with transnational networks. War machines emerged in Africa during the last quarter of the twentieth century in direct relation to the erosion of the postcolonial state's capacity to build the economic underpinnings of political authority and order. This capacity involves raising revenue and commanding and regulating access to natural resources within a well-defined territory. In the mid-1970s, as the state's ability to maintain this capacity began to erode, a clear-cut link emerged between monetary instability and spatial fragmentation. In the 1980s, the brutal experience of currency depreciation became more commonplace as several countries endured cycles of hyperinflation (which included such stunts as the sudden replacement of a currency). During the last decades of the twentieth century, monetary circulation influenced state and society in at least two different ways.

First, we saw a general drying up of liquidities and their gradual concentration within specific channels, access to which is subject to increasingly draconian conditions. As a result, the number of individuals endowed with the material means to control dependents through the creation of debts has abruptly decreased. Historically, capturing and fixing dependents through a debt mechanism was a central aspect of both the production of people and the constitution of a political bond.[65] Such bonds were crucial in determining the value of persons and gauging their utility. When their value and utility were not proven, they could be disposed of as slaves, pawns, or clients.

Second, the controlled inflow and fixing of money movements around zones in which specific resources are extracted has made possible the formation of *enclave economies*, shifting the old calculus between people and things. The concentration of activities connected with the extraction of valuable resources around these enclaves has, in return, turned the enclaves into privileged spaces of war and death. War itself is fed by the increased sales of the products extracted.[66] New linkages have therefore emerged between making war, war machines, and resource extraction.[67] War machines are involved in constituting highly transnational local or regional economies. In most places, the collapse of formal political institutions under the strain of violence tends to lead to the formation of militia economies. War machines (in this case militias or rebel movements) rapidly become highly organized mechanisms of predation, taxing the territories and the populations they occupy, and drawing on a range of transnational networks and diasporas that provide both material and financial support.

Correlated to the new geography of resource extraction is the emergence of an unprecedented form of governmentality that consists in *managing the multitudes*. The extraction and looting of natural resources by war machines goes hand in hand with brutal attempts to immobilize and spatially fix whole categories of people or, paradoxically, to free them as a way of forcing them to scatter over broad areas no longer contained by the boundaries of a territorial state. As a political category, populations are then disaggregated into rebels, child soldiers, victims, or refugees, or civilians who are incapacitated through mutilation or simply massacred on the model of ancient sacrifices, while, after enduring a horrific exodus, the "survivors" get confined in camps and zones of exception.[68]

This form of governmentality is different from colonial *commandement*.[69] Techniques of exercising police authority and discipline, the choice between obedience and simulation that characterized the colonial and postcolonial potentate, are gradually being replaced by an alternative that is more tragic because more extreme. Technologies of destruction have become more tactile, more anatomical and sensorial, in a context in which the choice is between life and death.[70] If power still depends on tight control over bodies (or on concentrating them in camps), the new technologies of destruction are less concerned with inscribing bodies within disciplinary apparatuses than with inscribing them, when the time comes, within the order of the maximal economy now represented by the "massacre." In turn, the generalization of insecurity has deepened the societal distinction between those who bear weapons and those who do not (*the law of weapons distribution*). Increasingly, war is no longer waged between the armies of two sovereign states but between armed groups that act behind the mask of the state against armed groups that have no state but control very distinct territories, with both sides having as their main targets civilian populations that are unarmed or organized into militias. In cases where armed dissidents have not completely taken over state power, they have provoked territorial partitions and succeeded in controlling entire regions, which they administer on the model of fiefdoms, especially if they contain mineral deposits.[71]

The methods of killing do not vary greatly. In the case of massacres in particular, lifeless bodies are quickly reduced to the status of simple skeletons. Their morphology henceforth inscribes them in the register of undifferentiated generality: simple relics of an unburied pain; empty, meaningless corporealities; strange deposits plunged into cruel stupor. In the case of the Rwandan genocide—in which a number of skeletons were, when not exhumed, kept in a visible state—what is striking is the tension between, on the one hand, the petrification of the bones and their strange coolness and, on the other, their stubborn will to mean, to signify something.

In these impassive bits of bone, there seems to be no *ataraxia*: nothing but the illusory rejection of a death that has already occurred. In other cases, in which physical amputation replaces immediate death, the severing of limbs paves the way for the deployment of techniques of incision, ablation, and excision that also have bones as their target. This demiurgic surgery leaves traces that persist for a long time, in the form of human shapes that are alive, to be sure, but whose bodily integrity has been replaced by pieces, fragments, folds, where even immense wounds do not easily heal. Their function is to hold forever the morbid spectacle of such severing before the eyes of the victim and the eyes of those around him.

Of Acts and Metal

Let us return to the example of Palestine, where we see a confrontation occurring between two apparently irreconcilable logics: the *logic of martyrdom* and the *logic of survival*. In examining these logics, I would like to reflect on the twin issues of death and terror, on the one hand, and terror and freedom, on the other.

In the confrontation between these two logics, terror and death do not stand on opposite sides from one another. Terror and death are the core of both logics. As Elias Canetti reminds us, the survivor is the one who, having stood in the path of death, having known many deaths and having been amid the fallen, is still alive. Or, more precisely, the survivor is the one who has taken on a whole pack of enemies and managed not only to escape alive but to kill his attackers. This is why killing is the lowest form of survival. Canetti points out that in the logic of survival, "each man is the enemy of every other." Even more radically, in the logic of survival the horror experienced upon seeing death turns into the satisfaction that the dead person is another. It is the death of the Other, the Other's physical presence as a corpse, that makes the survivor feel unique. And each enemy killed makes the survivor feel more secure.[72]

The logic of martyrdom proceeds along different lines. It is epitomized by the figure of the "suicide bomber," which itself raises a number of questions: What intrinsic difference is there between killing with a missile helicopter or a tank and killing with one's own body? Does the distinction between the weapons used to inflict death prevent the establishment of a system of general exchange between the manner of killing and that of dying?

The suicide bomber wears no ordinary soldier's uniform and brandishes no weapon. The candidate for martyrdom hunts down the targets; the enemy is a prey for whom a trap is set. Significant in this respect is the location of the ambush laid: the bus stop, the café, the discotheque, the marketplace, the checkpoint, the road—in sum, spaces of everyday life.

On top of the location of the ambush is the trap of the body. Candidates for martyrdom transform their bodies into a mask that hides the soon-to-be-detonated weapon. While a tank or a missile is clearly visible, the weapon carried in the shape of the body is invisible. Thus concealed, it forms part of the body. It is so intimately part of the body that at the time of detonation it annihilates the bearer's own body, which takes the bodies of others with it, when it does not reduce them to pieces. The body does not simply conceal a weapon. The body is transformed into a weapon, not in a metaphorical sense but in the truly ballistic sense.

In this instance, my death goes hand in hand with the Other's death. Homicide and suicide are accomplished in the same act. Resistance and self-destruction are largely synonymous. To mete out death is therefore to reduce the Other and oneself to the status of pieces of inert flesh, scattered about everywhere, and pieced back together with difficulty before the burial. In this case, war is the body-on-body war (*guerre au corps-à-corps*). To kill, one must get as close as possible to the body of the enemy. To detonate the bomb necessitates resolving the question of distance through the work of proximity and concealment.

How are we to interpret this manner of spilling blood, in which the death is not simply *my own* but always goes hand in hand with the other's death?[73] How does it differ from the death inflicted by a tank or a missile, in a context in which the cost of my survival is calculated in terms of my capacity and readiness to kill someone else? In the logic of "martyrdom," the will to die is fused with the will to take the enemy down with you, that is, to slam shut the door on the possibility of life for everyone. This logic seems contrary to another one, which consists in wishing to impose death on others while preserving one's own life. Canetti describes this moment of survival as a moment of power. In such a case, triumph develops precisely from the possibility of being there when the others (in this case the enemy) are no longer there. Such is the logic of heroism as classically understood: executing others while holding one's own death at a distance.

A new semiosis of killing emerges in the logic of martyrdom. It is not necessarily based on a relationship between form and matter. As I have already indicated, the body here becomes the martyr's uniform. But the body as such is not only an object to protect against danger and death. The body in itself has neither power nor value. Rather its power and value result from a process of abstraction based on the desire for eternity. In that sense, the martyr, having established a moment of supremacy in which the subject overcomes his own mortality, can be seen as laboring under the sign of the future. In other words, in death the future is collapsed into the present.

In its desire for eternity, the besieged body passes through two stages. First, it is transformed into a mere thing, mere malleable matter. Second, the manner in which it is put to death — suicide — affords it its ultimate signification. The body's matter, or again the matter which the body is, is invested with properties that can be deduced not from its character as a thing but from a transcendental *nomos* outside it. The besieged body becomes a piece of metal whose function is to bring eternal life into being through sacrifice. The body duplicates itself and, in death, literally and metaphorically escapes the state of siege and occupation.

Let me explore, in conclusion, the relation between terror, freedom, and sacrifice. Heidegger argues that the human's "being toward death" is the decisive condition of all true human freedom.[74] In other words, one is free to live one's own life only because one is free to die one's own death. Whereas Heidegger grants an existential status to being-toward-death and considers it an event of freedom, Bataille suggests that "sacrifice in reality reveals nothing." It is not simply the absolute manifestation of negativity. It is also a comedy. For Bataille, death reveals the human subject's animal side, which he refers to, moreover, as the subject's "natural being." He adds, "For man to reveal himself in the end, he has to die, but he will have to do so while alive — by looking at himself ceasing to exist." In other words, the human subject has to be fully alive at the very moment of dying, to be aware of his own death, to live with the impression of actually dying. Death itself must become self-awareness at the very time that it does away with the conscious being. "In a sense, this is what happens (what at least is on the point of taking place, or what takes place in an elusive, fugitive manner), by means of a subterfuge in the sacrifice. In the sacrifice, the sacrificed identifies himself with the animal on the point of death. Thus he dies seeing himself die, and even, in some sense, through his own will, at one with the weapon of sacrifice. But this is play!" And for Bataille, play is more or less the means by which the human subject "voluntarily tricks himself."[75]

How does the notion of play and trickery relate to the suicide bomber? In the case of the suicide bomber, the sacrifice doubtless consists in the spectacular putting of oneself to death, in becoming one's own victim (self-sacrifice). Self-sacrificers proceed to take power over their death by approaching it head-on. This power may be derived from the belief that destroying one's own body does not affect the continuity of being. The idea is that being exists outside us. Here self-sacrifice consists in the removal of a twofold prohibition: that of self-immolation (suicide) and that of murder. Unlike primitive sacrifices, however, there is no animal to serve as a substitute victim. Death here achieves the character of a transgression. But unlike crucifixion, it has no expiatory dimension. It is not related to the Hegelian paradigms of prestige or recognition. Indeed, a dead person cannot recognize his killer, who is also dead. Does this imply that death occurs here as pure annihilation and nothingness, excess and scandal?

Whether read from the perspective of slavery or that of colonial occupation, death and freedom are irrevocably interwoven. As we have seen, terror is a defining feature of both slave and late modern colonial regimes. Both regimes are also specific instances and experiences of unfreedom. To live under late-modern occupation is to experience a permanent condition of "being in pain": fortified structures, military posts, and roadblocks everywhere; buildings that bring back painful memories of humiliation, interrogations, and beatings; curfews that imprison hundreds of thousands in their cramped homes every night from dusk to dawn; soldiers patrolling the unlit streets, frightened by their own shadows; children blinded by rubber bullets; parents shamed and beaten in front of their families; soldiers urinating on fences, shooting at rooftop water tanks just for kicks, chanting loud and offensive slogans, pounding on fragile tin doors to frighten children, confiscating papers, or dumping garbage in the middle of residential neighborhoods; border guards kicking over vegetable stands or closing borders at whim; bones broken; shootings and fatalities—a certain kind of madness.[76]

In such circumstances, the discipline of life and the necessities of hardship (trial by death) are marked by excess. What connects terror, death, and freedom is an *ecstatic* notion of temporality and politics. The future, here, can be authentically anticipated, but not in the present. The present itself is but a moment of vision—a vision of the freedom not yet come. Death in the present is the mediator of redemption. Far from being an encounter with a limit, boundary, or barrier, it is experienced as "a release from terror and bondage."[77] As Gilroy notes, this preference for death over continued servitude is a commentary on the nature of freedom itself (or the lack thereof). If this lack is the very nature of what it means for the slave or the colonized to exist, the same lack is also precisely the way in which he takes account of his mortality. Referring to the practice of individual or mass suicide by slaves cornered by slave catchers, Gilroy suggests that death, in this case, can be represented as agency. For death is precisely that from and over which I have power. But it is also the space where freedom and negation operate.

In this chapter, I have argued that contemporary forms of subjugating life to the power of death (necropolitics) are deeply reconfiguring the relations between resistance, sacrifice, and terror. I have demonstrated that the notion of biopower is insufficient to account for contemporary forms of the subjugation of life to the power of death. Moreover, I have put forward the notion of necropolitics, or necropower, to account for the various ways in which, in our contemporary world, weapons are deployed in the interest of maximally destroying persons and creating *death-worlds*, that is, new and unique forms of social existence in which vast populations are subjected to living conditions that confer upon them the status of the *living dead*. I have also outlined some of the repressed topographies of cruelty (the plantation and the colony in particular) and suggested that today's form of necropower blurs the lines between resistance and suicide, sacrifice and redemption, martyrdom and freedom.

FOUR
VISCERALITY

In what ways can we problematize some of the constituent features of these times of ours, this peculiar moment our world is going through, a moment for which there doesn't yet seem to be a proper name? Since naming our time is part of what is at stake, I suggest that, in the midst of the current dread and confusion, one thing at least is clear—ours is a *time of planetary entanglement*. Worldwide, the combination of "fast capitalism," soft-power warfare, and the saturation of the everyday by digital and computational technologies has led to the acceleration of speed and the intensification of connections.

Technology and Eschatology

We inherited from Heidegger's *The Question concerning Technology* two ways of interrogating the technological.[1] Heidegger was concerned about technology in terms of what he called its "essence," or more precisely its double essence, that is, technology as an *instrumentum*, a means to an end, and technology as an anthropology, that is, as an activity performed by humans, one that sets humans apart from other species. He was also concerned about technology as, in and of itself, "a way of thinking" or, to use another one of his formulations, "a mode of revealing." He understood revelation as a certain kind of presence in that specific realm where "unconcealment takes place," "where truth happens."

As a way of thinking, technology's role was to prepare us to entertain with it a "free relationship." To experience the technological within its own bounds, Heidegger thought, was the only way to open our human existence to its essence, which is a means to truth and freedom. But what is precisely at stake in the invocation of terms such as "the essence of technology" or "to experience the technological within its own bounds"? Or when we suggest that the technological is the event through which truth and freedom come into being and manifest themselves as the ultimate Being and the ultimate dwelling of the human? The essence of technology, argues Heidegger,

> is by no means anything technological. . . . We shall never experience our relationship with the essence of technology so long as we merely conceive and push forward the technological, put up with it, or evade it. Everywhere we remain unfree and chained to technology, whether we passionately affirm or deny it. But we are delivered over to it in the worst possible way when we regard it as something neutral; for this conception of it, to which today we particularly like to do homage, makes us utterly blind to the essence of technology.[2]

Freedom is therefore the ground from which the question concerning technology must be posed. Heidegger assimilates freedom with something he calls "the open," a space where we are neither confined to "a stultified compulsion to push on blindly with technology" or—what amounts to the same—"to rebel helplessly against it and curse it as the work of the devil."[3] His insistence on approaching the technological from the vantage point of freedom, in terms of disclosure and opening and dwelling, is part of a long tradition in Western metaphysics when it comes to the relation between humans and artifacts or technical objects.

This tradition assumes that there is a division between the technical world of humans and the natural world of nonhuman animals. In privileging the human, this tradition conveniently forgets that the widespread use of tools among animals is a fact. The human in question is distinguished from the nonhuman because of his or her presumably larger cognitive capacity. Thanks to the latter, he has been able to free himself from a purely instinctive relationship with his environment. In this, he is not only distinct from the animal. He is also distinct from the primitive, that is, the class of original humans who still live under the rule of animism.[4]

At its core, this tradition harbors two kinds of anxieties. The first is a deep anxiety concerning the proper relation between people/humans, on the one hand, and things/objects, on the other. The belief is that people invent things but that people are not things. This being the case, the fear is of a time when things take the place of people and people are treated like things.[5] Such fear finds expression in questions like: How much of human activity should technical objects replace? Since much of human activity takes shape through the human body, how much of this body should technical objects replace? To what extent should technical objects be made in the image of the human and of his body?[6]

A second type of anxiety haunts this tradition. It manifests itself in the form of an acute nostalgia for a mythical time when humans could manipulate the environment directly and at will. This originary capacity, we are told, has been taken away by machines, and technological artifacts have become increasingly complex and autonomous. They now threaten to enslave us or to dehumanize us by turning us into mere extensions of the tools originally intended to serve us. Thus the desire for a return to a time of spontaneous and nonmediated relationship with the natural world. This second type of anxiety speaks to the loss of self-sufficiency and to the fear that industrial-technical objects are no longer mere tools and, furthermore, that they are now capable of inventing themselves independently of our intentions.

As a matter of fact, unprecedented numbers of human beings are now embedded in increasingly complex technostructures. Over the past decade, numerous algorithms have been developed. They are inspired by the natural world and ideas of natural selection and evolution. Such is the case of genetic algorithms — a subset of evolutionary algorithms that "mimic actions inspired in biological operators, such as cells." They "seek to optimize the responses to the problems of their environments by self-generating, and encompassing processes of mutation and natural selection."[7]

As Margarida Mendes powerfully argues, a shifting redistribution of powers between the human and the technological is unfolding.[8] Technologies, in turn, are more and more tied in, both metabolically and reproductively, with complex networks of extraction and predation, many of whose forms have led to the transgression of planetary boundaries such as those related to anthropogenic climate change, degenerative land-use change, biodiversity loss, the creation of novel entities and genetically engineered organisms.[9]

Mendes shows the broad extent to which the genetic codes of humans, plants, and animals are being cracked and publicly disseminated. This, in turn, is giving way to an exponential rise of biological patents. The human genome is in the process of being privately owned. Life itself is increasingly being perceived as a commodity to be replicated under the volatility of market consumption. Thousands of new molecules whose behavior cannot be predicted are being produced and released into the ecosystem. Seeds, chemical herbicides, GMOs, and pesticides are being patented by a handful of multinationals. Through widespread genetic modification of key elements in the food chain, corporations are intervening directly in the natural cycles of life and ecosystems. Patented GMO genes are absorbed into human bodies and the bodies of various other species, turning the latter into infrastructures as well as inscribing them into a proprietary relationship of biological subjugation.

As algorithmic forms of intelligence grow in parallel (and often in alliance) with genetic research, the integration of algorithms and big data analysis in the biological sphere brings with it a greater belief in techno-positivism. Increasingly, statistical thought, regimes of assessment of the natural world, and modes of prediction and analysis treat matter and life itself as finite and computable objects. The idea that life might be an open, nonlinear, and exponentially chaotic system is increasingly behind us. We might be far removed from Heidegger and his preoccupation with metaphysical questions of truth and freedom. Yet, the rapid advance in automated systems is threatening the exceptionalism of the human species. Concerns about the technological singularity of our age are increasingly couched in the eschatological and apocalyptic language of "human obsolescence or extinction."[10]

Planetary Disentanglement and the Hunt for Fugitives

But entanglement is not all that characterizes the now. Indeed, wherever we look, the drive is decisively toward contraction, containment, and enclosure.[11] By enclosure, contraction, and containment, I do not simply mean the erection of all kinds of walls and fortifications, gates and enclaves, or various practices of partitioning space, of offshoring and fencing off wealth. I am also referring to a *matrix of rules* mostly designed for those human bodies deemed either in excess, unwanted, illegal, dispensable, or superfluous.[12]

Indeed, perhaps more than at any other moment in our recent past, we are increasingly faced with the question of what to do with those whose very existence does not seem to be necessary for our reproduction, those whose mere existence or proximity is deemed to represent a physical or biological threat to our own life. Paradigmatic of this matrix of rule is present-day Gaza in Palestine. Gaza is a paradigmatic example on two counts. On the one hand, it is the culmination of spatial exclusionary arrangements that existed in an incipient state during the early phases of modern settler or genocidal colonialism. Such was the case of Native American reservations in the United States, as well as island prisons, penal colonies, camps, and Bantustans in South Africa in the not-so-distant past. On the other hand, Gaza might well prefigure what is yet to come.

Here, the control of vulnerable, unwanted, or surplus people is exercised through a combination of tactics, chief among which is the "modulated blockade." A blockade prohibits, obstructs, and limits who and what can enter and leave the Strip. The goal might not be to cut the Strip off entirely from supply lines, infrastructural grids, or trade routes. It is nevertheless relatively sealed off in a way which effectively turns it into an imprisoned territory. Comprehensive or relative closure is punctuated by periodic military escalations and the generalized use of extrajudicial assassinations. Spatial violence, humanitarian strategies, and a peculiar biopolitics of punishment all combine to produce, in turn, a peculiar carceral space in which people deemed surplus, unwanted, or illegal are governed through abdication of any responsibility for their lives and their welfare.[13]

But this is not all. These times of planetary entanglement are ripe for escalation and, consequently, for the renewed production of myths, fictions, and fantasies both baroque and dystopian, immaterial formations that strive to generate their own actuality through sheer excess and stupefaction.[14] Thus, once more, something extremely troubling is taking place at the heart of Europe. Unmistakably, an ever increasing multitude of voices are making themselves heard. Spurred on by the strength of fellow living souls, human chains of solidarity are forming. In the darkness of fear and denunciation, and faced with unrelenting waves of repression, compassionate men and women seek to awaken the sleeping fireflies of hospitality and solidarity. In the midst of an otherwise troubling anesthesia, an active minority is taking a stance. With renewed vigor they seek to denounce acts carried out in their name against the Other—who, it is claimed, is not one of us. Forced from their households, millions of desperate men, women, and children have set out on paths of exodus. Another great cycle of repopulation is taking place in the world. However, these people are not deserters. They are fugitives. Threatened by one calamity or another, they have escaped their places of birth and childhood — places where they lived but which one day became uninhabitable, impossible abodes. In response to this great upheaval, familiar, well-rehearsed refrains sound out in unison. "Demographic explosion." "Armed conflicts." "The rise of religious extremism." "Gold Rush, to Europe!" "The migrant crisis." "Why are they coming here?" "They should just stay put."

Resting on the fable of "foreign aid," many are still wont to believe in fairy tales. Despite the fact that between 1980 and 2009, net transfers of financial resources from Africa to the rest of the world reached the threshold of approximately 1,400 billion dollars, and illicit transfers totaled 1,350 billion dollars, the belief somehow holds firm that the countries of the North subsidize those of the South. Besides, it seems to count for little that the countries with weak or intermediate GDP have welcomed more than 90 percent of the 65.6 million refugees currently displaced and uprooted in the world. In this sector, as in others, an era of fantasy and closed-mindedness is upon us. Old prejudices are constantly recycled from the scrap heap, and in a cyclical process typical of racist discourses, new fantasies are suggested. "It's both cultural and civilizational," proclaim the erudite pseudo-experts. "They are fleeing because of intergenerational tensions." "The poorer they are, the more likely they are to leave, but as their condition of life improves, their desire to live elsewhere grows." From the depths of the shadows, an old specter returns to haunt people's minds with invasions of hordes from overpopulated lands — countries "where each woman still gives birth to seven or eight children."

The Solution?

We must close the borders. Filter those who make it across them. Process them. Choose who we want to remain. Deport the rest. Sign contracts with corrupt elites from the countries of origin, third world countries, transition countries. They must be turned into the prison guards of the West, to whom the lucrative business of administering brutality can be subcontracted. These states must become the protectorates of Europe — at once prisons for those seeking to leave and dumping grounds for those of whom it would be better to rid ourselves. And above all, we must make Europeans want to have more children.

This is the cornerstone of European migratory policy at the start of this century.

In truth, the problem is neither the migrants nor the refugees nor the asylum seekers. Borders. Everything begins with them, and all paths lead back to them. They are no longer merely a line of demarcation separating distinct sovereign entities. Increasingly, they are the name used to describe the organized violence that underpins both contemporary capitalism and our world order in general — the women, the men, and the unwanted children condemned to abandonment; the shipwrecks and drownings of hundreds, indeed thousands, weekly; the endless waiting and humiliation in consulates, in limbo; days of woe spent wandering in airports, in police stations, in parks, in train stations, then down onto the city pavements, where at nightfall blankets and rags are snatched from people who have already been stripped and deprived of virtually everything — bare bodies debased by a lack of water, hygiene, and sleep. In short, an image of humanity on a road to ruin.

In fact, everything leads back to borders — these dead spaces of non-connection which deny the very idea of a shared humanity, of a planet, the only one we have, that we share together, and to which we are linked by the ephemerality of our common condition. But perhaps, to be completely exact, we should speak not of borders but instead of "borderization." What, then, is this "borderization," if not the process by which world powers permanently transform certain spaces into impassable places for certain classes of populations? What is it about, if not the conscious multiplication of spaces of loss and mourning, where the lives of a multitude of people judged to be undesirable come to be shattered?

What is it, if not a way of waging war against enemies whose means of existence and survival we have previously destroyed — with the use of uranium warheads and banned weapons like white phosphorus; with high-altitude bombardment of basic infrastructures; with a cocktail of cancerous chemical substances deposited in the soil, which fill the air; the toxic dust in the ruins of towns razed to the ground; the pollution from burning hydrocarbons?

And what should we say of the bombs? In the last quarter of the twentieth century, are there any types of bomb to which civilian populations have not been subjected? Conventional blind bombs, reconverted with central inertial systems in the tail; cruise missiles with inbuilt infrared head-hunting systems; E-bombs destined to paralyze the enemy's electronic nerve centers; bombs that explode in towns, emitting rays of energy like lightning bolts; other E-bombs that, while not deadly, instead burn their victims and raise the temperature of their skin; thermobaric bombs that release walls of fire, absorbing all the oxygen from surrounding spaces, which kill with shockwaves, asphyxiating nearly everything that breathes; cluster bombs that devastate civilian populations as they break up in the air, dispersing mini-munitions designed to explode upon contact over vast areas; a plethora of bombs, absurd demonstrations of untold destructive power — in short, ecocide.

Under such conditions, no wonder that those who are able, that those survivors of a living hell, take flight and seek refuge in any corner of the world where their lives might be spared.

This kind of war of attrition, methodically calculated and programmed and implemented with new methods, is a war against the very ideas of mobility, circulation, and speed, while the age we live in is precisely one of velocity, acceleration, and increasing abstraction and algorithms. Moreover, the targets of this kind of warfare are not by any means singular bodies but rather great swaths of humanity adjudged worthless and superfluous, whose every organ must be specifically incapacitated in a way that affects generations to come — eyes, noses, mouths, ears, tongues, skin, bones, lungs, intestines, blood, hands, legs, all these maimed people, paralytics and survivors, all these pulmonary diseases like pneumoconiosis, all these traces of uranium on their hair, the thousands of cases of cancer, abortions, fetal malformations, birth defects, ruptured thoraxes, dysfunctions of the nervous system — all bear witness to a terrible devastation.

All of the above, it is worth repeating, belong to the current practice of remote borderization — carried out from afar, in the name of freedom and security. This battle, waged against certain undesirables, reducing them to mounds of human flesh, is rolled out on a global scale. It is on the verge of defining the times in which we live.

Often this battle either precedes, accompanies, or completes the campaigns that take place among us or at our doors — namely the tracking of those bodies that made the mistake of moving. Movement, incidentally, is the very essence of human bodies, but these bodies are assumed to have illegally broken into certain spaces and places where they should never have been — places that they now pollute by their presence alone and from which they must be expelled.

As the philosopher Elsa Dorlin has suggested, this form of violence sets its sights on a prey.[15] It bears a likeness to the great hunts of yesteryear, to both fox hunting and trapping and their respective techniques — research, pursuit, and entrapment, prior to driving the prey to a point at which it is surrounded, captured, or killed with the aid of foxhounds and blood-hounds.

But it also belongs to a long history of manhunts. Gregoire Chamayou has studied the modalities of these in his book *Manhunts*.[16] The targets are always roughly the same — Maroon slaves, Red Indians, blacks, Jews, the stateless, the poor, and, more recently, the homeless. These hunts target animated, living bodies, bodies that are mobile, fugitive, and endowed with a presence and intensity, yet which are marked and ostracized to the extent that they are no longer thought of as bodies of flesh and blood like our own. What's more, this hunt is rolled out at a moment in which the acceleration of technologies shows no sign of relenting, creating a segmented planet of multiple speeds.

The technological transformation of borders is in full swing. Physical and virtual barriers of separation, digitalization of databases, filing systems, the development of new tracking devices, sensors, drones, satellites and sentinel robots, infrared detectors and various other cameras, biometric controls, and new microchips containing personal details, everything is put in place to transform the very nature of the border phenomenon and to speed up the implementation of this new type of border — one that is mobile, portable, and omnipresent.

Migrants and refugees are thus not, as it stands, the main focus of the argument. Furthermore, they have neither proper names nor faces and possess no identity cards. They are merely a kind of hollowed-out entity, walking vaults concealed by a multitude of organs, empty yet menacing forms in which we seek to bury the fantasies of an age terrified of itself and of its own excess. The dream of perfect security, which requires not only complete systematic surveillance but also a policy of cleansing, is symptomatic of the structural tensions that, for decades, have accompanied our transition into a new technical system of increased automation—one that is increasingly complex yet also increasingly abstract, composed of multiple screens: digital, algorithmic, even mystical.

The world has ceased to present itself to us in the old terms/ways. We are witnessing the birth of a previously unseen form of the human subject-object relationship, as well as the emergence of new ways of conceiving space. Our phenomenological experiences of the world are being thoroughly shaken up. Reason and perception no longer tally. Panic ensues. We see less and less of what is given to us to see, and more and more of what we desperately want to see, even if what we desperately want to see does not correspond to any given reality. Perhaps more than ever before, others can present themselves to us in a physical and tactile, concrete way, while remaining in ghostly absence in a similarly concrete void, almost as phenomena. This is indeed the case with migrants, refugees, and asylum seekers. It is not only the way in which they appear among us that plunges us into a chronic, existential anxiety. It is also the matrix of their being, of which we suppose they are merely the mask, that plunges us into a state of agitation and radical uncertainty. For, after all, what really lies behind what we can see?

In an increasingly Balkanized and isolated world, where are the most deadly migrant routes? It is Europe! Who claims the largest number of skeletons and the largest marine cemetery in this century? Again, it is Europe! The greatest number of deserts, territorial and international waters, channels, islands, straits, enclaves, canals, rivers, ports, and airports transformed into iron curtain technologies? Europe! And to top it all off, in these times of permanent escalation—the camps. The return of camps. A Europe of camps. Samos, Chios, Lesbos, Idomeni, Lampedusa, Vintimille, Sicily, Subotica—the list goes on.

Refugee camps? Camps for displaced people? Migrant camps? Waiting rooms for people in process? Transit zones? Detention centers? Emergency accommodation centers? Jungles? Composite, heterogeneous landscapes, certainly. Let us sum up all of the above in a single phrase, the only one which paints a truthful picture of what is going on: camps for foreigners. In the end, that's all they are. Camps for foreigners, both in the heart of Europe and at its borders. This is the only suitable name for these devices and for the kind of penitentiary geography that they serve to enforce.

Some years ago, the anthropologist Michel Agier counted some four hundred such camps at the heart of the European Union. This was before the great influx of 2015. Since then, new camps and new sorting infrastructures have been created both in Europe and on its borders and, at its insistence, in third world countries. In 2011, this array of detention spaces contained up to thirty-two thousand people. In 2016, the total had grown to forty-seven thousand. The detainees are simply people without visas or indefinite leave to remain and thus judged ineligible for international protection. Essentially, they are places of internment, spaces of relegation, a means by which to sideline people considered to be intruders, lacking valid permits, rendering them illegal and ultimately undeserving of dignity.

Fleeing their worlds of places rendered uninhabitable, persecuted both at home and from afar, they have come to be in places where they were never supposed to be without invitation, and where their presence is undesired. It is very difficult to claim that rounding them up and sidelining them in this way is being done in their best interests. After detaining them in camps, placing them in limbo, and denying them the status of possessing human rights, the aim is to turn them into objects that can be deported, stopped in their tracks — or even destroyed.

It must be repeated that this war (which aims to hunt down, capture, round up, process, segregate, and deport) has only one end goal. It is not so much about cutting Europe off from the rest of the world or turning her into an impenetrable fortress, but rather about granting Europeans alone the privilege of the rights to possession and free movement across the whole of the planet — a planet on which, in truth, we should all have the same entitlements.

Will the twenty-first century prove to be the century of assessment and selection on the bias of security technologies? From the confines of the Sahara, across the Mediterranean, the camps are once more on their way to becoming the last step in a certain European project, a certain idea of Europe in the world, her macabre emblem, just as Aimé Césaire foretold in his *Discourse on Colonialism* only too recently.

One of the major contradictions of liberal order has always been the tension between freedom and security. Today, this question seems to have been cut in two. Security now matters more than freedom.

A society of security is not necessarily a society of freedom. A society of security is a society dominated by the irrepressible need for adhesion to a collection of certainties. It is one fearful of the type of interrogation that delves into the unknown, unearthing the risks that must surely be contained within.

This is why in a society of security, the priority is, at all costs, to identify that which lurks behind each new arrival—who is who, who lives where, with whom, and since when, who does what, who comes from where, who is going where, when, how, why, and so on and so forth. And moreover, who plans to carry out which acts, either consciously or unconsciously. The aim of a society of security is not to affirm freedom but to control and govern the modes of arrival.

The current myth claims that technology constitutes the best tool for governing these arrivals—that technology alone allows for the resolution of this problem, a problem of order, but also of awareness, of identifiers, of anticipation and predictions. It is feared that the dream of a self-transparent humanity, stripped of all mystery, might prove to be a catastrophic illusion. For the time being, migrants and refugees are bearing the brunt of it. In the long run, it is by no means certain that they will be the only ones.

Under such conditions, how else might we resist the claim by one province of the world to a universal right of predation, if not by daring to imagine the impossible—the abolition of borders, that is to say, giving all inhabitants of the Earth—human and nonhuman alike—the inalienable right to freedom of movement on this planet?

Negative Messianism

Moments of escalation can also be genuinely frightening. This is because, in the midst of the dread, many suddenly come to the realization that things could get yet uglier. They suddenly awaken to the consciousness that events they always imagined were all but improbable might in fact happen, and they might end up having to go through a lot more than they ever expected or were prepared for. Indeed throughout the world, including in the wealthiest parts of the globe, many are prepping for disaster. A significant number of techies and apocalyptic libertarians in places such as Silicon Valley actually believe that the world is going to end. They are convinced that the human species is moving toward a dark future, an eschatological moment that might signal either the end of its history on Earth or the return to some kind of idyllic past.[17]

As confidence in freedom and democracy erodes, paranoia is increasingly becoming the dominant language both of power and of those who oppose it. Opposition to popular suffrage, egalitarianism, and pluralism is the cornerstone of the "Dark Enlightenment," a political religion which bemoans what it perceives as the "excess of democracy." Thus the calls for the *exit from democratic society* and for total corporate and absolute dictatorship. Deploying the familiar tropes of white victimhood, this credo reaffirms the myth of "human biodiversity" and of the supposed differences in intelligence across races. It sustains the dreams of a future society integrally run by technology and specifically sets aside "a part of the world for unregulated experiment."[18]

Various quasi-metaphysical dispositions therefore characterize our times. Each is underpinned by a particular theology of the future. In the first constellation, the future is in the past. In the second, it fundamentally opens to Nothingness. The world is on the road to serfdom and the end is near. Destruction is inevitable, and since what is coming will destroy us all anyway, many are asking, "Why wait? Let's bring it on. Let's just end it all now." Another configuration celebrates the fact that human reason has seemingly reached its limits. The fundaments of truth can now better be expressed in the form of algorithmic thinking by machines of different kinds capable of making decisions.[19]

Many contemporary versions of the messianic take the form of American prosperity theology. Here, conspicuous consumption is both an act of faith and an investment in one's own future blessings.[20] The dichotomy between the sacred and the profane having been erased, miracles are the stock-in-trade. Spending is turned into a "higher calling and spiritual pathos into gaudy pageantry."[21] Healing miracles, it is claimed, are being performed, and tumors, sickle cell anemia, and emphysema squashed by prayer and daily baptisms. A form of casino-messianism, prosperity theology is set up as a theme park, a triumph of deception. Through evangelical entertainment, it lures consumers in and traps them with narcotizing spectacles before spitting them out, "their pockets noticeably lighter."[22]

In yet another constellation, which combines technophilia and millenarianism, the old quest for immortality is reactivated. The belief is that technology will overcome "the brute empirical facts of the human condition," that is, death itself.[23] The latter is no longer thought of as irreversible. It is believed that cryonic preservation (which involves the freezing of parts of corpses for later resurrection) might open the door to an unlimited lifespan. Digital replication of the human mind may eventually be downloaded and natural, social and biological limits to self-actualization and self-realization removed.[24] Notwithstanding the false hope that technology will one day revive humans who have been cryonically preserved and "vitrified," the times are therefore propitious for a *negative messianism*.[25]

The full force of messianism resides in the concept of a redemption still to come. The most dramatic instance of redemption in the history of humanity is that of the slave. Messianicity is originally tied to the purchasing of the slave by God. The human being formerly owned by a master, the slave is declared "bought" by God, who, in retrocessing full value to the captive, effectively redeems him. The act of redemption involves a price. In the Paulinian tradition, this price is Christ's blood. To free the slave, the ransom is supplied out of God's own blood.

Contrary to biblical messianism, contemporary avatars of messianism are not concerned about the fate of the slave. Negative messianism is a kind of messianism that has either forfeited the idea of redemption as such or has been reduced to a crude belief in the expiatory power of bloodshed. It is not about salvation. In its minor version, it is about survival and the willingness to sacrifice or to be sacrificed. Its aim is to turn a forgiving God into an ethnic and angry god. In its major version, it is about collective suicide before the Apocalypse. In its most tech-dystopian instantiation, "the future is an anxious bird, flying in circles over a hot, flat, crowded landscape, biding its time until an ISIS-operated drone sprays weaponized bird flu in its face. What else can it do? The clock is ticking down and nothing is sustainable. The seas are boiling, filthy with plastic bags and drowning polar bears; the smoggy air will soon be swarming with (more) U.S. military drones, rogue-states nuclear drones, homemade bioweaponry, and Amazon's fleet of robotic delivery devices."[26]

Stories about an increasingly dangerous and insecure world in turn feed a thirst to trace and mete out "justice" and retribution to dispersed anonymous and not-so-anonymous enemies: from terror cells manufacturing AK-47s on 3-D printers to freelance "assassins with termite-sized drone armies" to Google, Amazon, and Facebook, responsible for bundling "all our personal data—social security numbers, credit card numbers, nude photos, names of children, pets, and second cousins" before selling them to data brokers or peddling them to identity-theft crime rings and pedophiles."[27]

When it does not give rise to a renewed politics of pure violence (in the form of suicide, martyrdom, or technomillenarianism), negative messianism paves the way for a politics of survival. It is haunted by apocalyptic fantasies. A messianism of destruction, it seeks not to actually bring about a community. Nor does it seek compromises. Rather, it emphasizes purity and self-separation as ways of staving off the disasters of a "crackup civilization."[28]

The spirit of the times is not only about survival. It is also about a renewed *will to kill* as opposed to the *will to care*, a will to severe all relationships as opposed to the will to engage in the exacting labor of repairing the ties that have been broken.

The Return of Animism

Another key feature of this age is the advent of electronic reason and computational media as well as the *return of animism*.

In old African cognitive worlds, some objects and tools were thought to be a mirror image of humans. It was not as if, in interacting with them, humans were interacting with illusory entities situated on the other side of the mirror. In any case, in numerous circumstances, the impossibility of ever fixing such a boundary was universally recognized. It was also generally recognized that there will always be some degree of overlap and even reversibility between the human, his body, and the objects he invented, that agency was shared between different entities and co-agency was itself a key element in the nurturing and circulation of all kinds of vital forces. Whatever the case, human beings were never satisfied with simply being human beings. They were constantly in search of a supplement to their humanhood. Often, to their humanhood, they added attributes of animals, properties of plants and various animate and inanimate objects. Personhood was therefore not a matter of ontology. It was always a matter of composition and of assemblage of a multiplicity of vital beings. To convert one specific object into something else and to capture the force inherent in every single matter and being constituted the ultimate form of power and agency. The world itself was a *transactional world*. One was always transacting with some other force or some other entity just as one was always trying to capture some of the power invested in those entities in an effort to add the latter to one's own originary powers.

Modernity rejected such ways of being, such different ways of sensing and acting with objects and relegated them to the "childhood of Man." Today, the technological devices that saturate our lives have become extensions of ourselves. In the process, a new relationship between humans and other living or vital things has been instituted. This new relationship is not unlike what African traditions had long prefigured. Not long ago, it was understood that the human person (who the West mistook for the white man) was neither a thing nor an object. Nor was he an animal or a machine. Human emancipation was precisely premised on such a distinction. Today many want to capture for themselves the forces, energies, and vitalism of the objects that surround us, most of which we have invented. We think of ourselves as made up of various spare or animate parts. How we assemble them and for what purpose is the question that late modern identity politics raises so unequivocally.

Neoliberalism has created the conditions for a renewed convergence, and at times fusion, between the living human being and objects, artifacts, or the technologies that supplement or augment us and are in the process transfigured and transformed by us. This event, which we can equate to a *return to animism*, is nevertheless not without danger for the idea of emancipation in this age of crypto-fascism. What does it portend for the future of democracy—democracy understood not in national terms but as a kind of planetary and shared responsibility and agency in relation to the future of all inhabitants of the Earth, humans and other-than-humans?

A first reason has to do with science's having turned into fiction and fiction into the real—all of which has led to a profound destabilization of what, not so long ago, counted as the ground for knowledge and, by extension, power and accountability. After all, the fact is that today there is hardly any consensus concerning what constitutes reality and how to access it. In the absence of such a consensus, all that we are left with is *ontological difference*. Every form of difference—minor differences included—is imparted ontological attributes in a context in which we cannot refer to one and the same external deity who would have the last word when it comes to granting a singular truth or adjudicating between right and wrong.

A major consequence of this apparent collapse of the basic foundations of knowledge and cognition is the impossibility of accountability, the radical impossibility we increasingly find ourselves in, specifying what is true and what is false, what is right and what is wrong—and in fact the obsolescence of those very categories. No wonder pure violence is back on the agenda and is being willfully embraced by all sides as the final arbiter of any and every single *differend*.

This condition of epistemic obsolescence and indeterminacy is itself a consequence of—or has been exacerbated by—the overreliance, under late capitalism, on modes of production of knowledge that take for facts only that which can be measured and experimented with. The trend toward a relentless *impoverishment of the real* has only escalated during the second half of the twentieth century and the first decade of the twenty-first. It has reached a point where today, knowledge is increasingly defined as knowledge for the market. The market in turn is increasingly reimagined as the primary mechanism for the validation of truth. Since markets themselves are increasingly turning into algorithmic structures and technologies, the only useful knowledge today is supposed to be algorithmic. Instead of actual human beings with a body, history, and flesh, big data and statistical inferences are all that count, and both are mostly derived from computation.

As Matteo Pasquinelli explains, algorithmic reason is a form of rationality whose finality is about the understanding of vast amounts of data according to a specific vector, the recording of emerging properties, and the forecasting of tendencies.[29] To some extent, Pasquinelli's metadata society is characterized by the "accumulation of information about information." Algorithms mostly mine metadata for the purpose of measurement and forecasting, of establishing patterns of behavior, detecting anomalies, and recognizing an enemy. The enemy is constructed as a reality via statistics, modeling, and mathematics.

Power, thus, is increasingly about identifying patterns or connections in random data, in a context in which the opposition between information and knowledge, knowledge and data, data and image, thinking and seeing, appears to collapse. Computational and algorithmic logic is now found at the very source of general perception. As a result of the conflation of knowledge, computation, and markets, contempt has been extended to anyone who has nothing to sell and nothing to buy or anything that cannot be bought and sold. The Enlightenment notion of the rational subject capable of deliberation and choice is gradually being replaced by the consciously deliberating and choosing consumer. The more the real is deprived of enchantment, the more people yearn for enchantment. At the same time, we are witnessing the loss of authority of established forms of evidence-making, a growing disregard for scientific expertise, and the reduction of that expertise to numbers and codes, all of which throws into confusion the related forms of accountability. How do we know in the face of uncertainty?

The reason is that the very concept of evidence has been discredited, throwing into confusion the related forms of accountability, since there is no accountability without some form or other of evidence. How we are to get to the reality of reality is now the question at the center of public debate, as recently illustrated by the notion of a postfact. The main casualty of a "postfact world" is arguably democracy itself. Democracy has no future in a factless world or in a world without evidence, that is, accountability. Such a world is, by definition, hostile to the very idea of reason and freedom.

Democracy after Financialization

Let me now move to a second set of observations in relation to the future of democracy—this time in regard to the transformations of late capitalism. It doesn't help anybody to indulge in a facile—and ultimately counterproductive—denunciation of capitalism as such. Yet, it is increasingly difficult to deny that the logic of escalation embedded in the very structure of global capitalism is today running full steam ahead, almost unbridled.

In fact, the world liberal order as constituted since the end of the Second World War, the long years of decolonization, the cold war, and the defeat of communism is reaching its end. Another long and deadlier game has started. The main clash of the first half of the twenty-first century will not oppose religions or so-called civilizations. It will oppose liberal democracy and global capitalism. It will pit, in ways we have not seen before, the rule of finance against the rule of the people. It will oppose what we used to refer to as "humanism," on the one hand, and, on the other, technomillenarianism and its corollary, nihilism in all its many accents and dystopian forms of expression.

Capitalism and liberal democracy triumphed over fascism in 1945 and over communism in the early 1990s, when the Soviet Union collapsed. The conciliation of two divergent guiding principles — market competition, on the one hand, and, on the other, a set of entitlements and vested rights defined by social needs — gave the postwar liberal order a semblance of stability at least in the developed countries of the Western bloc.

An expanding welfare state, powerful unions, and the commitment of the political elites to full employment enabled democracy and capitalism to live in relative harmony — so long as the reconstruction of Europe and Japan generated robust rates of growth. With the dissolution of the Soviet Union and the advent of globalization, the fate of capitalism does not any longer depend structurally on liberal democracy. They are on a collision course, and we are now well along the way toward their disentanglement.

The last decades of the twentieth century have been marked by the universalization of the market principle. Capital, in particular finance capital, having reached its maximal capacity for velocity, circulation, and flight, is now more than just dictating its own temporal regime. It now seeks to reproduce itself on its own, in an infinite series of structurally insolvent debts. If yesterday's drama of the human subject was exploitation by capital, the tragedy of the multitude today is that they are unable to be exploited at all. Abetted by technological and military might, finance capital has achieved its hegemony over the Earth by annexing the core of human desires. In the process, it has turned itself into perhaps the first planetary secular theology.

The dogmas that modern forms of capitalism had reluctantly shared with democracy since the postwar period — individual liberty, market competition and the rule of the commodity and property, the cult of science, technology, and reason — are currently under threat. At its core, liberal democracy is not compatible with the inner logic of global finance capitalism. The clash between these two ideas and principles is likely to be the most significant event of the first half of a twenty-first-century political landscape, itself shaped less and less by the rule of reason and more and more by the general release of passions, emotions, and affect.

As a consequence of this logic of escalation, a number of institutions, ways of life, and organizational forms that previously served to contain the free market are being hollowed out, remodeled, and broken up in order to make possible what Schumpeter optimistically called "creative destruction" but which today must be more appropriately qualified as destruction without reserve.

Indeed, what other name could we possibly give to an entity whose very future has historically been constantly tied to the ability to draw on what exceeds it, on what tends to escape it—yesterday human beings not deemed human enough, vast territories subjected to conquest and occupation, new resources and new markets, and today entire "spheres of life, human activities that until now had not been subjected to market exchange, and even segments of our personality structures" like emotional needs, intimacy, social relationships, or even a simple activity such as sleep.

Muslims, Jews, migrants, foreigners, and all the wretched of the Earth are therefore not the main threat to the contemporary liberal order. The main threat to the contemporary liberal order is the widening bifurcation of democracy and global capital. Today, we are witnessing a shift to outright, direct *capture* and control of the state by elites with substantial private economic power.[30]

State capture takes various forms. In some instances, it is led by a coalition of businesspeople-turned-politicians who believe that erecting all kinds of walls and giving a new lease on life to apartheid-like formations is a good way to help society and the economy, all the while busying themselves with cutting taxes for the rich and raising them for almost everyone else.

State capture has been rendered possible by hyperglobalization, which puts emphasis on rules for governing intellectual property, capital flows, and investment protections, all of which are mainly designed to generate and preserve profits for financial institutions and multinational enterprises at the expense of other legitimate social goals. Everywhere, these trends have resulted in the deepening of social cleavages, the exacerbation of distributional problems, and the undermining of domestic social bargains.

Reason on Trial

It remains to comment on the fate of democracy in the age of electronic reason and the hallucinatory power unleashed by contemporary computational technologies. More than ever, if we are serious about the fate of democracy in our world, we now need a critique of technology—and of reason—that is up to the challenges posed by the advent of computational media. Properly understood, reason is not only about calculation. If yesterday the modern rational subject's *raison de vivre* was to fight against myth, superstition, and obscurantism, the work of reason nowadays is to allow for different modes of seeing and measuring to appear. It is to help human subjects to properly identify the threshold that distinguishes between the calculable and the incalculable, the quantifiable and the unquantifiable, the computable and the incomputable. It is to help them understand that technologies of calculation, computation, and quantification do present us with one world among many actual and possible worlds. Therefore, as Pasquinelli argues, different modes of measuring will open up the possibility of different aesthetics, of different politics of inhabiting the Earth, and, we may add, of sharing the planet.

As multiple wave fronts of calculation expand throughout the planet, incorporating more and more life and matter into systems of abstraction and "machine reasoning," and as politics increasingly turns into a mathematical object, it becomes urgent to oppose an epistemic hegemony that reduces the Earth to a financial problem and a problem of financial value. To be intelligent, one still needs consciousness. Were data to overcode the subject, to act without reasoning, to leave behind reflexive thinking, and to privilege data correlation, then formal language and inferential deductions would become the norm. Sociality would become totally automated. Reason as we know it would be swallowed within a computational matrix that trades on circular causality.[31]

I have just suggested that the main threat to the contemporary liberal order stems from the fact that global capitalism is less and less about the creation of social wealth. Partly fueled by processes of sudden devaluation and expendability, rapid supersession, ceaseless disinvestment, obsolescence and discard, it increasingly aspires to free itself from any social obligation and to become its own ends and its own means.

In this context, one of the many functions of computational media and digital technologies is not only to extract surplus value through the annexation and commodification of the human attention span. It is also to accelerate the disappearance of transcendence and its reinstitutionalization in the guise of the commodity. Formatting as many minds as possible, shaping people's desires, recrafting their symbolic world, blurring the distinction between reality and fiction, and, eventually, colonizing their unconscious have become key operations in the dissemination of micro-fascism in the interstices of the real.

Furthermore, neoliberal capitalism, computational technologies, and social media all speak to some of the deepest fantasies that the modern human being entertains, beginning with the fantasy of looking at oneself that was first experienced with the invention of the mirror. Before the advent of the mirror as a technology of self-gazing, we could not fully take ourselves as eminent objects of contemplation. We could see only our shadow or the refraction of our double through the surface of the water or as an effect of light. Today various auxiliary technologies and platforms including all kinds of nano-cameras have taken the mirror to its ultimate stage, with explosive effects. They have brought the history of the shadow to its knees by making us believe that there can be a world without opacity, a translucent world transparent to itself, without any nocturnal attribute.

We can finally become our own spectacle, our own scene, our own theater and audience, even our own public. In this age of endless self-curation and exhibition, we can finally draw our own portrait. Intimacy has been replaced by what Jacques Lacan called "extimacy." A different kind of human entangled with objects, technologies, and other living or animate things is therefore being constituted through and within digital technologies and new media forms. This is not at all the liberal individual who, not so long ago, we believed could be the subject of democracy.

This new order of things has serious implications for traditional understandings of reason, the political, freedom, and self-government. Since modernity, every project of genuine human emancipation has aimed at preventing the human from being treated as an object and ultimately from being turned into waste. If, under the empire of the digital and the Eros of consumption, the human also begins to desire to be an object or to have some of its attributes or to see to it that objects and other animate and in-animate entities are also endowed with the same rights as humans, what does this signal in terms of the future of the political as such?

Already in the making, a new kind of human being will triumph. This will not be the liberal individual who, not so long ago, we believed could be the subject of democracy. The new human being will be constituted through and within digital technologies and computational media. The computational age (the age of Facebook, Instagram, Twitter) is dominated by the idea that there are clean slates in the unconscious. New media forms have not only lifted the lid that previous cultural eras had put on the unconscious. They have become the new infrastructures of the unconscious.

Yesterday, human sociality consisted in keeping a tab on the unconscious. For the social to thrive at all meant exercising vigilance on ourselves or delegating to specific authorities the right to enforce such vigilance. This was called repression. Repression's main function was to set the conditions for sublimation. Not all desires could be fulfilled. Not everything could be said or enacted. The capacity to limit oneself was the essence of one's freedom and the freedom of all.

Thanks partly to new media forms and the postrepressive era it has unleashed, the unconscious can now roam free. Sublimation is no longer necessary. Language itself has been dislocated. The content is in the form, and the form is beyond, or in excess of, the content. We are now led to believe that mediation is no longer necessary. Direct, originary experience is the new norm. This explains the growing antihumanist stance that now goes hand in hand with a general contempt for democracy. Calling this phase of our history fascist might be misleading, unless by fascism we mean the normalization of a social state of warfare.

Such a state would in itself be a paradox since, if anything, warfare leads to the dissolution of the social. And yet under conditions of neoliberal capitalism, politics will become a barely sublimated warfare. This will be a class warfare which denies its very nature—a war against the poor, a race war against minorities, a gender war against women, a religious war against Muslims, a war against the disabled.

Neoliberal capitalism has left in its wake a multitude of destroyed subjects, many of whom are deeply convinced that their immediate future will be one of continuous exposure to violence and existential threat.

They genuinely long for a return to some sense of certainty, the sacred, hierarchy, religion, and tradition. They believe that nations have become akin to swamps that need to be drained and the world as it is should be brought to its end. For this to happen, everything should be cleansed. They are convinced that they can be saved only in a violent struggle to restore their masculinity, the loss of which they unfortunately attribute to the weaker among them, to the weak they do not want to become.

In this context, the most successful political entrepreneurs will be those who convincingly speak to the losers, to the destroyed men and women of globalization and to their ruined identities. In the street fight that politics will become, reason will not matter. Nor will facts. Politics will revert to brutal survivalism in an ultracompetitive environment. Under such conditions, the future of a progressive and future-oriented mass politics of the left is very uncertain. In a world set on objectifying everybody and every living thing in the name of profit, the erasure of the political by capital is the real threat. The transformation of the political into business raises the risk of the elimination of the very possibility of politics. Whether human civilization can give rise to any form of political life at all is the problem of the twenty-first century.

FIVE
FANON'S PHARMACY

The first four chapters have shown how enmity now constitutes the spirit of liberal democracies, and how hatred gives them the impression of experiencing a pure present, a pure politics, using means that are themselves pure. I have also made the case that, historically speaking, neither the republic of slaves nor the colonial and imperial regime was a body foreign to democracy. On the contrary, they were its phosphorescent matter, the very thing enabling democracy to leave itself behind, to place itself deliberately at the service of something other than that which it proclaimed in theory, and to exercise, when required, dictatorship over itself, its enemies, and those it rejected as different. The most significant emblems of this long repressive stasis were the task forces of the era of colonial conquest and the military campaigns during the counterinsurgency warfare of decolonization.

In the worst of cases, there is no liberal democracy except through this supplement of the servile and the racial, the colonial, and the imperial. This *inaugural redoubling* is typical of liberal democracy. Democracy incurs risks and threats that do not so much obliterate its message, or even eradicate its name, as turn it against itself by repatriating to the inside what one strives to discharge to the outside. Insofar as it is practically impossible today to delimit inside from outside, the peril that terror and counterterror place on modern democracies is one of civil war.

This long chapter directly tackles the tension between the *principle of destruction*—which serves as the cornerstone of contemporary policies of enmity—and the *principle of life*. In the reflection it contains, I make a specific appeal to Frantz Fanon, whose considerations on destruction and violence, on the one hand, and on the therapeutic process and desire for unlimited life, on the other, form the basis of his theory of radical decolonization. Indeed, Fanon's work envisages radical decolonization from the angle of a movement and a violent labor. This labor aims at the principle of life; it aims to enable the creation of the new. But does all violence create something new? What about the sorts of violence that found nothing, on which nothing can be founded, and whose unique function is to institute disorder, chaos, and loss?

The Principle of Destruction

To grasp the importance that Fanon grants to creative violence and its healing power, two reminders are necessary. Fanon's work participated directly in three of the twentieth century's most decisive debates and controversies: the debate on *human genuses* (racism), the debate on *dividing up the world and the conditions of planetary domination* (imperialism and the right of peoples to self-determination), and the debate on the *status of machines and the destiny of war* (our relation to destruction and death). These three questions have eaten away at European consciousness since the sixteenth century and, at the dawn of the twentieth, would pave the way for a deep cultural pessimism.

In many regards, the twentieth century truly began with the Great War. Freud would write about this war that never has an "event ever destroyed so much that is precious in the common possessions of humanity."[1] The reason, he adds, is not merely the perfecting of the offensive and defensive weapons that made this war "more bloody and more destructive than any war of other days," since it is

> at least as cruel, as embittered, as implacable as any that has preceded it. It disregards all the restrictions known in International Law, which in peace-time the state had bound themselves to observe; it ignores the prerogatives of the wounded and the medical service, the distinction between civil and military sections of the population, the claims of private property. It tramples in blind fury on all that comes in its way as though there were to be no future and no peace among men after it is over.[2]

"The first impression that the ward full of war neurotics made on me was one of bewilderment," related Sándor Ferenczi, for his part. He had around fifty patients in the ward, nearly all of whom seemed, he added, "to be seriously ill, if not crippled." Many were "incapable of moving about," whereas with others the least attempt at moving gave rise to "such violent tremors of knees and feet" that his voice was unable to "be heard above the noise of their shoes upon the floor." In his opinion, the most remarkable thing was the gait of "these tremblers." It created the impression of a spastic paresis, where the various combination of tremor, rigidity, and weakness produced "quite peculiar gaits, possibly only to be reproduced by cinematography."[3]

The Great War was a scene on which all language other than mirror speech stumbled, and it smashed to pieces—or at least profoundly challenged—several centuries' worth of attempts to define a "law of war," that is to say, a fundamental law prescribing what was permissible and what not in a war between Europeans. This law was the product of a long process of maturation, of countless trials and errors, as well as of intense debates that zeroed in on the very nature of war, what constituted it, and its relation to natural law and justice.

In relation to the problematic of interest to us here, namely the terror of democracy, in particular in colonial and postcolonial situations, it is worthwhile bearing in mind that European thought initially distinguished between several forms of law. Taken as an attribute of action, law was divided into the right of superiority and equal rights; into natural law and so-called human law (which itself included civil law, the law of peoples); into universal law and particular law. Law endeavored to resolve questions as complex as that of knowing how to distinguish between so-called solemn, or public, war and all other forms of war, in particular private war.

As all war by definition ran the lingering risk of bringing down the state, public war could be undertaken only upon an order from the person in the state holding sovereign power.[4] A public war was recognizable in that those who engaged in it were invested with a sovereign power and had to observe a certain number of formalities. Apart from this, it was understood that if blood was paid with blood, the use of weapons was never free from peril and that defending oneself was not the same thing as avenging oneself. On the philosophical level, the attempt to establish a law of war culminated with Grotius's seventeenth-century treatise *The Rights of War and Peace*.

The cultural pessimism engulfing Europe in the wake of the Great War led to a fairly unprecedented merging of nationalism and militarism.[5] In Germany in particular, the defeat was considered to be the result of a betrayal. The war had been lost, but it was not over. "Jewish traitors" were deemed guilty for the defeat, and country's revenge would not be complete until their extermination.[6] The new military nationalism found its wellspring in an unprecedented imaginary of devastation and catastrophe. Its emblematic figure was the soldier returning from the hell of the trenches. This figure had endured the unbearable experience of the mud. He had born witness to a world in tatters. He had lived close to death in all its forms.

Gas attacks had transformed the atmosphere itself into a deadly weapon. With the poisoning of the air itself, even breathing became perilous. Thousands of cylinders released thousands of tons of chlorine gas into the trenches. Many soldiers died from suffocation and choking on their own fluids against the backdrop of a thick, wind-borne, yellow-green cloud stretching for many kilometers.[7] For the returning soldier, nervous breakdown was an almost permanent threat. Beset with terror, this soldier had heard his comrades' screams of death and had witnessed their incommunicable distress. In danger of going mad, he felt himself to be entirely in thrall to chance and predestination.[8]

The "great disillusionment" (Freud) caused by the war did not stem from the persistence of the bellicose fact as such. Very few people at the time believed in a definitive cessation of war or in the utopia of a perpetual peace. War, Freud maintained, will not stop "as long as nations live under such varied conditions, as long as they place such different values upon the individual life, and as long as the animosities which divide them represent such powerful psychic forces."[9]

Neither did the disillusionment stem from the reality of war "between primitive and civilized nations and between those divided by color, as well as with and among the partly enlightened and more or less civilized peoples of Europe." "The great ruling nations of the white race, the leaders of mankind," which in addition enjoyed a "civilized community," had recently demonstrated "brutal behavior by individuals of the highest culture, of whom one would not have believed any such thing possible"—this was the scandal of the Great War.[10] In other words, the man of origins, the man of the early times, the very same who gladly endured the other's death, who had no scruples provoking it, who willingly practiced murder, and in whose eyes the enemy's death meant no more than the annihilation of that which he hated, this primitive man was "still preserved in each of us," but was hidden, "invisible to our consciousness, in the deeper layers of our psychic life."[11] The vast reorganization of the life of drives that the civilizing process was supposed to bring about had barely erased the capacities particular to returning to the past — a process Freud named regression.

The revelation of the Great War was, therefore, on the one hand, that "primitive conditions can always be reconstructed," the primitive psyche being, "in the strictest sense, indestructible."[12] On the other hand, if the death drive, or drive for destruction, can in large part be diverted toward the outside or directed at the objects of the outside world, many other parts of this same drive can always escape the taming process (the very aim of the civilizing endeavor). Further still, the drive to destruction (with all the sadistic and masochistic behavior it involves), once turned toward the outside or projected, can be turned anew toward the inside or introjected.

This drive begins by taking the internal Other as a target. This is the sense of the imperative to exterminate the Jewish people (*Ausrottung*), a parcel of rot supposedly inhabiting the body of the German people under the Nazi regime. But, before long, it invests the subject itself as its object. In this case, destruction "returns from the external world toward the subject" and pushes this latter to "do what is inexpedient, act against his own interests, ruin the prospects which open out to him in the real world, and, perhaps, destroy his own real existence."[13] Colonialism, fascism, and Nazism constitute three forms, now extreme, now pathological, of this *return of the presumed external world to the subject*.

In the war's aftermath, fascist movements and parties emerged on the scene, notably in Europe. The rise of fascism, and then of Nazism, continued in parallel to that of colonialism, and it is now established that colonialism, fascism, and Nazism entertained more than just circumstantial relations with one another.[14] Although markedly distinct, these three formations shared the same myth about the absolute superiority of so-called Western culture, understood as the culture of a race — the white race. Its supposed essence — the Faustian spirit — was, moreover, recognizable by its technological power. Whether it concerns the past or the present, this power is to have enabled the erecting of Western culture into a culture like no other. In the understanding of the era, the phrase "culture like no other" had a twofold meaning.

First, it referred to an essence. Western culture, so it was claimed, was not an ordinary component of the cultures of humanity. In the concert of human creations, it enjoyed a preeminent status that freed it from all dependency on other cultures and granted it an immunity, as a consequence of which it supposedly could not be "touched." It was "untouchable" because it was distinct from all the others. It was further "untouchable" because it alone had the ability to relate all the others to itself. It could never totally melt into the network of the world's other cultures because these other cultures existed only through and in relation to it.

Thus hypostasized and placed on a pedestal, Western culture or civilization became the zero point of orientation of the humanities. Such was, moreover, the place and the flesh that it assigned to itself—its "here," its metaphysical point, that which enabled it to abstract from existence, from the will and the desires of other bodies and other fleshes, from faraway places that were at once other than its place and implicated in it, but toward which it could hardly be transported in return. In the spirit of the times, the phrase "culture like no other" also meant it was the only one to have symbolically overcome death. Domesticating death came about by dominating nature, by worshiping limitless space and inventing the concept of force. This culture was not unable to engage in contemplation, though its project was to steer the world according to its will. The West, a vast Promethean program, was to have pried divinity of its secret and turned man into a God—therein lies its originality.

Colonialism, fascism, and Nazism shared a second myth. For each of these historical formations, the West was a natural living body. It had marrow and a soul. Paul Valéry proclaimed, "Other parts of the world have had admirable civilizations. . . . But no part of the world has possessed this singular *physical* property: the most intense power of *radiation* combined with an equally intense power of *assimilation*. Everything came to Europe, and everything came from it."[15]

This singular physical property, this "intense power of radiation" wedded to the "most intense power of assimilation," came to take, via the repression of wars of resistance against colonialism, a concrete form: the camp-form.[16]

For more than half a century, the interpretation of the camp-form was dominated by what ought to be called "extreme politics," that is to say, to adopt Aimé Césaire's expression, the *politics of de-civilization*, which, in line with mechanisms of a sometimes spectacular and sometimes invisible and more or less subterranean nature, came to be consubstantial with the colonial condition. A consequence of the destruction of Europe's Jews, in the wake of the Holocaust the camp was envisaged as the site of a radical dehumanization, the space where humans were made to experience their becoming-animal in the gesture by which other human existences were reduced to the state of dust. The camp was also interpreted as symptomatic of the process of expulsion of its victims of common humanity, the scene of a crime as secret as it was unfigurable and unsayable, inseparably doomed, at least with those who perpetrated it, to oblivion, since everything conspired, from the outset, to erase its traces.

It is possible that the intensive power of radiation and assimilation evoked by Valéry was the origin not of a unique crime that, recapitulating all others, would enjoy an elective status and carry meanings "outside humanity," but instead a *chain of crimes* and terrors whose complex genealogies we must think through. Indeed, colonial policies were situated on the diurnal side of the de-civilizing (or extreme or terrorizing) politics denounced by Césaire, together with their attendant wars of conquest, occupation, and extermination, genocides and other massacres, and their inevitable counterparts, the wars of liberation and of counterinsurgency, whose magnitude we are only now beginning to measure.[17] On the nocturnal side were situated the concentration camp and the exterminatory processes that so many survivors have borne witness to, including Jean Améry, a reader of Fanon, in whom he found more than an interlocutor and practically a parent.[18] And also, as Hannah Arendt and later Michel Foucault well saw, linking both sides together, race or, to be precise, racism.[19]

From a strictly historical viewpoint, the camp-form emerged on the cusp of the twentieth century (between 1896 and 1907) as part of colonial war in Cuba, the Philippines, South Africa, and the then-German-controlled African Southwest. The camp in its modern meaning is not the same thing as the policing of population displacement practiced by the English in India during the eighteenth century, in Mexico in 1811, or in the United States throughout the nineteenth century. In this context the camp was a war measure used by a colonial government for the mass repression of civil populations deemed hostile. In general fashion, the issue here was systematically to expose women, children, and the aged to hunger, torture, forced labor, and epidemics.[20]

In South America, the first camp experiences took place in Cuba during the Ten Years' War (1868–78). Later, in 1896, these categories of the population were concentrated in the provinces of Santiago and Puerto Principe by the Spanish general Valeriano Weyler. In certain regions, following the example of Santa Clara, mortality rates hit 38 percent.[21] As for the Americans, they built multiple concentration camps in the Philippines between 1899 and 1902, after the Filipino nationalist insurgents engaged in guerrilla warfare to assert their rights.

The concentration camps established in the Philippines pertain entirely to hard war—a term whose origins stem from the American Civil War. At the time, an array of punitive measures was adopted. These measures entered into the framework of the Lieber Code of 1863. This code enacted many distinctions between the diverse categories of populations against which the counterinsurgency wars were conducted, the most important being the one that split loyal citizens from disloyal ones or traitors.

Disloyal citizens were in turn divided between citizens who were perfectly well known to be sympathizing with the rebellion, albeit without contributing any concrete aid to it, and citizens that, without necessarily taking up arms, gave objective support to the rebel enemy despite not being in the least constrained to do so. According to the Lieber Code, commanders of the armed forces could bring the weight of the war to bear on disloyal citizens in the rebel provinces. It was natural for traitors to be subjected, on occasion, to exceptional punitive measures, which were not at all imposed on noncombatant enemies, above all in periods of regular war. The military governor could also expel these citizens, who, moreover, could be subject to transfer, imprisonment, or heavy fines.[22]

Brigadier General Arthur MacArthur adopted measures in December 1900, as did Brigadier General J. Franklin Bell later, in November 1911. The area concerned was chiefly the province of Batangas, where the Filipino resistance was particularly intense. Massive population transfers were carried out in rural areas. Concentration camps were opened and torture stepped up. Brigadier General Jacob H. Smith adopted the same methods in Samar province. To the panoply of atrocities already in use, General Smith added a genuine scorched earth policy coupled with mass executions.[23]

Concentration camp logic thus existed well before its systematization and radicalization under the Third Reich. In the South African case (from 1889 to 1902), the British crown was up against a guerrilla logic. Between

1899 and 1900, a largely conventional war set these two enemies against one another. Placed under unbearable pressure by English troops, the Boers soon changed tactics, and their commandos turned increasingly to guerrilla warfare. Instead of openly confronting the enemy in the form of a constituted army, the Boers donned their civil outfits and reinserted themselves among the local population. From this position, they could subject the English troops to inopportune harassment that, without leading to decisive military victories, nonetheless had the effect of considerably undermining army morale.

Under the leadership of Horatio H. Kitchener, the crown responded by ramping up the opening of concentration camps. Legalized by the government in December 1900, these camps were presented as exceptional measures aiming to separate the civil populations from the combatants that the colonial forces were seeking to isolate and destroy. Civil populations, notably women and children, were from then on confined in barbed-wire sites of desolation where mortality rates proved particularly high.

The Third Reich added a crucial dimension to these models of colonial origin: the planning of mass death. The Germans had, it so happens, already made plans for mass death in the African Southwest in 1904, when the Herero were the first to experience forced labor in a concentration camp system — the first genocide of the twentieth century. Outside the colonies, on European territory, the logic of the concentration camp did not only take on Nazi forms. It existed not only during but also before and after the Second World War. In 1942, for example, France had close to a hundred camps. The majority of them emerged under the Third Republic *finissante* of Édouard Daladier, prior to the Vichy regime. They accommodated all sorts of individuals adjudged "a hazard to national defense and public safety" — in the majority of cases people who had fled their countries and sought refuge in France (Germans and Austrians; Jews from 1933 on; and then Spaniards, former combatants of the republican cause, from 1939).[24] These sites and others that emerged under Vichy (Compiègne, Rivesaltes, Les Milles, Gurs, Pithiviers, Beaune, Drancy, etc.) served as laboratories where a certain radicalization of preventative, repressive, and punitive measures occurred.

It was thus a time in which multiple figures were produced for the purpose of scapegoating. Many foreigners were perceived as, if not enemies, then at least "useless mouths" of whom it was necessary to be rid. They were accused of "stealing the jobs and women of Frenchmen."[25] Under Vichy, the slow darkening of the figure of the foreigner hit its defining moment. The foreigner was now only a degraded biological element whose defects and pathologies directly threatened the integrity of the national body. In the fall of 1940, a new law was made to enable the revision of all naturalizations granted since 1927. Between 1940 and 1944, close to fifteen thousand persons were stripped of French nationality and "rendered stateless."[26]

Let's return to the colonial concentration camps; it should be made clear that they were not, initially, camps destined for extermination properly speaking. As regards the European case in particular, many historians suggest a distinction between the universe of *relocation camps, of concentration camps* destined for non-Jewish peoples, and that of *the extermination camps* in which the Judeocide was perpetrated—between the camps designed to receive political enemies and the death centers as such. Indeed, not all camps were about programming death. The distinction between concentration camp measures in the strict sense and the exterminatory machinery properly speaking is therefore important, even if, moreover, all camps (colonial camps included) were spaces over which hovered suffering and, potentially, diverse forms of death—slow death, by exhaustion, labor, or abandonment and indifference, or, as was the case in the very heart of Europe, disappearance by gas pure and simple—then smoke, ashes, and dust. In both cases, the camps held a humanity sometimes declared useless, sometimes harmful, sometimes perceived as an enemy, and in any case parasitic and superfluous. This is how, in modern philosophy, the world of the camps became inseparable from the world of a singular crime, perpetrated in apparent secrecy: *a crime against humanity.*

The colonial site was one of the clearest modern expressions of this problematic whereby a crime against humanity was committed and not necessarily acknowledged as such. Still today, it is not obvious to the eyes of all that the enslaving of the Negroes and colonial atrocities are part of our world memory; even less that this memory, as common, is not the property of the sole peoples that suffered these events, but of humanity as a whole; or again that our inability to assume the memories of the "All-World" will make it impossible to imagine what a truly common world, a truly common humanity, might be.

Admittedly, not every carceral space under colonization necessarily participated in the concentration camp system or in the extermination apparatus. But the camp was a central apparatus of colonial and imperialist wars. We must therefore bear in mind these origins of the camp—first, in the cauldron of imperialist and colonial wars (asymmetrical wars by definition), later in civil wars and their aftermath, and, last, in the horizon of the world war. This genealogy suggests that a project to divide humans is always to be found at the camp's origin. Division and occupation go hand in hand with expulsion and deportation, and often also with an avowed or disavowed program of elimination. When all is said and done, not for nothing will the camp-form have accompanied, practically everywhere, logics of the eliminatory settlement.

Of this division of humans and this eliminatory settlement, Frantz Fanon, who devoted a large part of his short life to treating the unwell, was the witness. He was the direct witness of unfathomable suffering, madness, human distress, and, above all, the seemingly senseless death of manifold innocent people, that is to say, of those whom one would expect to be spared, including in *situations of extremity.*

In fact, a potential situation of extremity is constituted by every situation of structural subjugation, at least for those subject to it. This was the case of the colonial experience. Wherever it was driven by a will to exterminate, the colonial undertaking left behind it only the remainders of the indigenous population that it had, for that matter, hastened to confine to enclaves. By restricting occasions for meeting and contact between settlers and the subjugated, both groups were set at a maximal distance—a prior condition for the banalizing of indifference. On the part of those tasked with implementing it, conquest and colonial occupation demanded not only an extraordinary aptitude for indifference but also norm-defying capacities to perform properly repugnant acts. Massacres, butchery, and the repression of resistance sometimes required hand-to-hand contact, meting out horrible forms of cruelty, assaults on bodies and goods—all acts designed to express, each and every time, the ignominy in which the so-called inferior races were held. Wherever necessary, aerial slaughter was used together with terrestrial demolition.[27] The panoply was completed with decapitations, dismemberings, torture, and forms of sexual abuse.[28]

Habituation to sadism, the implacable will to know nothing, to experience no empathy toward the victims, to be persuaded of the natives' villainy, to hold them responsible for the atrocities as well as the exactions and massive damages inflicted upon them—such was the law. As Fanon explains it, whenever colonialism was to be exonerated, the same subterfuges were unhesitatingly appealed to: the crimes were deeds performed by lone-acting individuals, who themselves were racked with fear owing to the animalistic behavior and the extreme, barbaric acts of their victims, and were thus overcome by the threat to their lives posed by these savages; the horrors experienced by the colonized scarcely carried any weight as regards the misery they would endure when left to their own devices; what had been accomplished in the name of civilization (economic development, technological progress, schooling, health, Christianization, and assimilation) worked to offset the negative—and allegedly inevitable— effects of the colonial project.[29]

Algeria was a particular case in point. As regards colonial war in general, Fanon maintained that it generated all sorts of pathologies and constituted a favorable terrain for hatching mental disorders. These war-time pathologies properly speaking came on top of all the various injuries that colonization had previously inflicted on the colonized during conquest and occupation. Colonized individuals who lived through colonial war, or again who participated as combatants in it, bore upon themselves, in themselves, and had in their possession its scars and other traces of originary cuts.

About the Algerian war in particular, Fanon argued that it often had all the aspects of a "genuine genocide."[30] In fact, in its structure as well as in its ornament—above all when it rested on racist and supremacist presuppositions—the colonial process always revolved around a genocidal drive. In many cases, this drive never materialized. But it was always there, in a latent state. It reached its maximal point of incandescence in times of war—of conquest, occupation, or counterinsurgency. This genocidal drive proceeded in molecular fashion. For the most part simmering, it crystalized from time to time by shedding blood (slaughters, massacres, repressions), events that continually recurred. Its point of paroxysm was war. It executed and revealed to all the threat that every colonial system is ready to wield when its survival is at stake: spill as much blood as possible, shatter piece by piece the worlds of the colonized and transform them into an undifferentiated pile of ruins, of bodies torn to shreds, of forever broken lives, an uninhabitable place.

Still on the subject of the Algerian war, Fanon said that the atmosphere into which it plunged people, victims and executioners, combatants and civilians alike, was notable for its gore factor. It threatened to transform everyone, to varying degrees, into statues of hatred and empty them of all human feelings—pity, for starters—as well as the capacity to let oneself be touched, to recall one's own vulnerability to misfortune and to the distress of Others. The eradicating of all feelings of pity: this zero degree of exchange between fellow humans had paved the way to a generalization of inhuman practices, creating the tenacious impression that people were "witnessing a veritable apocalypse."[31]

Faced with this undermining and its ensuing destruction, Fanon maintained the necessity of violence. Such violence had a twofold target: the colonial system as such and the systems of inhibitions of all sorts that kept the colonized under the yoke of fear, superstitions, and manifold persecution and inferiority complexes. By performing a tabula rasa of the oppressive order, the necessary field could be opened for the creation of something new. By rendering the colonial order null and void—ineffective—violence acted as an instrument of resurrection.

In Fanon's mind, at issue was not to conquer the state but instead to create another formation of sovereignty. As a privileged moment of the upsurge of the new, regenerative violence aimed to produce other forms of life. It had a dimension of incalculability, owing to which it was, by essence, unpredicted. Set loose, it was liable to become uncontrollable. From this viewpoint, it was at once that which was liable to save and that by which the peril penetrated the abode.

Society of Objects

Colonial societies were entities bereft of feelings of pity. Far from depicting themselves as *societies of fellow humans*, they were, in law and in fact, communities of separation and hatred. Paradoxically, this hatred was what held them together. The cruelty was all the more ordinary and the scorn all the more aggressive as the relations of enmity were by and large irrevocably internalized. Indeed, reciprocal relations of instrumentalization between the dominant and the dominated were such that distinguishing the part of the internal enemy and the part of the outside enemy with any clarity was almost impossible. On top of everything, racism was simultaneously the driver of this sort of society and its principle of destruction. And insofar as a self scarcely existed without an Other—the Other being only another me, including in the figure of denial—killing the Other was no longer separable from killing oneself.

Racism, according to Fanon, was almost never accidental. All racism—and in particular anti-Negro racism—is subtended by a structure. This structure was in the service of what he called a gigantic work of economic and biological subjugation. In other terms, racism ought to be analyzed *at once in relation to a bio-economy and to an ecobiology*. On the one hand, the racist act consists in an arbitrary and original declaration of superiority—a superiority destined to establish the supremacy of a group, a class, or a species of humans, over others. On the other hand, the nature of racism is always to try to avoid sclerosis. To maintain its virulence and its efficacity, each time it has to renew itself, to change its physiognomy, to metamorphose.

Fanon distinguished between two types of racism in particular. First, there was unadorned racism, vulgar, primitive, and simplistic, which he considered corresponds to "the period of brutal exploitation of man's arms and legs."[32] This racism belonged to times when skulls were compared, when one endeavored to identify the quantity and configuration of the encephalon's furrows, to grasp the logic of the Negro's emotional lability, to define the Arab's subcortical integration, to establish the Jew's generic guilt, to measure vertebrae, and to determine microscopic aspects of the epidermis. Though vulgar, this modality of racism strove to be rational, and even scientific. It sought to draw its authority from science, especially from biology and psychology.

Second, there is a rampant form of racism that Fanon calls cultural. Cultural racism was, in fact, the mere result of a mutation of vulgar racism. It did not rely on equations of a morphological order. It attacked particular forms of existing, which colonialism, in particular, then sought to liquidate. Short of destroying them, it made an attempt either to devalorize them or to turn them into exotic objects. The domains most exposed to this sort of insidious work were clothes, language, technologies, ways of eating, sitting down, resting, amusing oneself, and laughing and, above all, relations to sexuality.

Beyond these two forms of racism linked in a bio-economy, Fanon never stopped insisting on the nature of the injuries caused by racism. As he put it, "Racism bloats and disfigures the face of the culture that practices it."[33] In even more decisive fashion, he asserted that racism, at bottom, participates in an elementary form of neurosis. It always contained an element of passionate engagement such as can be seen in some psychoses. It was in league with delusion, notably of a passionate order. To this triple neurotic, psychotic, and delusional structure he added a dimension that criticism has left relatively unexplored: racism was a way for the subject to divert onto the Other the intimate shame he had of himself, to shift it onto a scapegoat.

Fanon called this mechanism of projection *transitivism*. By transitivism, he understood not the way in which a culture denies or disavows its inferior elements and its drives but the mechanism by which it ascribes to them an evil genius (the Negro, the Jew, the Arab), one that it has produced for itself and that it conjures up in its moments of panic or cruelty.

Thanks to this evil spirit, this culture creates an internal enemy for itself and, by way of social neurosis, undermines itself and destroys from within the values that it otherwise claims to hold. Standing opposed to primitive and coarse surface racism is another, more insidious form of racism, the point of which is to forever unburden oneself of all guilt. If this is so, according to Fanon, it is because every racist expression is always, somewhere, haunted by a bad conscience that it seeks to stifle. This is one reason why he maintains that in general the racist hides himself or tries to dissimulate himself.

It cannot be ruled out that this penchant for hiding and dissimulation is linked to a fundamental aspect of the relations that racist affect maintains with sexuality in general. For, says Fanon, a racist society is one that is worried about the question of losing its sexual potential. It is also a society inhabited by "an irrational nostalgia for the extraordinary times of sexual licentiousness, of orgiastic scenes, of unpunished rapes, of unrepressed incest."[34] Orgies, rape, and incest do not fulfill exactly the same functions in the constitution of racist fantasies. What they nonetheless have in common, Fanon maintains, is that they respond to the life instinct. This life instinct has a double, namely, fear of the Negro, whose supposed genital potency, unhindered by morality and prohibitions, constitutes a real biological danger.

Turning to the forms of suffering that racism produces: To what kinds of torment are those targeted by the aforementioned different forms of racism exposed? How can we characterize the wounds inflicted upon them, the cuts with which they are overrun, the traumas they undergo, and the sort of madness they experience? Replying to these questions obliges us to dwell closely on how racism works and how it constitutes the subject exposed to its fury from within.

First, the racialized subject is the product of the desire of a force outside oneself, a force one has not chosen but that paradoxically initiates and supports one's being. A very large part of the suffering described by Fanon is due to the reception that the subject reserves for that external force, which, this doing, is transformed into the constitutive moment of its inauguration. This constitution of the subject in the desire for subordination is one of the specific, internalized modalities of racial domination. Again we must take seriously what Fanon examines: the process whereby the colonial subject turns against itself and frees itself from the conditions of its emergence in and by subjection. Psychic life is strongly implicated in this *process of freeing* that, in Fanon, proceeds naturally from an absolute practice of violence and from a tearing from oneself — if required, by insurrection.

Second, to be reduced to the state of the subject of race is to be installed immediately in the position of the Other. The Other is the one who must, each time, prove to others that he is a human being, that he merits being taken for a fellow human, that he is, as Fanon did not stop repeating, "a man akin to others," "a man like others," who is like us, who is us, who is one of ours. To be the Other is to feel oneself always as being in an unstable position. The tragedy of the Other is that, due to this instability, the Other is constantly on the alert. He lives in the expectation of a repudiation. He does everything so that this repudiation does not take place, all the while knowing that it will necessarily come and at a time over which he has little control.

As a result, he fears showing himself such as he really is, preferring disguise and dissimulation to authenticity, and convinced that shame has been brought upon his existence. His ego is a knot of conflicts. Split and unable to face up to the world, how could he undertake to give it a form? How could he endeavor to inhabit it? "I wanted quite simply to be a man among men. . . . I wanted to be a man, nothing but a man." And yet "I find myself an object among objects."[35] The desire to be a human among others is countered by the decree of difference. On the subject of race, that is to say, defined by difference, racism demands the "conduct of a Negro," that is to say, of a human apart, since the Negro represents *this part of humans that are held apart — the part apart.* They constitute a sort of *remainder* ordained to dishonor and disgrace.

Body-object, subject-in-the-object, what sort of object are we speaking about? Is it a matter of a real and material object, such as a piece of furniture? Is it a matter of images of objects — the Negro as a mask? Or is it a matter of a spectral and phantasmatic object, at the limit of desire and of terror — the fantasy of the Negro that rapes me, whips me, and makes me yell without my knowing precisely whether the yell is of pleasure or dread? Probably all at once and, further still, a yell of partial objects, of disjoined limbs that, instead of uniting in a body, arise from who knows where: "My body was returned to me spread-eagled, disjointed, redone, draped in mourning on this white winter's day."[36]

Winter's mourning on this white day, winter's white on this day of mourning, in a void place, the time of a voiding, and curtain closes. The essential human person, witnessing its dissolution in the thing, is suddenly stripped of all human substantiality and imprisoned in a crushing objectality. Others have "fixed" me, "in the same way you fix a preparation with a dye." My "blood congealed," here I am henceforth the prisoner of a vicious circle.[37] A representative instance of the "white" took my place and made my consciousness its object. Henceforth, this instance breathes in my place, thinks in my place, speaks in my place, monitors me, acts in my place. At the same time, this master instance fears me. In it, I bring to the surface all the obscure feelings buried in the penumbras of culture — terror and horror, hatred, scorn, and insult. The master instance imagines that I could subject it to all sorts of shameful abuse, pretty much the same ones that it inflicts on me. In it, I feed an anxious worry inside this master instance that flows not from my desire for revenge, still less from anger and from the impotent rage occupying me, but instead from the status of phobogenic object it has attached to me. The white fears me not at all because of what I have done to it or of what I have given it to see, but owing to what he has done to me and thinks that I could do to him in return.

Racist formations, by definition, thus produce and redistribute all sorts of miniaturized madnesses. They contain within themselves the incandescent kernels of a madness that they strive to liberate in cellular doses — various modes of neurosis, psychosis, delirium, and even eroticism. At the same time, they secrete objective situations of madness. These situations of madness envelop and structure social existence in its entirety. As all are caught in the lure of this violence, its diverse mirrors, or in its different refractions, they are all survivors of this violence to varying degrees. The fact of being on one side or on the other does not at all mean, far from it, that one is outside the game or contravening the rules.

Racist Fears

Not only, then, does the racist have a penchant for dissimulation. Fear inhabits him just as much—in the case of concern to us here, fear of the Negro, that Other forced to live life under the sign of duplicity, need, and antagonism. This need is grasped generally in the language of nature and of organic and biological processes. Indeed, the Negro breathes, drinks, eats, sleeps, and expels. The Negro's body is a natural body, a body of needs, a physiological body. This body does not suffer in the manner of an expressive human body. At bottom, the Negro can scarcely fall ill, since, in any case, precariousness is its attribute. A healthy body was never at stake. Negro life is deficient, and therefore poor.

In the colonial situation, the racists have the power. But having power does not suffice to eliminate fear. The racist indeed fears the Negro all the while having already decreed the latter's inferiority. How can one fear someone that one has nevertheless devalued, one from whom one has beforehand removed all the attributes of strength and power? Moreover, it is a matter not only of fear but a mix of fear, hatred, and displaced love. Such is indeed the characteristic feature of anti-Negro racism—the fact that confronted with a Negro one is unable to behave oneself and act "normally." This impacts the Negro himself as much as the one confronting him.

Fanon observes of phobia that it is "a neurosis characterized by the anxious fear of an object (in the broadest sense of anything outside the individual) or, by extension, of a situation."[38] The Negro is an object that awakens dread and disgust. Dread, anxiety, fearing the Negro as object— all stem from an infantile structure. In other terms, an infantile structure of racism exists that is linked to a disconcerting (*désécurisant*) accident and, among humans in particular, to the mother's absence. The choice of phobogenic object, Fanon suggests, is determined. "Such an object does not come out of the void of Nothingness." An accident has taken place. This accident has provoked an affect in the subject. "The phobia is the latent presence of this affect on the core of the world of the subject. There is an organization that has been given a form." For "the object, naturally, need not be there, it is enough that somewhere the object *exists*: is a possibility." This object is "endowed with evil intentions and with all the attributes of a malefic power."[39] Thus, in the person who fears, something of magical thinking occurs.[40]

One who hates the black, who experiences dread in his regard, or that the real or phantasmatic encounter with the black engulfs in anxiety—this someone rehearses a disconcerting trauma. He acts neither rationally nor logically. He thinks not a bit. He is moved by an affect and obeys its laws. The Negro is, in the majority of cases, a more or less imaginary aggressor. A fearsome object, he awakens terror. Fanon goes on to examine the place occupied by sexuality in this dynamic of racist fear. Following Angelo Hesnard, he puts forward the hypothesis that the cause of terror stems from the fear that the Negro might "do all sorts of things to me, but not the usual ill-treatment: sexual abuses—in other words, immoral and shameful things."[41]

In racist imagery, the Negro as sexual subject is the equivalent of an aggressive and frightening object, capable of inflicting abuse and traumas on his victim. Since, with him, everything purportedly runs through the genital level, the abuses whose author he potentially is may prove especially shameful. Were he effectively to rape us or simply to whip us, this disgrace would not solely stem from our forced implication in a shamed existence. It would also be the result of the effraction of a purportedly human body by an object-body. And yet, what is more enchanting and more joyous, in a Dionysian and sadomasochistic perspective, than enjoyment *through* the object rather than enjoyment *through* the member of another subject?

Subsequently we can understand the privileged place that the two forms of Dionysiac and sadomasochist sexuality occupy in racist phantasmagoria. In bacchanal-type Dionysiac sexuality, the Negro is basically a member—not just any one: an alarming member. In sadomasochist-type sexuality, he is a rapist. The racist subject, from this point of view, is one who does not stop shouting, "The Negro is raping me! The Negro is whipping me! The Negro raped me!" But, says Fanon, we are essentially dealing here with an infantile fantasy. To say "The Negro is raping me" or "whipping me" does not mean "hurt me" or "The Negro hurt me." It means "I am hurting myself as the Negro would if indeed he were in my place, if he had the opportunity."

At the center of both forms of sexuality the phallus is to be found. The phallus is not only an abstract place, a simple signifier or differentiating sign—the detachable, divisible object available to symbolic retranscription, of which Jacques Lacan spoke. To be sure, the phallus does not reduce to the penis as such. But neither is it the organ without body so dear to a certain Western psychoanalytic tradition. On the contrary, in colonial—and therefore racist—situations, it represents that which, of life, is manifest in the purest fashion as turgescence, as thrust, and as intrusion. Clearly, it is impossible to speak about thrust, turgescence, and intrusion without restoring to the phallus if not its physicality, then at least its living flesh, its capacity to testify to domains of the sensible, to feel all sorts of sensations, vibrations, and quiverings (a color, a scent, touch, weights, an odor). In contexts of racial domination and thus of social minoritization, the Negro phallus is above all perceived as an enormous power of affirmation. It is the name of an at once totally affirmative and transgressive force that no prohibition holds in check.

As such, it radically contradicts the racial power that, in addition to defining itself first and foremost as the power of a prohibition, also represents itself as endowed with a phallus that functions as its emblem and its finery, as much as the central apparatus of its discipline. This power *is* phallus, and the phallus is the ultimate name of prohibition. As the ultimate name of prohibition, that is to say, as beyond all prohibition, it can blithely mount those subject to it. In this capacity, it pretends to act as a source of movement and energy. It can act as though it happened that the event occurred in and through the phallus, as if, in fact, the phallus were the event.

The belief according to which power is, when all is said and done, the effort that the *phallos* expends on itself to become Figure—this belief is at the basis of all colonial domination. In fact, it continues to function as the unsaid, the subsoil, and even the horizon of our modernity, even if we absolutely want to hear nothing of it. The same goes for the belief according to which the phallus is only phallus in the movement whereby it seeks to escape the body and endow itself with its own autonomy. And it is this breakaway attempt, or again this thrust, which produces spasms; moreover, in a colonial and racist situation power inflects its identity precisely through these spasmodic thrusts.

The spasms by means of which one believes one can recognize and identify power and its vibrations only work to sketch the hollow and flattened volume of this same power. For, though the phallus may dilate, this dilation is always followed by a contraction and a dissipation, by a detumescence. In addition, under colonial and racist conditions, the power that brings the Negro to yell and that wrests incessant cries from his chest can only be a power coupled with its beast—with its dog-spirit, its pork-spirit, its scoundrel-spirit. It can only involve a power endowed with a bodily material, with a carcass of which the phallus is the most brilliant manifestation as well as the darkened surface. A power that is *phallos*, in the sense that Fanon suggests, can only present itself to its subjects dressed up in a skull. This skull is what makes them give out such yells and makes the Negro's life a Negro life—a simple zoological life.

Historically, the lynching of black people in the South of the United States during the era of slavery and in the aftermath of the Emancipation Proclamation originates in part in the desire to castrate them. Anxiety-ridden as regards one's own sexual potential, the racist "little whites" and the plantation owner are seized with terror in thinking of the "black two-edged sword," dreading not only its presumed volume but also its penetrative and assailing essence.[42] The writer Michel Cournot said much the same thing in more sensual terms: "The Black's prick is a sword. When he has thrust it into your wife, she really feels something. It comes as a revelation. In the chasm it has left, your little bauble is lost."[43] And he compares the black man's member to the palm tree and to the breadfruit tree that would not lose its hard-on for an empire.

In the obscene act of lynching, the aim is thus to protect the supposed purity of the white woman by keeping the black level with his death. The desire is to bring him to contemplate extinction and the darkening of what, in racist phantasmagoria, is held to be his "sublime sun," his *phallos*. The gashing of his masculinity has to transpire by transforming his genital organs into a field of ruins—separating them from the powers of life. This is because, as Fanon puts it so well, in this configuration the Negro does not exist. Or rather, the Negro is above all a *member.*

To fear someone from whom one has previously removed all attributes of force does not mean, however, being unable to inflict violence upon him. The violence perpetrated against him is propped up on a myth that always accompanies the violence of the dominant. The dominant, Fanon never stops reminding us, have a relation to their own violence, that of which they are the authors, which generally passes via mythologization, that is to say, the construction of a discursive derealization, a discourse cut out of history. The function of the myth is thus to make the victims responsible for the violence whose victims they are. At the basis of this myth lies not only an originary separation between "them" and "us." The true problem is the following: It is not okay for them not to be like us. But it is also not okay for them to become like us. For the dominant, both options are absurd and intolerable in equal measure.

Consequently, a situation of madness is created, the perpetuation of which requires unceasing violence with a mythical function, insofar as it is ceaselessly derealized. It is not recognized by the dominant, who, for that matter, never stop denying it or euphemizing it. It exists, but those producing it remain invisible and anonymous. And even when its existence is proven, it has no subject. As the dominant bear no responsibility for it, the only possible initiator of it is the victim himself. Thus, if, for example, they are killed, it is owing to who they are. To avoid being killed, they only have to not be who they are. Or again, if they are killed, it can only be incidentally—as collateral damage. To avoid being killed, they only have to avoid being where they are at this precise time. Or again, if they are killed, it is because they pretend to be like us, our double. And by killing the double, we assure our survival. So they only have to be different from us. This permanent renewal of the division between "them" and "us" is one of the conditions of reproduction on a molecular scale of colonial- and racist-type violence. But, as we may observe nowadays, it is the nature of racial violence to survive the historical conditions of its birth.

Approaching racial violence in particular, Fanon began with a seemingly anodyne question: What happens during the encounter between the black and the white? According to Fanon, the encounter is performed under the sign of a shared myth—the myth of the Negro. In actual fact, Fanon clarifies, European culture possesses an *imago* of the Negro that Negroes themselves have internalized and reproduce faithfully, including in the most anodyne circumstances. What does that imago consist in? In this imaginary economy, the Negro is not a human but an object. More exactly, the Negro is a phobic object that, as such, arouses fear and terror. This phobic object is first discovered through the gaze.

Festival of the Imagination

Let us dwell, then, on this founding moment that, in Fanon, has a name: radical decolonization. In his work, this decolonization is likened to a force of refusal and it stands directly opposed to the passion of habituation. This force of refusal constitutes the first moment of the political and of the subject. In fact, the subject of the political — or the Fanonian subject period — is born to the world and to itself through this inaugural gesture, namely the capacity to say no. What is being refused if not subjugation, and firstly subjugation to a representation. For, in racist contexts, "to represent" is the same thing as "to disfigure." The will to representation is at bottom a will to destruction aiming to turn something violently into nothing. Representing thus participates at once in a play of shadows and in an act of devastation, even if, after this devastation, something still exists that belonged to the previous order.

As a symbolic operation, representation does not necessarily lead to the possibility of mutual recognition. First, in the consciousness of the representing subject, the represented subject always runs the risk of being transformed into an object or a plaything. By allowing himself to be represented, he denies himself the capacity to create himself, both for himself and for the world, a self-image. This subject is obliged to take to an image that will demand endless struggle. This subject grapples with an image that has been pinned on it, which it labors to rid itself of, whose author he is not and in which he scarcely recognizes himself. Then, and instead of being "fully what [he is]," supposing that to be possible, this subject is condemned to live its consciousness as a lack.[44] In the history of the encounter between the West and faraway worlds, a manner of representing the Other effectively does empty it of all substance and leave it lifeless, "in a bodily struggle with death, a death on this side of death, a death in life."[45]

This is the negative theory of representation subtending the idea that Fanon formed of racial violence. Such violence does not merely work through the gaze. It rests on all sorts of measures that include, for example, spatial division and segregation of the same name, a racist division of "dirty work" (at the end of which, by way of example, "Senegalese sharpshooters" were charged with ending the Malagasy insurgency through bloodshed), as well as technologies such as language, the radio, and even medicine, which are endowed, as befits the occasion, with a deadly power. Racial violence produces an entire series of survivors. These survivors are, essentially, men and women shut within a bodily struggle against the shadow having engulfed them, men and women who are at pains to rip it asunder and come to self-clarity.

If Fanon dwells so much on the shadowy face of life in situations of madness (racism being considered, from this point of view, a particular instance of psychic disturbance), it is always to sketch an affirmative and almost solar moment, one of mutual recognition announcing the advent of "a man like all others." The human "like all others" has a body. He has feet, hands, a chest, a heart. He is not a pile of organs. He breathes. He walks.

Just as a body is only ever animated and in movement—that is, a breathing and walking body—so, too, is the body always a *name*-bearing body. The name differs from the sobriquet: him, little matter who he is; we'll routinely call him Muhammad or Mamadou. The sobriquet, Fanon suggests, is the result of the falsification of an original name, based on the idea that we know is "repulsive" (*dégueulasse*).[46] The name combines with the *face*. No mutual recognition arises without a claim about the Other's face being, if not similar to mine, then at least close to mine. The gesture of claiming the Other's face as a visage whose guardian I am a priori stands directly opposed to the gesture of effacement seen in, for example, profiling his *facies*, or racial profiling.

Last, the Other is only Other insofar as he has *a place* among us, insofar as he finds some room among us, insofar as we make a place for him among us.[47] Recognition of the human that I am in the visage of the man or woman facing me, such is the condition under which the "man that lives on this earth"—this earth as the home of all—is more than a pile of organs and more than a Muhammad. And if it is true that this Earth is the home of all, then nobody at all can be required to return home.

Fanon's patient is recognized not only in his capacity of refusal. He distinguishes himself also by his disposition to struggle. To express struggle, Fanon has recourse to a series of terms: liberation, decolonization, absolute disorder, changing the world order, the upsurge, exiting the great night, coming to the world. Struggle is not spontaneous. It is organized and conscious. It is, he says, the fruit of a "radical decision."[48] It has a specific rhythm.

As the work of new humans, the struggle has a privileged actor, to wit, the people—a collective subject if ever there was one. It is at the origin of new languages. It aims to bring about a new humanity. It engages every-thing: muscles, bare fists, intelligence, the suffering from which one is not spared, blood. A new gesture, it creates new respiratory rhythms. The Fanonian fighter is a human who breathes anew, whose muscular tensions unclench, and whose imagination is in celebration.

The celebration of the imagination produced by struggle — this is the name that Fanon gives to culture. It is cadenced by the transmutation of picaresque figures, the resurgence of epic stories, an immense work on objects and on forms. Such is the case with wood and especially with masks, which range from despondency to animation, with faces in particu-lar. Such is also the case with ceramics (pitchers, earthenware jars, colors, and trays). Through dance and melodic song, the colonized restructure their perception. The world loses its accursed character, and the conditions come together for the inevitable confrontation. No struggle occurs that does not perforce entail the breaking apart of old cultural sedimentations. This sort of struggle is an organized collective work. It distinctly aims to overturn history. The Fanonian patient seeks to become, once more, the origin of the future.

The Relation of Care

Of the various patients that the society of enmity produces, Fanon was con-cerned in particular with people affected with impotence, raped women, torture victims; those struck with anxiety, stupor, or depression; many people (including children) who had killed or tortured; people having lost their parents; people suffering all sorts of phobias; combatants and civil-ians; French and Algerians; refugees affected with all sorts of puerperal psychoses; others on the edge of despair and who, unable to go on, had at-tempted suicide; profoundly broken people who, having lost their voices, began to yell, and whose agitations, he attested, could sometimes take the appearance of fury or delusions (notably of persecution).

That wasn't all. He took care of men and women of all ages and pro-fessions; patients with serious mental disturbances, with behavioral dis-orders; those inhabited by delusional ideas of persecution; those emit-ting raucous cries and screams at any place or time; those affected with intermittent psychomotor agitation, diurnal or nocturnal; sometimes ag-gressive patients, totally unaware of their illness; sthenic and unwilling patients; mad people who, moreover, could be racists; people, including missionaries, who had returned from Africa, where they had distinguished themselves by their violent and contemptuous conduct toward the natives, especially the children; hypochondriacs; human beings whose ego and relations with the rest of the world were subject to an alteration not allowing them any longer to find their "place among people."[49]

But these human persons were essentially engulfed in almost continuous depressive states, excited, irritable, stricken with anger and sometimes with rage, beset by tears, cries, lamentations, confronted with the impression of imminent death, face-to-face with (visible and invisible) executioners that they never stop pleading with. This world of hatred, misfortune, and war, woven with unanswered appeals to mercy, appeals to spare the innocent—such is the world to which Fanon lent his attention and strove especially hard to listen to. He patiently endeavored to reconstitute the narrative of this world and wanted to give it a voice and a face, well removed from all miserabilism.

A patient, Fanon said, is "first of all someone who suffers and who asks for some relief to be given." Because "suffering provokes compassion, tenderness," the hospital establishment, which is above all a "curative establishment, a therapeutic establishment," cannot be transformed "into a barracks." The loss of freedom, the loss of the sense of time, the loss of the capacity to watch over oneself and take care of oneself, the loss of relation and the loss of world, he thought, constituted the real drama of the ill person and the alienated individual. This is so because "the sane human being is a social human being." The illness "cuts him off" from other social beings and "isolates him from them." It separates him from the world, "leaving him powerless, alone with an evil that is strictly his." The total or partial collapse of the patient's biophysical, psychic, or mental integrity threatens the system of relations without which the patient is rejected from the world and placed in a barracks. For wherever others—or, more specifically, my neighbor or my fellow human—no longer reveal me to myself, and wherever I render myself unable to "encounter the other's face," unable to "be here with other humans," with my fellow beings, illness is nearby.[50]

As illness places me in a state that scarcely allows me to encounter my neighbor, my fellow human, other human persons, every authentic act of curing presumes the reconstitution of this link, and therefore of something that is common to us. The reconstitution of the common begins with an exchange of speech and a breaking of silence: "Language is what breaks the silence and silences. Then you can communicate or commune *with* this person. The neighbour in the Christian sense is always an accomplice. . . . To commune with means to commune with faced with something. . . . Creative intentions can emerge from out of the common."[51]

If, for the patient, communicating, communing with, and developing affinities with one's fellows are means for maintaining contact with the world and taking part in it, then returning to life necessitates remembering and projecting oneself into the future, as crucial elements of every therapeutic adventure. This relation with the passing of time — the date to be born in mind, a calendar enabling a schedule to be established, yesterday, tomorrow, the passing of days that are not alike, celebrating Aïd el-Kébir, the sounding of the Angelus, the hearing of Easter bells — is a key point in every healing gesture. For, once hospitalized, some patients "erect between the outside world and themselves a very opaque screen behind which they immobilize themselves."[52]

Overcome with inertia, they surrender. Hence, in the hospital's "oppressive and stifling" atmosphere, life is made of interminable disputes between patients that the orderlies must continually separate "at the risk of receiving blows themselves." The cramped nature of the premises and the patients' propensity to "throw food on the table or to the ground, to bend their iron plates or break their spoons" is such that "cleaning care takes up a considerable part of the staff's activity." Fear sets in. The orderly dreads the patient. The hairdresser demands that the patients be bound before being shaved. "Out of fear of patients, or in order to punish them, some patients were left in secure units, sometimes shirtless, without mattresses and without sheets," when, for the sake of prevention, they were not purely and simply "tied up with a belt."[53]

Squatting, lying down, asleep, or sitting down, not only does the patient surrender. His temporal bearings are deeply affected. That which, previously, made up his world suddenly comes crashing down. Added to the temporal leveling is the degeneration of language. The bifurcation between the functions of expression and the functions of meaning increases. Reference is neutralized and the signifier destroyed. The ability to get to the reality of the world and engage in an encounter with the other by means of discourse is diminished. The speech act is no longer necessarily the manifest sign of a conscious activity. Detaching itself from consciousness, language is from there on in only the reified status of the illness. Half lying down, eyes closed, the patient enters the zone of inaccessibility and forgetting—the forgetting of the big wide world.

Under these conditions, the care relation indeed consists in interrupting the inexorable course of degeneration. But it essentially aims to restore the patient to his being and his relations with the world. So that the illness and possibly death do not monopolize the future and life as a whole, the care relation must be about recognizing the ill person and accompanying the patient in his efforts to be reborn again in the world. It must prevent him from dying before time, from thinking and acting as if he were already dead, as if the time of daily life no longer counted. It must encourage him to cultivate his interest in life. Whence, Fanon maintains, "the constant concern to refer each gesture, each word, each facial expression of the patient" to the illness afflicting him.[54]

One of Fanon's patients, a policeman, simply does his job: torture. That's his work. So he tortures with equanimity. Torture, truly, is tiring. But after all, it is normal, has its logic and rationale, until the day he begins to do at home as he does at work. Though he was not previously like this, now he is. At the clinic, he meets one of the men he had tortured. This meeting is intolerable for both of them. How can he make it understood, to himself for starters, that he has not become mad? The violence that he was led to perform henceforth locks him within the personage of the madman. Perhaps, to cope with it, he will have to set fire to his own body?

Fanon's other patient is racked with anger and rage. But he is not inhabited by the complex of immolation by fire. His testicles were practically crushed during a hideous torture session. He is crippled by impotence, his masculinity is wounded. He is able only to perform the violence that he has inside him owing to the violence he was made to suffer. His own wife was doubtless raped. Two instances of violence, then—one inflicted from without, but which produces the other violence, which lives inside the subject and provokes in him rage, anger, and, occasionally, despair.

The endured rage and anger constitute primordial forms of suffering. But this suffering is far-reaching. It attacks memory in its very frameworks. The ability to remember is eroded. From now on, memory works only through fragments and residues, and somewhat pathogenically. Piles of repressed desires no longer appear in the light of day except in disguise—everything, or almost, has become unrecognizable. A chain of traumatic events grips the subject, arousing in him loathing, resentment, anger, hatred, and impotent rage. To leave it behind, Fanon suggests, one must walk back over the trace of the person who has been defeated and re-create a genealogy. Myth must be left behind and history written—history is to be lived not as a hysteria, but based on the principle according to which "I am my own foundation."

The Stupefying Double

This policeman does not want to hear any more screams. They prevent him from sleeping. To break free of this nocturnal clamor, he must close the shutters each night before going to bed; draft-proof the windows, including during the high heat of summer; and stuff his ears with cotton.

This detective never stops smoking. He has lost his appetite, and endless nightmares disturb his sleep.

> As soon as someone confronts me, I feel like hitting him. Even outside work I feel like punching the guy who gets in my way. For nothing at all. Take for example when I go to buy the paper. There's a line. So you have to wait. I hold out my hand to take the paper (the guy who runs the newsstand is an old friend of mine) and someone in the line calls out aggressively: "Wait your turn." Well, I feel like beating him up and I tell myself: "If I could get you, pal, for a few hours, you wouldn't mess with me!"

In fact, he is tormented by the desire to hit. Everyone. Everything. Everywhere, including at home. No one escapes this torment, not his children, not "even the twenty-month-old baby" and "with a rare savagery," even less so his own wife, who commits the wrong of calling out to him and naming the trouble eating him: "For goodness sake, you're crazy." In response, "he turned on her, beat her, and tied her to a chair shouting: 'I'm going to teach you once and for all who's the boss around here.'"[55]

A twenty-one-year-old Frenchwoman finds her father's funeral sickening. She hears officials paint a portrait of him bearing no likeness to her own experience. A death that was to be mourned is suddenly overlaid with outstanding moral qualities (self-sacrifice, devotion, love for the fatherland). It nauseated her. In fact, whenever she had gone to her father's to sleep, she had been kept up at night, troubled no end by the screams coming from downstairs: "They were torturing Algerians in the cellar and the disused rooms to get information out of them. . . . I wonder how a human being can put up with . . . hearing someone scream in pain."[56]

"For close to three years," Fanon wrote in his resignation letter addressed to the resident minister in 1956, "I put myself wholly at the service of this country and the people who inhabit it." Yet, he no sooner remarks, what value do "intentions [have] if their embodiment is made impossible by an indigence of heart, sterility of spirit and hatred for this country's natives."[57] These three terms — indigence of heart, sterility of spirit, hatred of the natives — describe in lapidary fashion what, in his eyes, forever characterized the colonial system. Time and again, and based on the firsthand observation of facts, he provided a detailed and multiform description of this system. And the more direct the experience he had of it, the more it appeared to him a leprosy that spared the body of no one, whether settlers or colonized — "all this leprosy on your body."[58]

Fanon's "Letter to a Frenchman" must indeed be read together with his "Letter to the Resident Minister."[59] Whether or not they were written at the same time, the one explains the other. One serves as a justification for the other. As a form of leprosy, colonization attacks bodies and deforms them. But its essential target is the brain and, incidentally, also the nervous system. To "decerebralize" is its goal.

Decerebralizing consists, of course, in performing if not an amputation of the brain, then at least in sterilizing it. The act of decerebralization also aims at rendering the subject "foreign to his environment." This process of creating a "systematic break with reality" leads in many cases to madness. Often, this madness is expressed in the mode of lying. One of the functions of the colonial lie is to nourish silence and induce conducts of complicity on the pretext that "nothing else is to be done" except, perhaps, to leave.

So why leave? At which moment does the settler begin to entertain the idea that it is perhaps preferable to depart? At the moment he realizes that things are not going well: "the atmosphere is getting rotten"; the "country bristles"; the roads "are no longer safe." The wheat fields have been "transformed into sheets of flame." The Arabs "are becoming hostile." They will soon rape our women. Our own testicles will be "cut off and rammed between our teeth." But if things have really taken a turn for the worse, it is because colonial leprosy has spread everywhere and, with it, "this enormous wound" buried under this "winding-sheet of silence," the combined silence of all, the so-called ignorant silence, and that consequently claims its innocence on the basis of a lie.

For how can it be that no one sees this country and the people inhabiting it? That no one wants in the slightest to understand what is going on around them every passing day? How can it be that one raises a hue and cry about one's concern for Humankind, "but singularly not for the Arab," daily denied and transformed into "Saharan furniture"? How has one never "shaken hands with an Arab," never "drunk coffee" with one, "never talked about the weather with an Arab"? For, ultimately, not a single European "does not rebel, is not indignant, or alarmed by everything, except the fate meted out to the Arab."

For Fanon, then, the right to indifference, or to ignorance, does not exist. For that matter, he considered that, beyond its purely technical aspects, the doctor's task in a colonial context was to rise up in revolt, become indignant, show alarm for the fate dealt to those whose backs are bent over and whose "lives are stopped," whose faces bear the marks of despair, in whose stomachs resignation can be read, in whose blood one diagnoses "prostrate exhaustion of a whole lifetime." The medical act aims to bring forth what he called a viable world. The doctor had to be able to answer the question "What is happening?"; "What has occurred?"

This *demand to be able to answer* entailed a similar duty to see (refuse self-blindness), not to ignore, not to fail to mention, not to dissimulate the real. It required mixing with those who had been spun-dry, with that world of people without dreams, and recounting with a clear and distinct voice about things whose actor and witness one was. "I want," Fanon stated for his part, "my voice to be harsh, I don't want it to be beautiful, I don't want it to be pure, I don't want it to have all the dimensions." On the contrary, he wanted it to be "torn through and through." "I don't want it to be amusing, for I am speaking of humans and their refusal, of the daily rottenness of humans, of their dreadful failure."

For only a voice "torn through and through" could have reported the tragic, heartrending, and paradoxical character of the medical institution in the colonial situation. If the purpose of the medical act is indeed to silence pain by fighting against the illness, how is it that the colonized perceive "the doctor, the engineer, the schoolteacher, the policeman, the rural constable, through the haze of an almost organic confusion"?[60] "But the war goes on. And for many years to come we shall be bandaging the countless and sometimes indelible wounds inflicted on our people by the colonialist onslaught."[61]

Both phrases immediately establish a relation of causality between colonization and the facts of injuries. They also suggest just how difficult it is to cure the victims of colonization once and for all. This difficulty does not only have to do with the almost interminable time that the effort of cure takes. In reality, some wounds, cuts, and lesions will never be healed owing to their depth; their scars will never be effaced; their victims will forever carry the marks. As for colonial war, it is tackled here from the angle of the mental disturbances that it generates, among both the agents of the occupying power and the native population.

This young twenty-six-year-old Algerian is a case in point. At first sight, he suffers from persistent migraines and insomnia, but, at bottom, the problem is sexual impotence. After having escaped from a sealing-off operation, he abandoned the taxi that he first used to transport leaflets and political leaders, and then, little by little, Algerian commandos engaged in the liberation war. Two submachine-gun magazines were left in the taxi. Having hastily joined the maquis, he had no news about his wife and his young daughter of twenty months, until the day his spouse reached him with a message in which she asked him to forget her.

The request to be forgotten can be explained through her having suffered a double rape: first by a leading French serviceman, alone; then by another, and in the view of some others, must we say witnesses? The double dishonor she has endured immediately raises the problem of shame and guilt. Whereas the first rape scene occurred almost in private, in a face-to-face encounter between the woman and her executioner, the second takes on aspects of a public sitting. At this scene of shame, a sole soldier is performing, but under the quasi-pornographic gaze of several others who experience the ordeal in the mode of a delegated enjoyment. Hovering over the scene is a physically absent figure, but one whose spectral presence urges the rapist soldier to intensify the fury. This figure is the husband. By raping his wife, the French soldiers target his phallus and seek to castrate him symbolically.

In this conflict between men, the woman serves above all as a substitute and, additionally, as an object for the satisfaction of the officer's sadistic drives. For this officer, at issue is perhaps not even enjoyment. At issue, on the one hand, is to deeply humiliate the woman (and her husband through her), to compromise irremediably their respective feelings of pride and dignity, as well as the idea they have of themselves and of their relationship. On the other hand, it is to set down, through the act of rape, something like a relation of hatred. Hatred is everything bar a relation of recognition. It is above all a relation of execration. One phallus execrates another phallus: "If you ever see that bastard your husband again, don't forget to tell him what we did to you."[62] Furthermore, the injunction issued, the unfortunate spouse complies.

By asking her husband to forget her, the woman puts her finger on the disgust and the humiliation that she must have felt. Her intimate and secret being was laid bare to the other's gaze, to the gaze of unknown individuals, to the occupier's gaze. Her desire, her modesty, and her hidden enjoyment, as well as her bodily form, were, if not profaned, then at least exposed, possessed against her will, offended, and made vulgar. She will never be able to exhibit them in their integrity again.

And since everything transpired in front of witnesses, or in any case voyeurs, she can no longer, by herself, hide anything at all. All she can do is confess. And since she is unable to rub out this affront, she has a single option left, to ask her husband to forget her — a pure gesture of breaking off relations. Here, woman being made for men and not for her own enjoyment, the offense to the man's honor is a stain that necessarily ends in a sacrifice: the loss of this same man.

As for the man, he is stricken with impotence. His dignity as a husband is besmirched. Does it not rest on the principle of the exclusive enjoyment of his wife? Does his phallic power not cherish this exclusivity? As his wife has "had a taste of a Frenchman" despite herself, the link of exclusivity has been broken. At present she drags around a flesh lived as a stain that cannot be cleaned up, wiped away, or removed. He emerges from the experience deeply shaken. This trauma now possesses him: "Every time he tried to have sexual intercourse, he thought of his wife."[63] His wife is that girl that he had to marry although he loved someone else, his cousin, who, as a result of family arrangements, married another man. His wife is the girl that he ended up marrying because his parents proposed it. His wife was nice, but he did not truly love her.

The fact that she was raped makes him angry. His anger is directed at "those bastards." But, who knows, perhaps it is also directed at his wife. Little by little, anger gives way to relief: "Oh, it's nothing serious; she wasn't killed. She can start her life again." To live in dishonor is better than not living at all. Things get complicated. Is he not, ultimately, responsible for his own wife's rape? Has he not witnessed, in the douars, sadistic rapes, sometimes the consequence of idleness? And what if his wife was raped because she had not wanted to "sell out her husband"? And what if the rape was the result of his wife's will to "protect the network": "She had been raped *because they had been looking for me*. In fact, she had been raped to punish her for keeping quiet."[64]

He is therefore responsible for his own wife's rape. She was dishonored because of him. To be dishonored is to be "rotten." And whatever comes from something rotten can itself only be rotten, including his daughter of twenty months, whose photo he wants to rip up before every sexual act. To take back his wife after independence means living with the rot for the rest of his life. For, "that thing, how can you ever forget it?" Indeed, he will never forget that his wife was raped. Similarly, never will a moment arise when he does not ask himself this question: "And did she have to tell me about it?"[65] Just say nothing, period. Carry the burden of the dishonor alone, even if this dishonor resulted from the desire to protect the man to whom one was married.

The second case concerns the undifferentiated drives of a survivor of the communal liquidation of a douar in Constantinois to commit homicide. With his own eyes, he saw people killed and wounded. He was not like those whom the idea of a person's death no longer rattled. The human form, in its death, was still liable to move him. In this case, as with the former one, the refusal to betray is to be found from the start. An ambush had taken place. All the douar inhabitants were rounded up and interrogated. Nobody said anything. For this lack of response an officer gave the order to destroy the douar, set fire to the houses, round up the remaining people, lead them to a wadi, and massacre them. Twenty-nine men were killed at point-blank range. The patient in question survived with two bullets and a fractured humerus.

A survivor, then. But a practically disabled survivor, who does not stop crying for a gun. He refuses to "walk in front of anybody. He refuses to have anyone behind him. One night, he grabbed one of the soldier's guns and clumsily fired on the sleeping soldiers."[66] He was forcibly disarmed. From then on his hands were bound. He is agitated and yells. He wants to kill everyone, indiscriminately. In a mimetic and repetitive gesture, he wants to carry out his own small massacre.

For "in life, it's kill or be killed," he explains. And, to be able to kill, you must first not have been killed yourself. My life or my survival therefore passes via the murder of others, and above all those who I suspect of being an external body that, having disguised themselves, now present the appearances of the fellow being or the congeneric:

> There are some French among us. . . . They're disguised as Arabs. . . . They've all got to be killed. . . . Give me a machine gun. All these so-called Algerians are French. . . . And they won't leave me alone. As soon as I try to get some sleep, they come into my room. But now I know what they're up to. I'll kill them all, every one of them. I'll slit their throats, one after the other, and yours as well.[67]

The survivor is therefore consumed by a violent desire to murder. He pays no heed to distinctions and strikes at the world of women and that of children, the world of poultry and that of domestic animals: "You all want to take me out, but you'll have to think of other ways. Killing you won't affect me in the slightest. The little ones, the grown-ups, the women, the children, the dogs, the birds, the donkeys . . . nobody will be spared. . . . Afterwards I'll be able to sleep in peace."[68] Once the desire for group murder is satisfied, the survivor will at last be able to enjoy the sleep he so craves.

Life Fading Away

Then there is the nineteen-year-old soldier of the National Liberation Army, who has effectively killed a woman by whose phantom he is endlessly haunted. Fanon notes the details of the encounter. The patient before him seems "deeply depressed, [with] dry lips, and constantly moist hands."[69] Fanon finds his breathing concerning, a series of "constant sighs" that continuously puff up his chest. The patient having already committed a murder, he expresses no desire to commit another one. On the contrary, this time it is his own life that he has tried to take — to take his own life after having first taken someone else's. Similar to the aforementioned survivor, he is tormented by an absence of sleep.

Fanon observes his gaze, the way in which it "fixed for a few moments at a point in space while his face lit up, giving the impression he was seeing something." Then he dwells on what the patient says: "The patient talked of his blood being spilled, his arteries drained, and an abnormal heartbeat.

He begged us to stop the haemorrhaging and not let them come into hospital to 'suck the lifeblood' out of him. From time to time, he could no longer speak and asked for a pencil. Wrote: 'Have lost my voice, my whole life is fading away.'"[70]

The patient is still endowed with a body. But this body and all that it bears are assailed by active forces that sap its vital energies. Racked by intolerable suffering, this drifting body no longer constitutes a sign. Or if it still retains the marks of the sign, this sign is one that no longer forms a symbol. That which ought to have been contained from now on equivocates, overflows, and scatters. The body of the suffering subject is no longer a dwelling. If it remains a dwelling, it is hardly inviolable. It is no longer able to preserve anything at all. Its organs let go and its substances are on the loose. It can now be expressed only under the sign of the void or mutism—fear of collapse, the difficulty to inhabit language anew, to return to speech, to make oneself heard and, consequently, live life. The suffering subject understood it perfectly well. No doubt this is why he tried on two occasions to commit suicide, to take charge himself of his death, to appropriate it for himself in the manner of a self-offering.

Behind the feeling of bodily expropriation lies a story of murder. Its context is a colonial war. Colonial war, like other forms of war, rests upon a funerary economy—killing and getting killed. Men, women, children, livestock, poultry, plants, animals, mountains, hills and valleys, streams and rivers, an entire world is placed in the situation laden with the atmosphere of their having seen death. They had been there when others were put to death. They had witnessed the murders of presumably innocent people. In reply, they enlisted in the struggle.

One of the functions of struggle is to convert the economy of hatred and the desire for vengeance into a political economy. The aim of the liberation struggle is not to eradicate the drive to murder, the desire to kill, or the thirst for revenge, but to bend this drive, this desire, and this thirst to the commandments of a superego of a political nature, namely the advent of a nation.

The struggle consists in channeling this energy (the will to kill), without which it is merely sterile repetition. The gesture that consists in killing, the body that one kills (the enemy's), or the body that is put to death (the combatant's or the martyr's) must be able to find a place in the order of this signifier. The drive to kill must no longer be rooted in the primitive force of instincts. Transformed into an energy of political struggle, it must now be symbolically structured.

In the case at hand of a man whom the vampire haunts and who is imperiled with losing his blood, his voice, and his life, this arrangement is unstable. His mother was "killed at point blank range by a French soldier." Two of his sisters were "taken to the barracks," and he is unaware what has become of them, or even of the treatment to which they were subjected, in a context in which interrogations, torture, and, possibly, detentions and rapes are part of daily life. His father having "died some years back," he was the "only man" in the family, and his "sole ambition" was to make life easier for his mother and sisters.

The drama of the struggle attains its point of incandescence where an individual framework is articulated, at a given moment, to a political line. From then on it is difficult to untangle the threads. Everything becomes muddled, as the following story indicates well. A settler who is very committed to countering the liberation movement indeed slaughters two Algerian civilians. An operation is set up against him.

It takes place during the night. "Only his wife was in the house. On seeing us, she begged us not to kill her. . . . We decided to wait for the husband. But I kept looking at the woman and thinking of my mother. She was sitting in an armchair and her thoughts seemed to be elsewhere [in his eyes, she's already gone]. I was asking myself why we didn't kill her."[71] Why kill her? Has she not already in her plea made it perfectly clear that she has, on several occasions, asked her husband not to be mixed up in politics? And, in her second plea, has she not just pleaded for her life in the name of her children? ("Please don't kill me. . . . I've got children.") But neither the argument of responsibility nor the humanitarian argument manage to shake her interlocutor, who, moreover, simply does not answer.

In his works, Fanon did not stop emphasizing one of the major traits of master-subject relations in colonies, namely their poverty in terms of world. From this viewpoint, life in the colonial world might be likened to animal life. The link that colonial masters and their subjects maintain never leads to a living affective community. It never brings about the constitution of a common realm. The colonial master practically never lets himself be *touched* by the speech of his subject.

The poverty of the relation that the master keeps with the native (his *subject* from a juridicolegal viewpoint at the same time as his *thing* from a racial and ontological viewpoint) is reproduced here, but the other way around. In her husband's absence, the circle closes in on his wife, who, from this point forward, is confronted with the strength of drive of someone who, soon, will become her murderer. No sooner was the supplication over, "the next minute she was dead." Despite the final appeal to a certain humanity and compassion, to feelings that supposedly all share. No detonation. No distance either. The narrow play of proximity, almost in a clinch, closed circuit, the relation of an object to another object: "I'd killed her with my knife."

But who had he just killed? This woman who implored him to spare her life and who, ultimately, lost it? Or that woman who, at bottom, is merely the effigy of another woman, the mirror of his mother about whom he thought at the very moment when he looked at his potential victim: "But I kept looking at the woman and thinking of my mother."

Let us recapitulate by paraphrasing: "She began pleading with us not to kill her. The following moment, she was dead. I had killed her with my knife. I was disarmed. Some days later I underwent an interrogation. I thought I was going to be killed. But I couldn't have cared less." It might be thought that everything would stop there. Someone had spilled the blood of his mother. A French soldier, the generic name of an enemy without a proper face, with multiple faces.

Responding to this blood's crying out for vengeance, he spills the blood of another woman who, for her part, has spilled no one's blood, but who finds herself indirectly implicated in the infernal circle of war despite herself, owing to her husband, who is effectively responsible for the assassination of two Algerians, but who escapes retribution yet loses his wife. On both sides, a mother is lost, and, for the man absent at the time of the murder, the loss of a wife. Orphans on both sides, and, on that of the man to whom death was originally destined, a widower. The women do not only pay the price of acts set down by men. They constitute the bargaining chip of this funerary economy.

Due to this excess-presence of woman, whether in the figure of the mother or in that of the spouse or sister, no longer can it be known with complete clarity who exactly was put to death. Who is presumed to have been the recipient of death? How can one be sure that by disemboweling the woman, one was not killing one's own mother? The vampire threatening to empty our bodies of all blood, this symbol of interminable hemorrhaging, is it not basically the name of this double disemboweling, one spectral (that of his mother) and the other real (that of the wife of my enemy)? The clamor of those women who, all of them, "had a gaping hole in their stomachs"; the pleas of all these women who were "bloodless, sickly pale and terribly thin," asking to be spared death for want of protection — is this not what, now, disturbs the murderer with terror, prevents him from sleeping, forces him to vomit after meals? Is this not why, as evening arrives, right as he goes to bed, the room is "invaded by women," all the same ones, demanding that their spilled blood be returned to them?

"At that moment," Fanon noted, "the sound of rushing water filled the room and grew so loud it seemed like a thundering waterfall, and the young patient saw the floor of his room soaked in blood, his blood, while the women slowly got their color back and their wounds began to close. Soaked in sweat and filled with anxiety, the patient would wake up and remain agitated until dawn."

SIX
THIS STIFLING NOONDAY

When Fanon died, his eyes were fixed on Africa or, precisely, on what he called "this Africa to come." Born in Martinique, passing through France, he tied his fate to Algeria's very own. Through Algeria he at last accomplished, as from the rear, the tour of the Triangle. "To participate in the ordered movement of a continent," he maintained, "that was ultimately the work I had chosen." The Africa he discovered in the aftermath of decolonization is a maze of contradictions. The Congo is at a standstill. The great "colonialist citadels" of southern Africa (Angola, Mozambique, South Africa, Rhodesia) are still in place. The specter of the West hovers everywhere. New national bourgeoisies are already on the path of predation. And if one listens "with one ear glued to the red earth one very distinctly hears the sounds of rusty chains, groans of distress, and the bruised flesh is so constantly present in this stifling noonday." Break the moorings, open new fronts, set Africa swinging, and give birth to a new world—such is nevertheless the project. This new world is inseparable from the advent of a new human. Difficult work? "Fortunately, in every corner arms make signs to us, voices answer us, hands grasp ours."[1]

Having essentially begun in the mid-eighteenth century, modern African and diasporic reflection on the possibility of a "new world" took place largely as part of the humanist thinking that has prevailed in the West over the past three centuries. That a number of autobiographies figure among the very first Afro-American writings is, from this viewpoint, revealing.[2] Is not saying "I" the first of all spoken words by which humans seek to make themselves exist as such?

Also significant is the place that religious narrative occupies in the narration and interpretation of their history. In conditions of terror, impoverishment, and the social death brought on by slavery, for the community that has been debased and struck with the mark of a stain, having recourse to theological discourse to pronounce oneself and state one's past must be understood as an attempt to reclaim a moral identity.[3] Ever since, via successive junctions, this reflection has continued to examine the conditions for forming a properly human world, in which the subject would be given on the basis of an ideal from which life would draw its resilience.[4]

Deadlocks of Humanism

This effort of self-explanation and self-comprehension would bring out two things. First—and it is not useless to recall this—that the history of Negroes is not a separate history. It is an integral part of the history of the world. Negroes are legatees of this history of the world in the same way as the rest of the human genus.[5] In addition, if retracing the chains of their distant origins almost inevitably leads back to Africa, their sojourn in the world has, by contrast, unfolded by way of displacement, circulation, and dispersion.[6] As movement and mobility have been structuring factors of their historical experience, today they find themselves spread across the face of the Earth. And so there is no past of the world (or any region of it) that must not also account for the past of the Negroes, just as there is no Negro past that ought not to inform the history of the world as a whole.

Thus, Negroes constitute part of the West's past, even if their presence in this self-awareness of this West often crops up only in the mode of obsessive fear, denegation, and effacement.[7] In this relation, James Baldwin maintained that, concerning America, the Negroes are integral to the history of this New World, which they have contributed to shaping and have accompanied all along its course. Negroes are constitutive subjects of this New World, even if, in the Negro, as figure of the absolute outside, this world does not recognize its "proper."[8] Premising his argument on the works of several historians, Paul Gilroy shows the value of their involvement in the emergence of the modern world, which stops being structured around the Atlantic at the beginning of the eighteenth century.[9]

Side by side with humanity's other rejects (those expropriated after the enclosure of the commons, peons and deported criminals, impressed sailors on board military and commercial marines, reprobates of radical religious sects, pirates and buccaneers, those absent without leave and deserters of every name under the sun), Negroes are located throughout the length and breadth of the new commercial routes, in ports, on boats, everywhere that forests must be cut back, tobacco produced, cotton grown, sugar cane cut, rum made, ingots transported, and furs, fish, sugar, and other products manufactured.[10]

African slaves—modernity's real "drudges," together with the multitude of other anonymous individuals—were at the heart of the quasi-cosmic forces released by European colonial expansion at the dawn of the seventeenth century and by the industrialization of Atlantic metropoles at the beginning of the nineteenth.[11] If their inscription in the modern course of human history is carried out under the veil of anonymity and effacement, it nonetheless conserves a triple dimension—planetary, heteroclite, and polyglot—that will deeply stamp their cultural productions.[12]

If the planetary dimension of the Negro fact is more or less acknowledged, the "Negro question" as posed in the framework and terms of Western humanist thinking continues to be subject to critiques—some internal, others external. Indeed from the vantage point of continental African and African American history, Western humanism, racial slavery, and racial capitalism are the cauldrons in which the idea of black difference, of blackness, was produced. To be sure, capitalism must be understood as an economic system. But it is also an apparatus of capture and a regime of signs, a certain kind of compulsion, that is, a certain mode of organization and redistribution of power: the compulsion to put things in order as a precondition for extracting their inner value. It is the compulsion to categorize, to separate, to measure, and to name, to classify and to establish equivalences between things and between things and persons, persons and animals, animals and the so-called natural, mineral, and organic world.

Whenever an order is manufactured and value is extracted, that which is deemed valueless is made redundant. It is forced to lose its face and its name, that which gives substance to the signifier, and to wear a mask. This does not simply apply to objects. It applies to people as well. This is what ordering is all about under slavery, colonialism, and capitalism. It is about separating what is useful from waste, from the detrituses. As a result, any critique of humanism in the context of black life must take as its point of departure not so much what some have called "social death" as this matter of waste, as how to retrieve the human from a history of waste or, to put it differently, a history of desiccation. Furthermore, African and African American history is not so much about "social death" as it is about the permanent generation, re-creation and resignification of life flows in the face of the forces of capture, extraction, and desiccation. To be sure, the two poles of re-creation and desiccation are inseparable. The "body-of-extraction" that is supposed to work is the same body that is continually under attack or made redundant. At different times and under various circumstances, the ropes are drawn tight. Ribs are shattered. Victims are mercilessly sodomized. In the process, various organs are sucked dry or destroyed. It becomes impossible to breathe with one's lungs. At the same time, the endless labor of restoring that which has been destroyed goes on. Many have been defeated in this peculiar struggle. But sewing up the holes, preventing the destroyed body from being completely torn apart, reconnecting the tissues, unblocking the points of blockage, getting out of the hole, breaking through the wall have been key parts of the dialectics, the line of writing that historically prevented many from drowning in the ocean of pessimism, despair, and nihilism. Underlying this process has been the question of unreason and unfreedom. For those who, for centuries, were condemned to live their lives in a cage or in a monstrous hood, humanism often took the face of an inhuman head and the form of wolves' jaws, a machine geared toward the elimination of certain classes of human beings located at the interface of the human and the nonhuman, or the human, the commodity, the object, the thing, the black thing, the black as a thing, the burning fossil that fueled capitalism during its primitive era.[13]

But this is not all. In practice, the critique of Western humanism also took the form of attempts to reassemble some form of the social and of community and, as such, the form of attending to matters of care and matters of repair. Flight itself had no other function except to create conditions under which to attend to the permanent labor of repairing that which had been broken. Wherever African slaves happened to be settled, the work of producing symbols and rituals, languages, memory, and meaning—and therefore the substance necessary to sustain life—never stopped. Nor did the interminable labor of caring for and repairing that which had been broken. The Sisyphus-like effort to resist being turned into waste partly explains why plantation slavery differs from other forms of genocidal colonialism. In the regime of capture that historically characterized the black experience in America, the capacity to develop multiple modalities of agency and different figures of personhood was crucial. The much used concept of fugitivity hardly exhausts the repertoires of practices of survival actually required. For once, to get out of the hole, and to break through the wall, the captured subject actively engaged in a relation of multiple doubles and multiple selves. He developed an extraordinary capacity to become imperceptible and unassignable, to shift continually from one self to its alternate, to inhabit the tiniest of cracks and fissures.

He had to know how and when to become like everybody else, how and when to be nobody, when to be alone, when to hide and when to no longer have anything to hide, when to become unfindable and when to rush to the other side in order to meet his double. These micro-movements and micro-postures were essential because survival depended on being able to inhabit multiple selves, often at one and the same time. Agency was therefore not so much a matter of fugitivity, flight, or escape. Since many objectively couldn't flee or escape, it became a matter of knowing when and how to cross over, to become somebody else (self-separation) in the face of what Deleuze and Guattari once called "an overcoding machine." Obviously there were all kinds of risks attached to this dizzying state of endless crossing and becoming whose end was simply to stay alive.

Whether with Césaire or with Fanon, the internal critique tends to emphasize the death drive and the desire to destroy at the very core of the Western humanist project, notably when this project is shut within the convolutions of colonialist and racist passion.[14] In general fashion, whether with Césaire or Fanon, or with Senghor or Glissant, the question of repudiating the idea of "man" as such once and for all never arises. More often the concern is to point up the deadlocks of the Western discourse on "man" with the aim of amending it.[15] The point then amounts either to insisting on the fact that the human is less a name than a praxis and a becoming (Wynter), or else to appeal to a new, more "planetary" humanity (Gilroy), to a poetics of the Earth, and to a world made of the flesh of All (Glissant), within which each human subject could once more be the bearer of his speech, his name, his acts, and his desire.[16]

Césaire, Senghor, Fanon, Wynter, Glissant, and Gilroy seek to speak with as full a voice as possible from an incomplete, partial, and fragmented archive. For an incomplete archive to speak with the fullness of a voice, it has to be created, not out of nothing but out of the debris of information, on the very site of the ruins, the remains and traces left behind by those who passed away. For this to happen, the voice must shift because it must confront something not so much unique as soiled, wasted lives it must attempt to retrieve from a broken existence. It must provide them with a home or place where they might be at peace. In such a context, the critique of Western humanism is not a mere historical account of what happened—the book of atrocities. It is also the mourning of what was lost, in a way that does not dwell in the trauma, in a way that allows the survivor to escape the curse of repetition, to put the debris together again. In this tradition, to mourn what has been lost (the critique of Western humanism) is akin to returning to life the harvest of bones that have been subjected to the forces of desiccation in an attempt to render the world habitable again and for all.

As for the external critique, it comes in three versions. The first, Afrocentric, sets out to demystify the universalist pretensions of Western humanism and lay the foundations for a knowledge endowed with categories and concepts drawn from the history of Africa itself. On this view, the notion of humanism essentially reduces to a structure that effaces historical depth and Negro originality. Humanism's function, it is argued, lies in arrogating the power of self-recounting and of defining, in the place of others, where these same others come from, what they are, and where they must go. Humanism is thus a myth that does not want to say its name.[17] As a mythology, humanism would be perfectly indifferent to the falsity of its own contents. Whence, for example in Cheikh Anta Diop, the will to counter European mythologies with others held to be more veridical and more apt to open onto different genealogies of the world. But if Afrocentrism formulates the question of humanism based on the possible debt of civilization that the world would owe to Africa, this line of thought nonetheless advocates no less than what Diop calls the "general progress of humanity," the "triumph of the notion of the human species" (the "human race"), and the "hatching of an era of universal understanding."[18]

The Other of the Human

The second and third objections—the ones on which we shall focus our attention here—stem from the so-called Afropessimist and Afrofuturist trends. Racial pessimism is, to a large extent, a product and an outcome, a key affect of liberalism. Liberalism has historically generated various forms of racial anger, rage, or frustrations. In turn, in certain instances, pessimism has been taken up as a self-understanding. In *Democracy in America*, volume 2, Alexis de Tocqueville examines race relations in the context of American democracy. He ends up concluding that an American democracy that accommodated blacks in particular is an impossibility. He then argues for one form or another of repatriation of the Negroes to Africa. Repatriation is not the same as reparation. Deportation and repatriation are always animated by a genocidal unconscious, an unrealized genocidal pathos. Tocqueville's democracy and humanism is not one of connections between different parts or segments. It is a humanism of extrication. It is underpinned by a line of purity.

In fact, liberal democracy and racism are fully compatible. At the same time, historically, liberal democracy has always needed a constitutive Other for its legitimation, an Other who is and is not at the same time part of the polis. We recognize pessimism wherever the language of impossibility and repatriation saturates speech or becomes the final word in any utterance. With Tocqueville, pessimism is articulated in the language of indivisibility and the impossibility of sharing. From a Tocquevillian perspective, the freedom of the "white race" is both absolute and indivisible. It cannot be shared with any nonwhite entity. If necessary, it will be secured by murderous or suicidal organizations. In this case, racial pessimism is anchored to white America's deep belief and conviction that the freedom and security of the white race can be guaranteed only at the expense of the life of nonwhites, even if this prospect might lead to catastrophe. The white race might need that Other. It might depend on him, and yet, there is not much to share with this Other.

Racial pessimism is based on the belief that for white America to exist at all, it must continuously produce a complex of bodies in chains (Niggers). "Niggers" are not only the condition of possibility of America; they are also a class of people America cannot live with, people America doesn't want to share anything with, although without them America means nothing or not much. America, in this sense, means the impossibility of sharing freedom with others—which "whiteness," properly understood, is. Embedded in Tocqueville's vibrant apology of liberal democracy is therefore a virulent racial pathos. Contemporary liberal democracies have not departed from this constitutive pessimism. This pessimism stems from a fantasy, that of an enemy in the body and of a body (a racially circumscribed commons) that aims to remain closed.

This racially circumscribed body is built on a politics that disavows passages, bridges, conjunctions of intensities. As it happens, certain strands of Afropessimism are also premised on the idea of a racial categorical antagonism, one that cannot be transcended, or can be transcended only through a war that is and is not a mere civil war, a war that would be waged against the very concept of humanity since this concept is indeed the Trojan horse that has trapped the Negro in a permanent state of death, social or otherwise. As a matter of fact, there is a mimetic relationship between two forms of asymmetrical racism, a hegemonic racism and a subaltern racism, both of which speak the same language but with different accents. They do not operate on the same plane and do not wield the same amount of power, but they do share the same fantasy of a freedom that is freedom only for oneself, indivisible and absolute in the face of an absolute Outside. This kind of metapolitics privileges shock and destruction. It calls for the burning of memory in the belief that what might emerge from the ashes can never be worse than what we already endure.

Afrofuturism is a literary, aesthetic, and cultural movement that emerged among the diaspora during the second half of the twentieth century. It combines science fiction, reflections on technology in its relations with black cultures, magic realism, and non-European cosmologies, with the aim of interrogating the past of so-called colored peoples and their condition in the present.[19] Afrofuturism rejects outright the humanist postulate, insofar as humanism can constitute itself only by relegating some other subject or entity (living or inert) to the mechanical status of an object or an accident.

For Afrofuturism does not rest with denouncing the illusion of the "specifically human." In its eyes, the Negro experience put paid to the idea of the human species. Product of a history of predation, the Negro is effectively the human that was forced to don the apparel of the thing and share the destiny of the object and the tool. This doing, the Negro bears within him the human's tombstone. He is the phantom haunting Western humanist delirium. Western humanism thus stands as a sort of vault haunted by the phantom of the one who had been forced to share the destiny of the object.

Armed with this rereading, the Afrofuturist current declares that the category of humanism is now obsolete. If the aim is to adequately name the contemporary condition, its spokespersons suggest, it will be necessary to do so based on all the assemblages of *objects-humans* and of *humans-objects* of which, since the advent of modern times, the Negro is the prototype or prefiguration.[20] For, ever since the irruption of Negroes on the stage of the modern world, no "human" exists that does not immediately participate in the "nonhuman," the "more-than-human," the "beyond human," or the "elsewhere-than-human."

In other terms, the human could be talked about only in the future tense and always coupled with the object, henceforth the human's double, or even its sarcophagus. The Negro is this future's prefiguration, as the history of the Negro refers to the idea of a quasi-infinite potential of transformation and plasticity.[21] Borrowing from fantasy literature, science fiction, technology, music, and the performing arts, Afrofuturism attempts to rewrite this Negro experience of the world in terms of more or less continuous metamorphoses, of multiple inversions, of plasticity, including anatomical, and of corporeality, if required machinic.[22]

On its own, the Earth could not be the sole place of habitation of this form to come of the living, whose prefiguration the Negro is. The Earth in its historical configuration would essentially become a vast prison for that metal-man, that silver-man, that wood-man, and that liquid-man, that body of extraction destined for endless transfiguration. A vessel both metaphorical and plastic, his dwelling could only be the whole wide Universe. The earthly condition is thus replaced by *the cosmic condition*, the stage of reconciliation between the human, the animal, the vegetal, the organic, the mineral, and all the other forces of the living, be they solar, nocturnal, or astral.

The Afrofuturist repudiation of the idea of "man" stemming from modernity may seem surprising. Does this repudiation not, ultimately, reinforce traditions of thought that prospered by flagrantly denying Negro humanity? This would be to forget that, since the advent of modern times, we have been inhabited by the dream of becoming masters and possessors of ourselves and nature. To achieve this, it was necessary for us to come to know ourselves, nature, and the world. The idea we inherited from the late seventeenth century was that the condition of really knowing ourselves, nature, and the world would require the integration of all fields of knowledge and the development of a science of order, according to which calculation and measure would make it possible to translate natural and social processes into arithmetic formulae.[23]

Using algebra to model nature and life, a modality of knowing thus gradually imposed itself that consisted essentially in flattening out the world, that is to say, homogenizing the entirety of the living, rendering its objects interchangeable and manipulable at will.[24] A good part of modern knowledge will thus have been governed by this centuries-long movement of flattening out.

It is a movement that, to varying degrees and with incalculable consequences, has accompanied that other historical process typical of modern times, namely the constitution of worlds-spaces under the aegis of capitalism. From the fifteenth century on, this new planetary adventure, propelled by the mercantilist slavery system, has had the Western Hemisphere as its privileged motor. On the basis of this system's triangular trade, the Atlantic world as a whole got restructured; the great colonial empires of the Americas saw the light of day or were consolidated, and a new era of human history began.

Two emblematic figures marked this new historical cycle: first, the shadowy figure of the Negro slave (during the mercantilist period that we refer to as the "first capitalism"); second, the solar and glowing red figure of the worker, and, by extension, the proletariat (during the industrial phase originating between 1750 and 1820). We are only just starting to understand the ecological metabolisms (matter, energy) involved in those "manhunts," and without which the Atlantic slave trade would have been impossible.[25]

More precisely, the slaves were the product of a dynamic of predation within an economy in which profit creation on one shore of the Atlantic depended closely on a system combining raids, wars of capture, and diverse forms of "manhunt" on the other shore.[26] During the times of Negro slave trading, capitalism operated by taking and consuming what could be called a biostock, at once human and vegetal.

The ecological disturbances brought about by this vast draining of humans and its procession of violence have yet to be systematically studied. But the New World plantations could hardly have operated without the massive use of "ambulant suns," that is, African slaves. Even after the Industrial Revolution, these real human fossils continued to serve as coal for producing energy and provided the necessary dynamism for economically transforming the Earth System.[27] An enormous capital manifestly had to be mobilized and expended to perpetrate such multiform depredations. In return for which, the slave owner could extract labor from slaves for a relatively reduced cost, since this labor was unpaid. He could also, now and again, sell the slaves to a third party. The slave's assignable and transferable character made him a private good open to a monetary evaluation or a market exchange.[28]

In the Atlantic economy, numberless paradoxes nevertheless characterized the worlds of slaves. On the one hand, while useful for harvesting profits, these slaves were subject to a deep symbolic and social devaluation through their abasement. Forced to share the destiny of the object, they remained human to the core. They had bodies. They breathed. They walked. They spoke, sang, and prayed. Some of them learned, occasionally in secrecy, to read and write.[29] They fell ill, and, in the course of therapeutic practices, they strove to reestablish a community of healing.[30] They experienced lack, pain, and sadness. They revolted when they were at the end of their tether, and the uprising of slaves is a motif of absolute terror for their masters.

In addition, although deeply sullied and stigmatized, these fundamentally *human* beings constituted reserves of value in the eyes of their owners. In the same way as money or again commodities, they served as a medium for all sorts of economic and social transactions. As movable objects and extended matter, theirs was the status of that which circulates, is invested in, and is expended.[31] From this point of view, pro-slavery worlds are worlds in which the production of matter is performed by means of living flesh and daytime sweat. This living flesh has an economic value that can be, as suits the occasion, measured and quantified.[32] A price can be attached to it. The matter produced from the brow sweat of slaves also has an active value insofar as the slave transforms nature, converts energy into matter, is himself at once a material and an energy-giving figure. Slaves are, from this viewpoint, more than simple natural goods enjoyed by the master, from whom he draws revenues or can sell without restriction on the market. At the same time, what distinguishes them from all the others is their fundamental alienability. The explanation for this fundamental alienability must be sought in *the principle of race.*[33]

The Zero World

In addition, life under the sign of race has always been equivalent to life in a zoo. In practice, two or three processes lie at the basis of the constitution of a zoo. First, the abduction, capture, and caging of the animals. These animals are taken from their natural habitat by humans who, having seized them, do not kill them but instead assign them to a vast subdivided enclosure, if required into several mini-ecosystems. In this space of entrapment, the animals are deprived of an important part of the resources that granted their lives their natural qualities and their fluidity. They are unable to freely move about. To get food, they are henceforth entirely dependent on those assigned to their daily upkeep.

Second, the animals thus tamed are the object of an implicit prohibition. They are unable to be killed except in exceptional circumstances and almost never for the purpose of direct consumption. Their bodies thus lose the attributes of meat, nonetheless without being transformed into pure human flesh. Third, such captive animals are not subjected to a strict regime of domestication. A lion at the zoo is not treated like a cat. It does not share in the private life of humans. As the zoo does not belong to the domestic realm, the distance between humans and animals is maintained. Indeed, their exhibition is permitted by this distance, as exhibition makes no sense except in the separation between the spectator and the exhibited object. For all that, the animal lives in a state of suspension. It is henceforth neither this nor that.

The Negroes exhibited in the human zoos of the West throughout history were neither animals nor objects. For the duration of their exhibition, their humanity was suspended. This *life in suspension* between the animal and its world, the world of humans, and the world of objects is still, in several respects, the law of our times — that of the economy. Now, it may well be that the economy — every economy — ultimately comes down to these two activities, hunting and gathering, and that despite appearances, we have never truly left them behind.

In the ancient economy, hunting and gathering were not only two categories of activity whose goal was to meet the needs of human beings. They were also two modes of relation with oneself and with others, as well as with nature, objects, and other species, living or otherwise. This was particularly the case of the relation with the animal and vegetal worlds. These latter worlds were perceived as external entities subject to the will of humans and were appropriated in line with their availability. Concessions were made to them if required, but when necessary nobody hesitated to fight against them, even if it meant purely and simply destroying them in the process.

The destruction did not take place in a single blow. It occurred as a chain with multiple stations. For animals caught in traps or slaughtered during the hunt, being cut open followed capture. This operation was necessary to transforming the animal into meat, which was consumed either raw or after treatment by fire (that is, cooked). The consumption process was crowned by the meat's devouring, digestion, and excretion. The paradigm of hunting and gathering is not specific to the primitive economy.

At bottom, every economy—the capitalist economy in particular—maintains a stock of primitiveness that forms its hidden and, occasionally, manifest wellspring. Destruction or liquidation is, incidentally, its key moment, its condition of possibility, on a par with the creation of tools, the invention of new technologies and systems of organization, and the cycles of accumulation. Destruction occurs at the last station, the end point of the line, at least before the cycle is, possibly, begun again.

The inevitability of destruction in the ancient regime of hunting and gathering has also been shown to operate in modern economic systems—it is a condition of the reproduction of social and biological life. But to say destroy or liquidate is first to indicate the confrontation between humans and matter—physical and organic matter, biological, liquid and fluid matter, human and animal matter, made flesh, bones, and blood, vegetal and mineral matter. It also refers to the confrontation with life—the life of humans, the life of nature, the life of animals, and the life of the machine. It refers to the work necessary to producing life—work that also includes the production of symbols, languages, and meanings. It refers to the processes whereby machine-captured human beings are transformed into matter—the matter of humans and the humans of matter. It refers further to the conditions of their withering away.

This withering away of life and matter is not the equivalent of death. It is an unfolding onto an extreme outside that I shall refer to as *the zero world*. In this zero world neither matter nor life ends as such. They do not return to nothingness. They merely pursue a movement of exiting toward something else, with the end being deferred each time and the very question of finitude left hanging. The zero world is a world in which becoming is difficult to figure because the time of which it is woven cannot be captured through the traditional categories of the present, past, and future. In this fragmented and crepuscular world, time constantly oscillates between its different segments.

Diverse types of exchanges tie together terms that we customarily oppose. The past is in the present. It does not necessarily redouble it. But it is sometimes refracted in it, sometimes insinuates itself into its interstices, that is, when it does not simply climb back up to time's surface, which it assails with its grayness, tries to saturate, to make illegible. The executioner is in the victim. The immobile is in movement. Speech is in silence. The beginning is at the end, and the end is in the middle. And all, or nearly all, is interlacing, incompletion, expansion, and contraction.

This world also wears the cuts of the machine in its flesh and its veins. Crevasses, chasms, and tunnels. Crater lakes. The sometimes ocher, sometimes lateritic red, and sometimes copper colors of the Earth. The cross-sections, the open cuts, the terracing, the play of depths. The acrid blue of still waters that no wave skims over, as if these waters were already dead. The road along the escarpment in this lunar landscape. Humans-ants, humans-termites, laterite-red humans that dig directly into the slopes, that dive into these tunnels of death, that, in an act of self-burial, make one body and color with these sepulchers from which they extract ore. They come and go, like ants and termites, carrying on their heads or on their backs the weight of the burden, with body and feet in the mud. And, at the surface, blast furnaces and smokestacks, and then tumuli of which we know not if they are pyramids, mausoleums, or one inside the other.

Something, manifestly, has been extracted from the ground and crushed here, in the guts of the machine. Machine-with-teeth. Large-intestine-machine. Anus-machine-that-swallows-and-crunches-and-digests-the-rock, leaving behind it the traces of its monumental defecation. At the same time, there is a pile of iron and steel. Red bricks, abandoned sheds, dismantled piece by piece and laid bare by ant-humans, termite-humans. Workshops now standing in a field of skeletons, adorned with their scrap iron and such like. Enormous blind machines, corroded by bad weather, mound-witnesses to an unrepeatable, idle past, which, however, it seems just as difficult to forget.

But the machine has aged and become a piece of rag, a stump, a skele-ton, a statue, a monument, a stela, and even a phantom. Today, this world of the machines that cut, perforate, and extract has collapsed. It stands no longer, unless under the sign of emptiness. However, in its verticality, the machine, with its roughcast stripped, continues to dominate the scenery, hanging over it with its mass and its seal, bearing a sort of power that is at once phallic, shamanic, and diabolical — the architrace in its pure facticity. In order to capture this triple phallic, shamanic, and diabolical power, the artist makes many a shadowy figure — witnesses without witnesses, epi-taph figures of an era slow to disappear — return to the *stage*.

In this theater of appearing, chained-up humans, barefoot captives, convicts, porters, half-naked people, with wild expressions, emerge from the night of slave caravans and forced labor in the colonies. They urge us to relive the traumatic scene, as if yesterday's nightmare was suddenly re-peating, being reproduced in the reality of the present. It is to them to give voice once more — and on this stage that is abandoned only in ap-pearance — to a language, a voice, and words that seem to us to have been hushed up, reduced to silence, just like the slave's voice.

Anti-Museum

By "slave" it is necessary to understand a generic term that covers diverse situations and contexts that historians and anthropologists have well de-scribed. The Atlantic slave complex, at the heart of which lay the system of the plantation in the Caribbean, Brazil, or the United States, was a mani-fest link in the constitution of modern capitalism. This Atlantic complex did not produce either the same type of societies or the same type of slaves as the Islamo-trans-Saharan complex. And if something distinguishes the transatlantic regimes of slavery from the indigenous forms of slavery in precolonial African societies, it is indeed that these societies were never able to extract from their captives a surplus value comparable to that ob-tained in the New World.

The slave of the New World, one of whose particularities was to be an essential cog in a planetary-scale process of accumulation, is therefore of particular interest.

This being so, the entering of this figure — a figure that is at once the ma-nure and silt of history — into the museum is undesirable. Besides, no museum exists that is liable to welcome it. To this day, most attempts to stage the history of transatlantic slavery in museums have stood out through their vacuity. In them, the slave appears, at best, as the appendix to another history, a citation at the bottom of a page devoted to someone else, to other places, to other things. For that matter, were the figure of the slave really to enter into the museum, such as it exists nowadays, the museum would automatically cease to be. It would sign its own death warrant, and it would be necessary, as it were, to transform it into something else, another scene, with other dispositions, other designations, even another name.

For, despite appearances, the museum has historically not always been an unconditional place of reception for the multiple faces of humanity taken in its unity. On the contrary, since the modern age the museum has been a powerful device of separation. The exhibiting of subjugated or humiliated humanities has always adhered to certain elementary rules of injury and violation. And, for starters, these humanities have never had the right in the museum to the same treatment, status, or dignity as the conquering humanities. They have always been subjected to other rules of classification and other logics of presentation. Added to this logic of separation, or of sorting out, has been that of assignation. The primary conviction is that because different forms of humanities have produced different objects and different forms of culture, these objects and forms of culture ought to be placed and exhibited in distinct places and assigned different and unequal symbolic statuses. The slave's entry into such a museum would doubly hallow the spirit of apartheid that lies at the source of this cult of difference, hierarchy, and inequality.

Moreover, one of the museum's functions has also been the production of statues, mummies, and fetishes—indeed objects deprived of their breath and returned to the inertia of matter. Mummification, statuefication, and fetishization all correspond perfectly to the aforementioned logic of separation. The point is generally not, it so happens, to offer the sign that has long accommodated the form some peace and rest. It was first necessary to chase out the spirit behind the form, as occurred with the skulls gathered during the wars of conquest and "pacification." In order to acquire a right to the city in the museum as it exists today, the slave necessarily had to be emptied—as did all the primitive objects that had gone before—of all force and primary energy.

The threat that this manure-figure and this silt-figure might represent, or again its potential to create a scandal, was thus domesticated, as a prior condition of exhibition. From this viewpoint, the museum is a space of neutralization and domestication of forces that were once living forces — flows of power — prior to their museumization. Such remains the essential aspect of its cultish function notably in the de-Christianized societies of the West. This function (which is also political and cultural) might be necessary for the very survival of society, similar to the function of forgetting within memory.

Now the slave's power of scandal ought precisely to be preserved. This power paradoxically originates in the refusal to recognize the scandal as such. Even in the refusal to recognize it, this scandal is what gives to this figure of humanity its insurrectional power. To preserve this scandal's power is the reason this slave ought not to enter into the museum. What the history of Atlantic slavery urges us to do is thus to found a new institution — *the anti-museum*.

The slave must continue to haunt the museum such as it exists today but do so by its absence. It ought to be everywhere and nowhere, its apparitions always occurring in the mode of breaking and entering and never of the institution. This is how the slave's spectral dimension will be preserved. This is also how facile consequences will be prevented from being drawn from the abominable event of the slave trade. As for the anti-museum, by no means is it an institution but rather the figure of another place, one of radical hospitality. A place of refuge, the anti-museum is also to be conceived as a place of unconditional rest and asylum for all the rejects of humanity and the "wretched of the earth," the ones who attest to the sacrificial system that will have been the history of our modernity — a history that the concept of archive struggles to contain.

Autophagy

Every archive, being always linked to a past and having necessarily dealt with a history of memory, has a sort of slit. It is at once a breaching (*frayage*), an opening, and a separation, a fissure and a breaking, a crazing and a disjunction, a crevasse and a rift, or indeed a tear. But the archive is above all a fissile material, its specificity being that, at its source, it is made of cuts. Indeed, no archive exists without its cracks (*lézardes*). One enters into it as though through a narrow door, with the hope of penetrating in depth the thickness of the event and its cavities. To penetrate archival material means to revisit traces. But above all it means to dig right into the slope. A risky effort, since, in our case, often the point has been to create a memory by obstinately fixing shadows rather than real events, or rather historical events submerged in the force of shadow. Often it has been necessary to outline, on preexisting traces, our own silhouette, to grasp for ourselves the contours of the shadow, and to try to see ourselves from the shadow, as shadow.

The result has sometimes been disconcerting. Here we see ourselves depicted in a painting on which we are about to shoot ourselves in the head. Further on, we see ourselves as children of Ethiopia at the height of the famine that took millions of human lives. We are on the verge of being devoured by a scavenger that is none other than ourselves. An autophagy, one ought to say. And this is not all. A Negro in the southern United States in times of racial segregation, a rope around the neck, here we are hanged from a tree, alone, without witnesses, at the mercy of vultures. We strive to stage an unfigurability that we want to present as constitutive if not of our person, then at least of our personage.

Through all these gestures, we cheerfully straddle time and identities, excise history and place ourselves firmly on both sides of the mirror. Doing so, we do not seek to efface prior traces. We seek to assail the archive by fastening our multiple silhouettes onto these traces. For, left to itself, the archive does not necessarily produce visibility. What the archive produces is a specular device, a fundamental and reality-generating hallucination. Now, the two originary reality-creating fantasies are most certainly race and sex. And both fantasies were of primary significance in the processes that led to our racialization.

The body of the Negress is a particular case in point. To grasp its meaning, it is perhaps important to recall that to be black means to be placed by the force of things on the side of those that go unseen, but that one nevertheless always permits oneself to represent. Negroes—and in particular Negresses—go unseen because we consider there is nothing to see and that we have basically nothing to do with them. They are not one of us. Telling stories about the men and women one does not see, drawing them, representing them, or photographing them has been an act of supreme authority throughout history, the manifestation par excellence of the relation without desire.

Contrary to the Negro bodies caught in the cyclone of racism and rendered invisible, disgusting, bloody, and obscene by the colonial eye, our own do not suffer from any spiriting away. Our bodies are modest without being so. This is the case in Senghor's poetry. Plastic and stylized bodies, they shine through their beauty and the gracious character of their lineaments. There is no need to metaphorize here, even when they are practically bare or when they are staged under the sign of sensuality. Almost mischievous, the poet deliberately seeks to seize the instant at which the men and women who run the risk of looking at such sensuality are no longer on their guard.

Images of bodies, of Negro bodies, indeed invite a *chassé-croisé* of feelings. From whoever looks at them, they invite now a game of seduction, now a fundamental ambiguity, now repulsion. Is the person one sees exactly the same, and from every angle? One looks at him, but does one really see him? What does this black skin mean with its gleaming and slippery surface? This body placed before others' eyes, viewed from everywhere, and that has placed itself in the bodies of others, at what moment does it pass from a self to the status of an object? How is this object the sign of a forbidden enjoyment?

In addition, and contrary to their prior traces, which they strive to inhabit, and even to hijack, there are images of Negresses that do not inspire any compassion. They embody, first, an extraordinary beauty, which, as Lacan might say, plays on the extreme edges of what he called the "forbidden zone." Beauty's specificity lies in the pacifying effects it exercises on the person experiencing it. In these images pain appears secondary. Nothing in them encourages us to look away. They are far from the hideous, bloody, and repugnant images of historical lynchings. No gaping mouths. No twisted and contorted faces.

This is the case because they pertain to an intimate movement: the body's work on itself. It is sometimes a matter of photographs, sometimes of specular images, and sometimes of effigies or even of reflections. But above all it is a matter of indexical icons whose relation to the subject is at once physical (in the sense that these images are faithful to the objective appearance of their author) and analogical (in the sense that they are but the indexical traces of the subject). They are created to capture those who look at them and compel them to lay down their arms.

From this point of view, they have something to do with the pacifying effect that Lacan attributes to painting. Far from deactivating desire, they enhance it by neutralizing and disconnecting the resistance of those who view them and by kindling their fantasies. An originary beauty flows from the body color of the night. This is a forbidden beauty, and so it generates manifest desires. But also masculine anxieties. Such beauty can only castrate. It cannot be the object of consumption. It can only be the object of a courteous and chaste delectation.

The force of the images of Negress bodies stems from their capacity to disarm the archive. Through these images, Negresses accept seeing themselves as Others. But do they really manage to expatriate from themselves? They have their bodies worked on. Now, all bodies, no matter which, are never entirely self-determining. A body is always also determined by the Other, the one who looks at it, contemplates it, as well as by the body parts that one looks at or that one gives to be looked at or to contemplate. The Self always rediscovers its own desire in the Other's gaze, albeit in an inverted form.

By thus allowing desire to surface, including the desire for self, but by assigning it to a forbidden enjoyment, do we not remove these images' power of historical signification? Does what was initially destined to deconstruct the thing and create a new term within the order of the archive — and therefore of the signifier — not become simple self-contemplation, simple hyperbole of the Self? By exhibiting us in this manner, do we look at ourselves as others look at us? And what do they see when they look at us? Do they see us as we see ourselves? Or do they not ultimately stare at a mirage?

In the light of these considerations we understand better the premises of the Afrofuturist critique. At present the issue is to know if this critique can be radicalized and if this radicalization necessarily presupposes the repudiation of every idea of humanity. In Fanon's work, no such repudiation is necessary. Humanity is forever in creation. Its common content is its vulnerability, beginning with that of the body exposed to suffering and degeneration. But this vulnerability also belongs to the subject exposed to other existences that threaten its own, or possibly. Without a reciprocal recognition of this vulnerability, there is no place for solicitude, and even less of one for care.

Allowing oneself to be affected by others — or to be defenselessly exposed to another existence — constitutes the first step toward that form of recognition that will not be contained in the master-slave paradigm, in the dialectic of powerlessness and omnipotence, or in that of combat, victory, and defeat. On the contrary, the kind of relation that arises from it is a *relation of care*. So, recognizing and accepting vulnerability—or even admitting that to live is always to live exposed, including to death—is the point of departure of every ethical elaboration whose aim, in the last instance, is humanity.

According to Fanon, this humanity-in-creation is the product of the encounter with "the face of the other," this person here, who, in addition, "reveals me to myself." It begins with what Fanon calls a "gesture," that is to say "that which makes a relationship possible."[34] Humanity in effect arises only when a gesture—and thus the relation of care—is possible; when one allows oneself to be affected by the faces of others; when a gesture is related to speech, to a silence-breaking language.

But nothing guarantees direct access to speech. Instead of speech, what is heard may be the mere expressing of raucous cries and yells—hallucination. The unique thing about slavery, or colonialism, is to produce beings of pain, people whose existence is forever overrun by threatening Others. Part of the identity of these beings involves enduring the ordeal of constriction, being constantly exposed to the Other's will. For the most part, their speech suffers from hallucinations.

This speech grants a central importance to play and mime. This speech, proliferating, unfolds in the manner of a whirlwind. Being both vertiginous and vehement in its aggressiveness and its protest, this speech is "replete with anxieties linked to infantile frustrations." With the process of hallucination, Fanon explains, what is witnessed is the world's collapse: "Hallucinatory time as well as hallucinatory space do not make any claims to reality" since at issue is a time and space "in permanent flight."[35]

Letting these injured people speak means reviving their weakened capacities. In the medical cases that Fanon treated, reviving weakened capacities transpired, when and as needed, through annihilation.[36] Taking the place of the narcosis sessions was a direct confrontation with the undercover part of the subject, the one that, veiled, slips into the interstices of speech, the cry, or the yell. This aggressive confrontation, at the limit of violating the personality, aims to break down defenses, to expose the part-waste and part-dregs of the subject divided in its radical nudity.

After this, the subject undergoes deep sleep therapy, which is the royal road to the amnesiac confusional stage. By precipitating the subject into the amnesiac confusional stage, the aim is to return him to his origins, to the moment of his "coming into the world," to the beginnings of consciousness. Using electroshocks and insulin therapy, it undertakes a reverse path, seeking out a primitive situation that every human has previously experienced: the return to a state of absolute vulnerability, the child-mother relationship, hygiene needs, the suckling infant, one's first words, first faces, first names, first steps, and first objects. Thus understood, resurrection is a process of "dissolution-reconstruction" of the personality. Its ultimate goal is the rediscovery of self and world.

Capitalism and Animism

Apart from this, the Afrofuturist critique of humanism can only be deepened by combining it with an equivalent critique of capitalism.

Three sorts of drives have effectively impelled capitalism since its origins. The first is the constant manufacturing of races, or species (as it happens, *Negroes*); the second is the seeking to calculate and convert everything into exchangeable commodities (law of *generalized exchange relations*); and the third is the attempt to maintain a monopoly over the manufacture of the living as such.

The "civilizational process" will have consisted in tempering these drives and in preserving, with varying degrees of success, a certain number of fundamental separations, in the absence of which "the end of humanity" would become a frank possibility: a subject is not an object; not all can be arithmetically calculated, bought and sold; not all is exploitable and substitutable; a certain number of perverse fantasies must necessarily undergo sublimation if they are not to lead to the pure and simple destruction of the social.

The age of neoliberalism is that in which all these dikes collapse, one after the other. It is no longer certain that the human person is very distinct from the object, the animal, or the machine. It may be that the human person aspires, with respect to content, to become an object.[37] It is no longer certain that the manufacturing of species and subspecies within humanity is taboo. The abolition of taboos, and the more or less complete liberation of all sorts of drives, followed by their transformation into so many materials in an endless process of accumulation and abstraction—all these are fundamental features of our time. These events and several others of the same nature indicate that the merging between capitalism and animism is well and truly advanced.

This is especially true as the raw materials of the economy are no longer really territories, natural resources, and human persons.[38] Of course territories, natural resources, and human persons are still indispensable, but the natural setting of the economy is now the world of processors and biological and artificial organisms. It is the astral universe of screens, fluid shifts in meaning, glimmerings and irradiation. It is also the world of human brains and automatized computations, of working with always smaller, increasingly miniaturized instruments.

In these conditions, producing Negroes no longer consists exactly in manufacturing a social link of subjection or of a *body of extraction*, that is to say, a body integrally exposed to the will of a master and from which one seeks to extract maximum profit. In addition, if, yesterday, the Negro was the human being of African origin marked by the sun of his looks and the color of his epidermis, today this is no longer necessarily the case. We are now witnessing a tendency to universalize the condition previously reserved for Negroes, but this condition is undergoing a reversal. This condition consisted in reducing the human person to a thing, an object, a sellable, buyable, or possessable commodity.

The production of "subjects of race" presses ahead, certainly, but using new modalities. Today's Negro is no longer only the person of African origin, marked by the sun of his color ("the surface Negro"). Today's Negro is a "depth Negro," a subaltern category of humanity, a *genus of subaltern humanity*, which, as a superfluous and almost excessive part for which capital has no use, seems destined for zoning and expulsion.[39]

This "depth Negro," qua genus of humanity, is making its appearance on the world stage even though, more than ever, capitalism is establishing itself in the modality of an animist religion, as yesteryear's flesh-and-bones human yields to a new digital-flux human, infiltrated from everywhere by all sorts of synthetic organs and artificial prostheses. The "depth Negro" is the Other of this software humanity, the new figure of the species and typical of the new age of capitalism, in which self-reification constitutes the best chance of self-capitalization.[40]

Last, if the accelerated development of technologies for the massive exploitation of natural resources was part of the old project of mathematizing the world, this project itself ultimately aimed at a single goal, namely to administer the living, a process that tends nowadays to operate mostly in digital mode.[41] In the technetronic age, the human appears more and more in the form of flux, of increasingly abstract codes, of increasingly fungible entities. As the idea is henceforth that everything is manufacturable, including the living, existence is taken as manageable capital and the individual as a particle within a system (*dispositif*), or again as a piece of information that must be translated into a code and connected with other codes, according to a logic of ever-greater abstraction.

In this universe of megacalculations, another regime of intellection is in the process of springing up, which ought probably be characterized as anthropomachinic. We are thus in the process of entering into a new human condition. Humanity is in the process of leaving behind the grand divisions between the human, the animal, and the machine so typical of the discourse on modernity and on humanism. Today's human is now firmly wedded to its animal and its machine, to a set of artificial brains, of linings and interfacings (*de doublures et de triplages*) that form the base of the extensive digitalization of its life.

This being the case, and contrary to the masters of yesteryear, today's masters no longer need slaves. As the burden of having slaves became too great, masters mostly sought to dispense with them. The great paradox of the twenty-first century is therefore the appearance of an ever-growing class of slaves without masters and of masters without slaves. Certainly, both human persons and natural resources continue to be squeezed to boost profits. This reversal is logical, after all, since the new capitalism is above all specular.

Having understood this, the erstwhile masters now strive to get rid of their slaves. With no slaves, it is thought, no revolt can take place. To nip insurrectional potentialities in the bud, it is deemed enough to liberate the enslaved's mimetic potential. So long as the newly emancipated slaves expend themselves in wanting to become the masters they will never be, things will never be able to be other than as they are. The repetition of the same, always and everywhere: such will be the rule.

Emancipation of the Living

It remains to address racism's future within such a configuration. Historically, at least in the settler colonies or the pro-slavery states, racism always served as a *subsidy* for capital. This was its function only yesterday. Class and race were mutually constitutive. In general, one belonged to a given class by virtue of one's race, and belonging to a given race in turn determined one's possibilities of social mobility and access to this or that status. Class struggle was inseparable from the struggle between races, even if both forms of antagonism were driven by sometimes autonomous logics.[42] Indeed, the process of racialization inevitably operated through practices of discrimination. Race made it possible to naturalize social differences and to confine unwanted people in frameworks that they were prevented, by law, and even by force, from leaving behind.

Today new varieties of racism are emerging that no longer need to appeal to biology for legitimation. They are content, for example, to resort to chasing away foreigners, content to proclaim the incompatibility of "civilizations," to assert that we do not belong to the same humanity, to declare that cultures are incommensurable, or to claim that any God that is not the god of their religion is a false god, an idol calling for sarcasm, or is unreservedly profanable.

In the current conditions of crisis in the West, this type of racism shapes up as a supplement for nationalism, at a time when, moreover, neoliberal globalization is emptying nationalism, and indeed democracy period, of all real content, and shifting the real decision-making centers to remote places. Additionally, recent progress in the domains of genetics and biotechnology confirms the meaninglessness of race as a concept. Paradoxically, far from giving renewed impetus to the idea of a race-free world, they are reviving, totally unexpectedly, the old classificatory and differentiating project so typical of the previous centuries.

Thus under way is a complex process of unification of the world as part of capitalism's limitless (albeit unequal) expansion. This process goes hand in hand with the reinvention of differences, a re-Balkanization of this same world and its division along a variety of lines of separation and disjunctive inclusions. These lines are at once internal to societies and states, and vertical, insofar as they reveal lines of division pertaining to planetary-scale domination. The planetarization of apartheid, as such, shapes up as the immediate future of the world, just when awareness of the Earth system's finitude has never been as vivid and the human species' involvement with other forms of the living never as manifest.

How, from thereon in, are we to pose in new terms the question of the liberation of the enslaved's emancipatory potential in the concrete conditions of our times? What does it mean to construct oneself, to trace one's own destiny, or again to fashion oneself at a time when "the human" is no longer anything but a force among several other entities endowed with cognitive powers that will, perhaps, soon exceed our own? What does it mean, then, that the human figure, split into multiple fragments, has to deal with a tangle of artificial, organic, synthetic, and even geological forces? Is it enough to disqualify the old concept of an abstract and undifferentiated humanism, one blind to its own violence and to its racist passions? And what are the limits of invoking a supposed "human species," whose relationship to itself it may rediscover only because it is exposed to the peril of its own extinction?

Moreover, in contemporary conditions, how are we to foster the emergence of a thinking able to help consolidate a world-scale democratic politics, a thinking of complementarities rather than of difference? We are indeed living through a strange period of the history of humanity. One of contemporary capitalism's paradoxes is simultaneously to create and annul time. This twofold process of creating, accelerating, and exploding time has devastating effects on our ability to "forge memory," that is to say, at bottom, to build together spaces of collective decision-making, to experience a truly democratic life. Instead of memory, we have increased tenfold our abilities to relate stories, and all sorts of histories. But increasingly we are dealing with obsessional stories wherein the aim is to prevent ourselves from having an awareness of our condition.

What is this new condition? Hoping for a possible victory over the master is no longer appropriate. We no longer expect the master's death. We no longer believe he is mortal. As the master is no longer mortal, a sole illusion prevails over us, namely that we ourselves participate in the master. We are now living only a single desire, increasingly so on screens, from screens. The screen is the new scene. The screen does not only seek to abolish the distance between fiction and reality. It has become reality-generating. It forms part of the conditions of the century.

Democracy is in crisis almost everywhere, including in the old countries that have laid claim to it for so long. It is undergoing, probably more so than yesterday, enormous difficulties in recognizing the full and complete value of memory and speech as foundations of a human world that we will all share together and of which it is up to the public sphere to take care.

Evoking speech and language here is important not only thanks to their power of revelation and their symbolic function but above all to their materiality. In every truly democratic regime, a materiality of speech exists that stems from the fact that, at bottom, all we have is speech and language for giving utterance to ourselves, to the world, and for acting upon this world. Now, speech and language have been made tools, nano-objects, and technologies. They have become instruments that, absorbed in a cycle of infinite reproduction, continually self-instrumentalize.

As a result, the incessant flows of events that strike our consciousness hardly register in our memories as history. This is because events do not register in the memory as history except after a specific labor, which is psychic as much as social, in short symbolic, and democracy no longer takes care to ensure this labor on the technological, economic, and political conditions of our civilization.

This crisis of relations between democracy and memory is aggravated by the twofold injunction under whose sign we live our lives—the injunction to mathematize the world and to instrumentalize—an injunction that would have us believe that we as human beings are in fact digitalized unities and not concrete beings, that the world is ultimately a set of problems-situations to be resolved, and that the solutions to these problems-situations are to be found among the specialists of experimental economics and game theory, to whom, besides, we ought to leave the care to decide in our stead.

What are we ultimately to say about this confluence between capitalism and animism? As the anthropologist Philippe Descola recalls, animism was defined at the end of the nineteenth century as a primitive belief. Primitive peoples, it was thought, imputed to inanimate things a force and an almost mysterious power. They believed that nonhuman natural and supernatural entities, such as animals, plants, and objects, possessed a soul and intentions similar to those of humans. These nonhuman existents were endowed with a spirit with which humans could enter into communication or again with which they could entertain very close relations. In this, the primitives were different from us. For, contrary to the primitives, we were aware of the difference between ourselves and the animals. What separated us from animals, as well as from plants, was the fact that we possessed an interiority as subjects, a capacity for self-representation, and intentions that were peculiar to us.

This confluence shows up in the contemporary revival of a neoliberal ideology that manufactures all sorts of fictions. Thus, with the fiction of a neuro-economic human—a strategizing, cold, calculating individual, internalizing the norms of the market and governing his conduct as if in a game of experimental economics, instrumentalizing himself and others to optimize his shares of enjoyment, and whose emotional competences are held to be genetically predetermined. Born at the intersection of the economic sciences and the neurosciences, this fiction leads to the liquidation of the tragic subject of psychoanalysis and political philosophy—that is, the divided subject in conflict with itself and others, and nonetheless the actor of its destiny by means of narrative, struggle, and history.

CONCLUSION
ETHICS OF THE PASSERBY

The twenty-first century opens onto an avowal about the extreme fragility of all. And of the All. Beginning with the idea of the "All-World," whose poet Édouard Glissant has recently shown himself to be.

The terrestrial condition was never the unique lot of humans. Tomorrow, it will be far less so than today. Henceforth, power will exist only as fissured, divided into several nuclei. Does this fission of power represent a chance for the human experience of freedom, or will it rather lead us to the limit of disjunction?

In the ordeal of extreme vulnerability, many are tempted by some repetition of the originary, while others are attracted by the void. Both believe that re-engendering will occur through radicalizing difference, and salvation, through the force of destruction.

They believe that our horizon is about preserving, conserving, and safeguarding, that these activities form the very condition of existing, at a time when the sword, now again, resolves all. Indeed, there is no politics over which the threat of abolition does not hang.

As for the democracies, they have not ceased to be emptied out and to be altered in their regime. As fantasies and accidents are now their sole subject matter, they have become unpredictable and paranoid, anarchic powers without symbols, devoid of meaning or destiny. Lacking in justification, only ornament remains to them.

Nothing, henceforth, is inviolable; nothing is inalienable; and nothing is imprescriptible. Except, perhaps, property — still.

In these conditions, it might well be that, at bottom, no one is the citizen of any state in particular.

The countries that saw us emerge: we carry them in our innermost selves — their faces, their landscapes, their chaotic multiplicities, their rivers and their mountains, their forests, their savannas, seasons, bird songs, insects, air, sweat and humidity, mud, city noise, laughter, disorder and indiscipline. And stupidity.

But as the march progresses, these countries also become unfamiliar to us, and now we occasionally glimpse them silhouetted, set in a bad light.

However, there are also days when one starts to sing their names again, in silence, wanting anew to walk along our childhood paths, in those countries of our birth from which we ended up distancing ourselves, though without ever having been able to forget them, without ever having been able to sever ourselves from them once and for all, without their ever having stopped being a concern to us. In this way, in the midst of the Algerian war, Fanon was reminded of Martinique, his island of birth.

This rememoration is simultaneously a taking of distance, a self-examination, and is thus the alleged price to pay for living and thinking freely, that is to say, doing so on the basis of a certain destitution, a certain detachment, located in the position of one who has nothing to lose since, to a certain extent, he has, from the outset, renounced the possession of anything whatsoever for himself, or again has already lost everything or nearly everything.

But why ought freedom, the capacity to think, and the renunciation of all forms of loss — and therefore a certain idea of calculation and gratuity — all come to be united in such a narrow relation?

Is losing everything or nearly everything — better, letting go of everything, or renouncing everything or nearly everything — the condition, then, under which we may win some serenity in this world and age of turbulence, a world in which, oftentimes, what one has does not tally with what one is and what one earns entertains only a distant relation with what one loses?

In addition, does not letting go of everything or nearly everything, renouncing everything or nearly everything, mean that one is henceforth "nowhere," that one no longer answers to anything or to any name?

And so what is freedom if one cannot really break with this accident of being born somewhere — the relation of flesh and bones, the double law of soil and blood?

How can who we are, how we are perceived, and how others take us, come to be indicated, and so irrevocably, by this accident? Why does this accident so decisively determine not only what we have rights to but also everything else, that is, the sum of proofs, documents, and justifications we are always obliged to supply if we are to hope for anything in the slightest, starting with the right to exist, the right to be wherever life ultimately takes us, including the right to move about freely? To traverse the world; to take the measure of the accident represented by our place of birth, with its weight of arbitrariness and constraint; to wed the irreversible flow comprising the time of life and existence; to learn to assume our status as passersby as the condition, in the last instance, of our humanity, as the base from which we create culture — these are perhaps, ultimately, the most untreatable questions of our time, questions that Fanon will have bequeathed to us in his pharmacy, *the pharmacy of the passerby* (*passant*).

In fact, few terms are as laden with meanings as *passant* is.

But, for starters, this word *passant* contains several others within in, beginning with *pas* ("not" as well as "step") — at once a negative instance (that which *is* not or does not yet exist or exists only through its absence), and a rhythm, cadence, and even speed, along a course or a march, or through a displacement — that which is (in) movement. Following this, as if from behind, is *passé* — not the past as a trace of what has already taken place, but the past in the process of happening, such as one can grasp it there, at the moment of breaking and entering, in the very act by which it happens, at the very instant when, arising as if via the crack, it strives to be born in the event, to become an event.

Next, there is *passant* as "passerby," that figure of the "elsewhere," since the passerby is only passing by, because, precisely, arriving from another place, he is moving toward other skies. He is "passing" through — and therefore enjoins us to welcome him, at least momentarily.

But there is also *passeur* (smuggler) and, further still, *passage* (way/gangway) and *passager* (passenger). The passerby is, then, all at once the vehicle, the bridge or gangway, the planking that covers the row of beams in a ship, the one who, having roots elsewhere, is passing through somewhere he stays temporarily (even if it means) returning home when the time comes. What would happen, however, if he did not return and if, by any chance, he continued his journey, going from one place to another, retracing his steps if necessary, but always at the periphery of his birthplace, yet not calling himself a "refugee" or a "migrant," and less still a "citizen" or a "native"—the pureblood human?

In evoking, apropos of the question of our times, the passerby, that is to say, the fugitive character of life, no praise is being made either of exile or of refuge, flight, or nomadism.

Nor is this a celebration of a bohemian and rootless world.

In current conditions, simply no such world exists. Instead, the aim is to convoke, as I have tried to throughout this long essay, the figure of a human out to make great strides up a steep path—who has left, quit his country, lived elsewhere, abroad, in places in which he forges an authentic dwelling, thereby tying his fate to those who welcome and recognize their own face in his, the face of a humanity to come.

Becoming-human-in-the-world is a question neither of birth nor of origin or race.

It is a matter of journeying, of movement, and of transfiguration.

The project of transfiguration demands that the subject consciously embrace the broken up part of its own life; that it compel itself to take detours and sometimes improbable connections; that it operates in the interstices if it cares about giving a common expression to things that we commonly dissociate. Fanon passed through each of these places, but he did so not without a reserve of distance and astonishment, in a bid to fully adopt the unstable and shifting cartography in which he found himself. For him, a "place" was any experience of encountering others, one that paved the way to becoming self-aware, not necessarily as a singular individual but as a seminal fragment (éclat) of a larger humanity, a fragment grappling with the inevitability of a never-ending time, the main attribute of which is to flow—a passing par excellence.

One can inhabit a place, however, only by allowing oneself to be inhabited by it. Yet inhabiting a place is not the same thing as belonging to this place. Being born in one's country of origin is a mere accident; nevertheless it does not dissolve the subject of all responsibility.

For that matter, there is no secret that birth as such conceals. Birth offers but the fiction of a world that is past despite all our attempts to attach it to everything that we venerate: custom, culture, tradition, rituals, the set of masks with which each of us is decked out.

At the limit, a "human's specificity" is not to belong to any particular place, since this human, which is a compound of other living beings and other species, belongs to all places together.

Learning to pass constantly from one place to another—this ought, then, to be its project, since it is, in any case, its destiny.

But passing from one place to another also means weaving with each one of them a twofold relation of solidarity and detachment. This experience of presence and distance, of solidarity and detachment, but never of indifference—let us call it the ethics of the passerby.

It is an ethics that says that it is only by moving away from a place that one is better able to name and inhabit it.

Do not one's being able to sojourn and to move about freely constitute the sine qua non conditions of sharing the world, or again of what Édouard Glissant has called the "World Relation"? What could the human person resemble beyond the accidents of birth, nationality, and citizenship?

It would have been good to be able to give an exhaustive reply to all these questions. Let us be content to observe that future thinking will necessarily be about passage, crossing, and movement. This thinking will be about flowing life, about passing life, which we strive to translate as an event. This thinking will not be about excess but about surplus, that is to say, about that which, as it has no price, must escape sacrifice, expenditure, loss.

If such thinking is to be articulated, it is further to be recognized that Europe, which has given so much to the world and taken so much in return, often by force and by ruse, is no longer the world's center of gravity. No longer is Europe that place over there to where we must go to find the solutions to the questions we have posed over here. It is no longer the pharmacy of the world.

But does saying it has ceased to be the world's center of gravity mean that the European archive is exhausted? For that matter, was this archive only ever the product of a particular history? As the history of Europe has been confounded over several centuries with the history of the world, and the history of the world in turn has been confounded with Europe's own, it follows, does it not, that this archive does not belong to Europe alone?

As the world no longer has only one pharmacy, so the matter essentially concerns how we might inhabit all its assemblages (*faisceaux*), how we might escape from the relation without desire and the peril of the society of enmity. Starting from a multiplicity of places, the concern is then to traverse them, as responsibly as possible, given the entitled parties that we all are, but in a total relation of freedom and, wherever necessary, of detachment. In this process, which entails translation but also conflict and misunderstandings, certain questions will be resolved. What will then emerge in relative clarity are the demands, if not of a possible universality, then at least of an idea of the Earth as that which is common to us, as our communal condition.

This is one reason why it is practically impossible to read Frantz Fanon and come out unscathed. It is difficult to read him without being interpellated by his voice, by his writing, his rhythm, his language, his sonorities and his vocal resonances, his spasms, his contractions, and, above all, his breath.

In the era of the Earth, we will effectively require a language that constantly bores, perforates, and digs like a gimlet, that knows how to become a projectile, a sort of full absolute, of will that ceaselessly gnaws at the real. Its function will not only be to force the locks but also to save life from the disaster lying in wait.

Each of the fragments of this terrestrial language will be rooted in the paradoxes of the body, the flesh, the skin, and nerves. To escape the threat of fixation, confinement, and strangulation, as well as the threat of dissociation and mutilation, language and writing will have to be ceaselessly projected toward the infinity of the outside, rise up and loosen the vice that threatens the subjugated person with suffocation as it does his body of muscles, lungs, heart, neck, liver, and spleen, that dishonored body, made of multiple incisions, that divisible, divided body, in struggle against itself, made of several bodies that confront each other within one and the same body—on the one hand, the body of hatred, of appalling burden, the false body of abjection crushed by indignity, and, on the other, the originary body, which, upon being stolen by others, is then disfigured and abominated, whereupon the matter is literally one of resuscitating it, in an act of veritable genesis.

Rendered to life and thereby different to the fallen body of colonized existence, this new body will be invited to become a member of a new community. Unfolding according to its own plan, it will henceforth walk along together with other bodies and, doing so, will re-create the world.

This is why, with Fanon, we address it in this final prayer:[1]

O my body, always make me a man who questions!

NOTES

Introduction

1 Chinua Achebe, *Things Fall Apart* (1958; New York: Knopf Doubleday, 1995).

One Exit from Democracy

1 Paul Gilroy, *The Black Atlantic: Modernity and Double-Consciousness* (New York: Verso, 1993).

2 For a general overview, see Parkakunnel Joseph Thomas, *Mercantilism and East India Trade* (London: Frank Cass, 1963); William J. Barber, *British Economic Thought and India, 1690–1858* (Oxford: Clarendon Press, 1975).

3 See Walter Johnson, *River of Dark Dreams: Slavery and Empire in the Cotton Kingdom* (Cambridge, MA: Belknap Press of Harvard University Press, 2013).

4 A comparative analysis of this institution is to be found in Richard S. Dunn, *A Tale of Two Plantations: Slave Life and Labor in Jamaica and Virginia* (Cambridge, MA: Harvard University Press, 2014).

5 Antoine de Montchrestien, *Traité d'économie politique* (1615; Geneva: Droz, 1999), 187.

6 See, for example, Josiah Child, *A New Discourse of Trade* (London: J. Hodges, 1690), 197; Charles Davenant, "Discourses on the Public Revenue and on the Trade" (1711), in *The Political and Commercial Works: Collected and Revised by Sir Charles Whitworth* (London: R. Horsfield, 1967), 3.

7 See Christophe Salvat, *Formation et diffusion de la pensée économique libérale française: André Morellet et l'économie politique du XVIIe siècle* (Lyon: Thèse, 2000); Francis Demier and Daniel Diatkine, eds., "Le libéralisme à l'épreuve: De l'empire aux nations (Adam Smith et l'économie coloniale)," *Cahiers d'économie politique*, nos. 27–28 (1996).

8 See Jean-Pierre Bardet and Jacques Dupâquier, eds., *Histoire des populations de l'Europe: I. Des origines aux prémices de la révolution démographique* (Paris: Fayard, 1998).

9 On the scale of these new forms of movement, see World Bank, *Development Goals in an Era of Demographic Change: Global Monitoring Report 2015–2016*, 2016, http://pubdocs.worldbank.org/en/503001444058224597/Global-Monitoring-Report-2015.pdf.

10 See Seyla Benhabib and Judith Resnik, eds., *Migrations and Mobilities: Citizenship, Borders, and Gender* (New York: New York University Press, 2009); Seyla Benhabib, *The Rights of Others: Aliens, Residents, and Citizens* (Cambridge, UK: Cambridge University Press, 2004).

11 The term "new inhabitants" does not mean that they were not already there. "New" is the change of their status in our systems of representation. On these questions, see Bruno Latour, *Facing Gaia: Eight Lectures on the New Climatic Regime*, trans. Catherine Porter (Cambridge, UK: Polity Press, 2017).

12 Claire Larsonneur, ed., *Le Sujet digital* (Paris: Les Presses du Réel, 2015), 3.

13 Pierre Caye, *Critique de la destruction créatrice* (Paris: Les Belles Lettres, 2015), 20.

14 Norbert Elias, *The Court Society*, trans. Edmund Jephcott (New York: Pantheon, 1993); Norbert Elias, *The Civilizing Process: Sociogenetic and Psychogenetic Investigations*, trans. Edmund Jephcott (1939; Oxford: Basil Blackwell, 2000).

15 Erving Goffman, *Interaction Ritual* (Garden City, NY: Doubleday, 1967).

16 W. E. B. Du Bois, *Black Reconstruction in America, 1860–1880* (1935; New York: Free Press, 1998).

17 Alexis de Tocqueville, *Democracy in America* (1835), ed. Edourdo Nolla, trans. James T. Schleifer (Indianapolis, IN: Liberty Fund, 2010), 554–55.

18 Tocqueville, *Democracy in America*, 565.

19 Kenneth C. Barnes, *Journey of Hope: The Back to Africa Movement in Arkansas in the Late 1800s* (Chapel Hill: University of North Carolina Press, 2004).

20 Tocqueville, *Democracy in America*, 555.

21 At about the same period in France, for example, an opposite tendency took shape. Democracy sought, if not to obtain violence without necessarily having recourse to direct violence, at least to relegate the most inhumane demonstrations to increasingly out-of-sight spaces. See Emmanuel Taieb, *La Guillotine au secret: Les exécutions publiques en France, 1870–1939* (Paris: Belin, 2011).

22 See Ida B. Wells-Barnett, *On Lynchings* (New York: Arno Press, 1969); Robyn Wiegman, "The Anatomy of Lynching," *Journal of the History of Sexuality* 3, no. 3 (1993): 445–67; David Garland, "Penal Excess and Surplus Meaning: Public Torture Lynchings in Twentieth-Century America," *Law and Society Review* 39, no. 4 (2005): 793–834; Dora Apel, "On Looking: Lynching Photographs and Legacies of Lynching after 9/11," *American Quarterly* 55, no. 3 (2003): 457–78.

23 Joyce Appleby and Terence Ball, eds., *Jefferson: Political Writings* (1775; Cambridge, UK: Cambridge University Press, 2004), 481.

24 Simon Gikandi, *Slavery and the Culture of Taste* (Princeton: Princeton University Press, 2015), 149.

25 See Sidney W. Mintz, *Sweetness and Power: The Place of Sugar in Modern History*

(New York: Penguin Books, 1986); K. N. Chaudhuri, *The Trading World of Asia and the English East India Company, 1660–1760* (Cambridge, UK: Cambridge University Press, 1978).

26 See Klauss Knorr, *British Colonial Theories, 1570–1850* (Toronto: Toronto University Press, 1944), 54; Joyce Oldham Appleby, *Economic Thought and Ideology in the Seventeenth-Century England* (Princeton: Princeton University Press, 1978); William Letwin, *The Origin of Scientific Economics: The English Economic Thought 1660–1776* (London: Methuen, 1963).

27 Romain Bertrand, "Norbert Elias et la question des violences impériales : Jalons pour une histoire de la 'mauvaise conscience' occidentale," *Vingtième siècle* 106 (2010): 127–40.

28 Mikhail Bakunin, "Federalism, Socialism, Anti-Theologism," in *Bakunin on Anarchy*, ed. Sam Dolgoff (New York: Vintage Books, 1971).

29 For a critique of right, see Carl Schmitt, *The Crisis of Parliamentary Democracy*, trans. E. Kennedy (Cambridge, MA: MIT Press, 1985).

30 Georges Sorel, *Reflections on Violence*, trans. T. E. Hulme, in *Cambridge Texts in the History of Political Thought*, ed. Jeremy Jennings (Cambridge, UK: Cambridge University Press, 1999), 165, 170.

31 See Romain Ducoulombier, *Ni Dieu, ni maitre, ni organisation? Contribution à l'histoire des réseaux sous la Troisième République (1880–1914)* (Rennes: Presses Universitaires de Rennes, 2009); Miguel Chueca, ed., *Déposséder les possédants: La grève générale aux 'temps héroïques' du syndicalisme révolutionnaire (1895–1906)* (Marseille: Agone, 2008).

32 Odile Krakovich, *Les Femmes bagnardes* (Paris: O. Orban, 1990).

33 Krokovich estimates the number of convicts from 1852 to 1938 to be 102,100 (*Les Femmes bagnardes*, 260). See, in addition, Danielle Donet-Vincent, "Les 'bagnes' des Indochinois en Guyane (1931–1963)," *Crimino Corpus*, January 2006, https://journals.openedition.org/criminocorpus/182.

34 Ruth Gilmore, *Golden Gulag: Prisons, Surplus, Crisis, and Opposition in Globalizing California* (Berkeley: University of California Press, 2007).

35 On these debates, consult Marie Gottschalk, *The Prison and the Gallows: The Politics of Mass Incarceration in America* (Cambridge, UK: Cambridge University Press, 2006); Michelle Alexander, *The New Jim Crow: Mass Incarceration in the Age of Colorblindness* (New York: New York University Press, 2010); Lorna A. Rhodes, *Total Confinement: Madness and Reason in the Maximum Security Prison* (Berkeley: University of California Press, 2004).

36 Daniel R. Headrick, *The Tools of Empire: Technology and European Imperialism in the Nineteenth-Century* (New York: Oxford University Press, 1981); Philip D. Curtin, *Disease and Empire: The Health of European Troops in the Conquest of Africa* (Cambridge, UK: Cambridge University Press, 1998); Marie-Noëlle Bourquet and Christophe Bonneuil, eds., "De l'inventaire du monde à la mise en valeur du globe: Botanique et colonisation (fin 17e siècle–début 20e siècle)," *Revue française d'Histoire d'Outre-Mer* 86 (1999): 322–23.

37 Bouda Etemad, *La Possession du monde: Poids et mesure de la colonisation* (Brussels: Complexe, 2000).

38 Laurent Henninger, "Industrialisation et mécanisation de la guerre, sources majeures du totalitarisme (XIXe–XXe siècles)," *Astérion*, no. 2 (2004): 1.

39 Iain R. Smith and Andreas Stucki, "The Colonial Development of Concentration Camps (1868–1902)," *Journal of Imperial and Commonwealth History* 39, no. 3 (2011): 417–37.

40 Olivier Le Cour Grandmaison, *Coloniser, exterminer: Sur la guerre et l'État colonial* (Paris: Fayard, 2005).

41 For the case of Cameroon, see Thomas Deltombe, Manuel Domergue, and Jacob Tatsitsa, *Kamerun! Une guerre cachée aux origines de la Françafrique (1948–1971)* (Paris: La Découverte, 2011).

42 See, for example, Kevin Kenny, *Peaceable Kingdom Lost: The Paxton Boys and the Destruction of William Penn's Holy Experiment* (New York: Oxford University Press, 2009).

43 A. Dirk Moses, ed., *Empire, Colony, Genocide: Conquest, Occupation, and Subaltern Resistance in World History* (New York: Berghahn, 2008); Martin Shaw, "Britain and Genocide: Historical and Contemporary Parameters of National Responsibility," *Review of International Studies* 37, no. 5 (2011): 2417–38.

44 For more details, see Elizabeth Kolsky, *Colonial Justice in British India: White Violence and the Rule of Law* (Cambridge, UK: Cambridge University Press, 2010).

45 Lisa Ford, *Settler Sovereignty: Jurisdiction and Indigenous People in America and Australia, 1788–1836* (Cambridge, MA: Harvard University Press, 2010).

46 See, in particular, Martin Thomas, "Intelligence Providers and the Fabric of the Late Colonial State," in *Elites and Decolonization in the Twentieth Century*, ed. Josh Dulfer and Marc Frey (Basingstoke, UK: Palgrave Macmillan, 2011), 11–35.

47 Priya Satia, *Spies in Arabia: The Great War and the Cultural Foundations of Britain's Covert Empire in the Middle East* (Oxford: Oxford University Press, 2008); Martin Thomas, *Empires of Intelligence: Security Services and Colonial Disorder after 1914* (Berkeley: University of California Press, 2008).

48 See Simon Frankel Pratt, "Crossing Off Names: The Logic of Military Assassination," *Small Wars and Insurgencies* 26, no. 1 (2015): 3–24; and, more generally, Nils Melzer, *Targeted Killing in International Law* (New York: Oxford University Press, 2008); Grégoire Chamayou, *Théorie du drone* (Paris: La Fabrique, 2013).

49 Arthur Kroker and Michael A. Weinstein, "Maidan, Caliphate, and Code: Theorizing Power and Resistance in the 21st Century," *Ctheory*, March 3, 2015, https://journals.uvic.ca/index.php/ctheory/article/view/15127/6106.

50 Thomas Gregory, "Dismembering the Dead: Violence, Vulnerability and the Body in War," *European Journal of International Relations* 21, no. 4 (December 2015): 944–65.

51 Denis Retaillé and Olivier Walther, "Guerre au Sahara-Sahel: La reconversion des savoirs nomades," *L'Information géographique* 75, no. 3 (2011): 4.

52 Achille Mbembe, "Necropolitics," *Public Culture* 15, no. 1 (2003): 11–40.

53 Wendy Brown, *Undoing the Demos: Neoliberalism's Stealth Revolution* (New York: Zone Books, 2015).

54 Achille Mbembe, "Epilogue: There Is Only One World," in *Critique of Black Reason* (Durham, NC: Duke University Press, 2017).

55 Aimé Césaire, *Discourse on Colonialism*, trans. Joan Pinkham (1955; New York: Monthly Review Press, 2000); Frantz Fanon, *The Wretched of the Earth*, trans. Richard Philcox (1961; New York: Grove Press, 2004).

56 Frédéric Lordon, *Imperium: Structures et affects des corps politiques* (Paris: La Fabrique, 2015), 16.

Two The Society of Enmity

1 As Freud argued in 1915, history "is essentially a series of murders of peoples." Sigmund Freud, "Our Attitude towards Death," in *The Standard Edition of the Complete Psychological Works of Sigmund Freud*, vol. 14 (1914–16): *On the History of the Psycho-Analytic Movement, Papers on Metapsychology, and Other Works*, trans. James Strachey et al. (London: Vintage, 2001), 292. Lacan went further in the 1950s, remarking that "our civilization is itself sufficiently one of hatred." Jacques Lacan, *The Seminar of Jacques Lacan, Book I: Freud's Papers on Technique, 1953–1954*, trans. John Forrester (New York: Norton, 1991), 277.

2 Carl Schmitt, *The Crisis of Parliamentary Democracy*, trans. Ellen Kennedy (Cambridge, MA: MIT Press, 2000), 10.

3 Schmitt, *The Crisis of Parliamentary Democracy*, 10–16.

4 Wendy Brown speaks of "de-democratization" in *Les Habits neufs de la politique mondiale* (Paris: Les Prairies Ordinaires, 2007). See also Jean-Luc Nancy, *The Truth of Democracy*, trans. Pascale Anne-Brault and Michael Naas (New York: Fordham University Press, 2010).

5 Wendy Brown, *Walled States, Waning Sovereignty* (New York: Zone Books, 2014).

6 Eyal Weizman, "Walking through Walls: Soldiers as Architects in the Israeli-Palestinian Conflict," *Radical Philosophy* 136 (March–April 2006): 8–22.

7 Eyal Weizman, *Hollow Land: Israel's Architecture of Occupation* (New York: Verso, 2012).

8 Amira Hass, "Israel Closure Policy: An Ineffective Strategy of Containment and Repression," *Journal of Palestinian Studies* 31, no. 3 (2002): 5–20.

9 Cédric Parizot, "Après le mur: Les représentations israéliennes de la séparation avec les Palestiniens," *Cultures et Conflits* 73 (2009): 53–72.

10 Idith Zertal, *Israel's Holocaust and the Politics of Nationhood* (Cambridge, UK: Cambridge University Press, 2010); Jacqueline Rose, *The Question of Zion* (Princeton: Princeton University Press, 2007); Judith Butler, *Parting Ways: Jewishness and the Critique of Zionism* (New York: Columbia University Press, 2012).

11 See Saree Makdisi, "The Architecture of Erasure," *Critical Inquiry* 36, no. 3 (2010): 519–59. See also Mick Taussig, "Two Weeks in Palestine: My First Visit," *Critical Inquiry*, n.d., https://criticalinquiry.uchicago.edu/two_weeks _in_palestine/.

12 See especially Ariella Azoulay, *Civil Imagination: A Political Ontology of Photography* (New York: Verso, 2015), 125–73.

13 Adi Ophir, Michal Givoni, and Sari Hana, eds., *The Power of Inclusive Exclusion: Anatomy of Israeli Rule in the Occupied Palestinian Territories* (New York: Zone Books, 2009); Neve Gordon, *Israel's Occupation* (Berkeley: University of California Press, 2008).

14 James Belich, *Replenishing the Earth: The Settler Revolution and the Rise of the Angloworld* (Oxford: Oxford University Press, 2009).

15 See especially A. Dirk Moses, ed., *Empire, Colony, Genocide: Conquest, Occupation, and Subaltern Resistance in World History* (New York: Berghahn, 2008); Patrick Wolfe, "Settler Colonialism and the Elimination of the Native," *Journal of Genocide Research* 8, no. 4 (2006): 387–409.

16 Cornelis W. De Kiewiet, *A History of South Africa: Social and Economic* (Oxford: Oxford University Press, 1957); Nigel Penn, *The Forgotten Frontier: Colonists and Khoisan on the Cape's Northern Frontier in the 18th Century* (Athens: Ohio University Press, 2006).

17 See Peter L. Geschiere, *Sorcellerie et politique en Afrique: La viande des autres* (Paris: Karthala, 1995).

18 See Mohamedou Ould Slahi, *Les Carnets de Guantanamo* (Paris: Michel Lafon, 2015).

19 Carl Schmitt, *The Concept of the Political*, trans. George Schwab (Chicago: University of Chicago Press, 2007), 26.

20 Schmitt, *The Concept of the Political*, 35.

21 Talal Asad, *On Suicide Bombing* (New York: Columbia University Press, 2007).

22 Sigmund Freud, *Mass Psychology and Other Writings*, trans. J. A. Underwood (London: Penguin, 2004), 26.

23 Gustave Le Bon, *Psychologie des foules* (Paris: PUF, 2013).

24 See Jean Comaro, "The Politics of Conviction: Faith on the Neo-liberal Frontier," *Social Analysis* 53, no. 1 (2009): 17–38.

25 Nicola Perugini and Neve Gordon, *The Human Right to Dominate* (Oxford: Oxford University Press, 2015).

26 On these developments, see Éric Sadin, *L'Humanité augmentée: L'administration numérique du monde* (Paris: L'Échappée, 2013).

27 The following remarks are largely inspired by Frédéric Lordon's *Willing Slaves of Capital: Spinoza and Marx on Desire*, trans. Gabriel Ash (New York: Verso, 2014).

28 Freud, *Mass Psychology*, 26.

29 Freud, *Mass Psychology*, 26.

30 The following remarks reproduce in part my "Nanoracisme et puissance du

vide," in *Le Grand Repli*, ed. Nicolas Bancel, Pascal Blanchard, and Ahmed Boubeker (Paris: La Découverte, 2015), 5–11.

31 See David Theo Goldberg and Susan Giroux, *Sites of Race* (Cambridge, UK: Polity Press, 2014); David Theo Goldberg, *Are We All Postracial Yet?* (Cambridge, UK: Polity Press, 2015).

32 Michel Agier, ed., *Un monde de camps* (Paris: La Découverte, 2014), 11.

33 Nacira Guénif-Souilamas and Éric Macé, *Les Féministes et le garçon arabe* (Paris: Éditions de L'Aube, 2004); Joan Wallach Scott, *The Politics of the Veil* (Princeton: Princeton University Press, 2009).

34 Michel Foucault, "Confronting Governments: Human Rights," in *Power: The Essential Works of Michel Foucault*, vol. 3, *1954–1984*, trans. Robert Hurley et al. (New York: Penguin, 2002), 475.

Three Necropolitics

1 The essay departs from the traditional accounts of sovereignty to be found in political science and international relations. For the most part, these accounts locate sovereignty within the boundaries of the nation-state, state-empowered institutions, or supranational institutions and networks. See, for example, "Sovereignty at the Millennium," special issue of *Political Studies* 47 (1999). My own approach builds on Foucault's critique of the notion of sovereignty and its relation to war and biopower in *Society Must Be Defended: Lectures at the Collège de France, 1975–1976*, ed. Mauro Bertani and Alessandro Fontano, trans. David Macey (New York: Picador, 2003), 65–86, 87–114, 141–66, 239–64. See also Giorgio Agamben, *Homo Sacer: Sovereign Power and Bare Life*, trans. Daniel Heller-Roazen (Stanford: Stanford University Press, 1998), 15–67.

2 Foucault, *Society Must Be Defended*, 239–64.

3 On the state of exception, see Carl Schmitt, *Dictatorship*, trans. Michael Hoelzt and Graham Ward (Malden, MA: Polity Press, 2014), 181–94, 200–201, 205–7, 218–19; Carl Schmitt, *Theory of the Partisan: A Commentary on the Concept of the Political*, trans. A. C. Goodson (East Lansing: Michigan State University Press, 2004).

4 Hannah Arendt, *The Origins of Totalitarianism* (New York: Harvest, 1966), 444.

5 Giorgio Agamben, *Means without End: Notes on Politics*, trans. Vincenzo Binetti and Cesare Casarino (Minneapolis: University of Minnesota Press, 2000), 39–40.

6 On these debates, see Saul Friedlander, ed., *Probing the Limits of Representation: Nazism and the "Final Solution"* (Cambridge, MA: Harvard University Press, 1992); and, more recently, Bertrand Ogilvie, "Comparer l'incomparable," *Multitudes*, no. 7 (2001): 130–66.

7 See James Bohman and William Rehg, eds., *Deliberative Democracy: Essays on Reason and Politics* (Cambridge, MA: MIT Press, 1997); Jürgen Habermas, *Between Facts and Norms* (Cambridge MA: MIT Press, 1996).

8 James Schmidt, ed., *What Is Enlightenment? Eighteenth-Century Answers and Twentieth-Century Questions* (Berkeley: University of California Press, 1996).

9 Cornelius Castoriadis, *The Imaginary Institution of Society*, trans. Kathleen Blamey (Oxford: Blackwell, 1987); and *Figures of The Thinkable*, trans. Helen Arnold (Stanford: Stanford University Press, 1999).

10 See, in particular, Paul Gilroy, *The Black Atlantic: Modernity and Double Consciousness* (Cambridge, MA: Harvard University Press, 1993), especially chap. 2.

11 G. W. F. Hegel, *Phenomenology of Spirit*, ed. and trans. Terry Pinkard and Micheal Baur (Cambridge, UK: Cambridge University Press, 2018). See also the critique by Alexandre Kojève, *Instruction to the Reading of Hegel* (Ithaca, NY: Cornell University Press, 1947), especially appendix II, "The Idea of Death in the Philosophy of Hegel"; Georges Bataille, *Oeuvres complètes XII* (Paris: Gallimard, 1988), especially "Hegel, la mort et le sacrifice," 326–48 (In English: "Hegel, Death and Sacrifice," trans. Jonathan Strauss, "On Bataille," special issue of *Yale French Studies*, no. 78 [1990]: 9–28), and "Hegel, l'homme et l'histoire," 349–69.

12 See Jean Baudrillard, "Death in Bataille," in *Bataille: A Critical Reader*, ed. Fred Botting and Scott Wilson (Oxford: Blackwell, 1998), especially 139–41.

13 Georges Bataille, *Visions of Excess: Selected Writings, 1927–1939*, trans. A. Stoekl (Minneapolis: University of Minnesota Press, 1985), 94–95.

14 Fred Botting and Scott Wilson, eds., *The Bataille Reader* (Oxford: Blackwell, 1997), 318–19. See also Georges Bataille, *The Accursed Share: An Essay on General Economy*, vol. 1, *Consumption*, trans. Robert Hurley (New York: Zone, 1988), and *Erotism: Death and Sensuality*, trans. Mary Dalwood (San Francisco: City Lights, 1986).

15 Georges Bataille, *The Accursed Share*, vol. 2, *The History of Eroticism* and *Sovereignty*, trans. Robert Hurley (New York: Zone Books, 1992).

16 On the state of siege, see Schmitt, *Dictatorship*, chap. 6.

17 See Foucault, *Society Must Be Defended*, 61–62, 65–80.

18 "Race is, politically speaking, not the beginning of humanity but its end . . . not the natural birth of man but his unnatural death." Arendt, *Origins of Totalitarianism*, 157.

19 Foucault, *Society Must Be Defended*, 256, 241.

20 Foucault, *Society Must Be Defended*, 240–45.

21 See Jürgen Habermas, *The Philosophical Discourse of Modernity: Twelve Lectures*, trans. Frederick G. Lawrence (Cambridge, MA: MIT Press, 1987), especially chaps. 3, 5, 6.

22 Enzo Traverso, *La violence nazie: Une généalogie européenne* (Paris: La Fabrique Editions, 2002).

23 Michel Foucault, *Discipline and Punish: The Birth of the Prison* (New York: Pantheon, 1977).

24 See Robert Wokler, "Contextualizing Hegel's Phenomenology of the French Revolution and the Terror," *Political Theory* 26 (1998): 33–55.

25 David W. Bates, *Enlightenment Aberrations: Error and Revolution in France* (Ithaca, NY: Cornell University Press, 2002), chap. 6.

26 Karl Marx, *Capital: A Critique of Political Economy* (London: Lawrence and Wishart, 1984), 3:817. See also *Capital*, trans. Ben Fowkes (Harmondsworth, UK: Penguin, 1986), 1:172.

27 Stephen Louw, "In the Shadow of the Pharaohs: The Militarization of Labour Debate and Classical Marxist Theory," *Economy and Society* 29 (2000): 240.

28 On labor militarization and the transition to communism, see Nikolai Bukharin, *The Politics and Economics of the Transition Period*, trans. Oliver Field (London: Routledge and Kegan Paul, 1979); Leon Trotsky, *Terrorism and Communism: A Reply to Karl Kautsky* (Ann Arbor: University of Michigan Press, 1961). On the collapse of the distinction between state and society, see Karl Marx, *The Civil War in France* (Moscow: Progress, 1972); Vladimir Il'ich Lenin, *Selected Works in Three Volumes*, vol. 2 (Moscow: Progress, 1977). For a critique of "revolutionary terror," see Maurice Merleau-Ponty, *Humanism and Terror: An Essay on the Communist Problem*, trans. John O'Neill (Boston: Beacon, 1969). For a more recent example of "revolutionary terror," see Steve J. Stern, ed., *Shining and Other Paths: War and Society in Peru, 1980–1995* (Durham, NC: Duke University Press, 1998).

29 See Saidiya V. Hartman, *Scenes of Subjection: Terror, Slavery, and Self-Making in Nineteenth-Century America* (Oxford: Oxford University Press, 1997); Manuel Moreno Fraginals, *The Sugarmill: The Socioeconomic Complex of Sugar in Cuba, 1760–1860* (New York: Monthly Review Press, 1976).

30 Gilroy, *Black Atlantic*, 57.

31 See Frederick Douglass, *Narrative of the Life of Frederick Douglass, an American Slave*, ed. Houston A. Baker (New York: Penguin, 1986).

32 The term "manners" is used here to denote the links between *social grace* and *social control*. According to Norbert Elias, manners embody what is "considered socially acceptable behavior," the "precepts on conduct," and the framework for "conviviality." *The History of Manners*, vol. 1, *The Civilizing Process*, trans. Edmund Jephcott (New York: Pantheon, 1978), chap. 2.

Douglass, *Narrative of the Life*, 51. On the random killing of slaves, see 67–68: "The louder she screamed, the harder he whipped; and where the blood ran faster, there he whipped longest," says Douglass in his narration of the whipping of his aunt by Mr. Plummer. "He would whip her to make her scream, and whip her to make her hush; and not until overcome by fatigue, would he cease to swing the blood-clotted cowskin. . . . It was a most terrible spectacle."

33 Susan Buck-Morss, "Hegel and Haiti," *Critical Inquiry* 26 (2000): 821–66.

34 Roger D. Abrahams, *Singing the Master: The Emergence of African American Culture in the Plantation South* (New York: Pantheon, 1992).

35 In what follows I am mindful of the fact that colonial forms of sovereignty were always fragmented. They were complex, "less concerned with legitimizing their own presence and more excessively violent than their European forms."

As important, "European states never aimed at governing the colonial territories with the same uniformity and intensity as was applied to their own populations." T. B. Hansen and Finn Stepputat, "Sovereign Bodies: Citizens, Migrants and States in the Post-Colonial World," unpublished manuscript, 2002.

36 In *The Racial State* (Malden, MA: Blackwell, 2002), David Theo Goldberg argues that from the nineteenth century on, there are at least two historically competing traditions of racial rationalization: naturism (based on an inferiority claim) and historicism (based on the claim of the historical "immaturity" — and therefore "educability" — of the natives). In a private communication (August 23, 2002), he argues that these two traditions played out differently when it came to issues of sovereignty, states of exception, and forms of necropower. In his view, necropower can take multiple forms: the terror of actual death or a more "benevolent" form — the result of which is the destruction of a culture in order to "save the people" from themselves.

37 Arendt, *Origins of Totalitarianism*, 185–221.

38 Etienne Balibar, "Prolegomena to Sovereignty," in *We, the People of Europe? Reflections on Transnational Citizenship*, trans. James Swenson (Princeton: Princeton University Press, 2003), 133–54.

39 Eugene Victor Walter, *Terror and Resistance: A Study of Political Violence with Case Studies of Some Primitive African Communities* (Oxford: Oxford University Press, 1969).

40 Arendt, *Origins of Totalitarianism*, 192.

41 For a powerful rendition of this process, see Michael Taussig, *Shamanism, Colonialism, and the Wild Man: A Study in Terror and Healing* (Chicago: University of Chicago Press, 1987).

42 On the notion of "enemy," see "L'ennemi," special issue of *Raisons politiques*, no. 5 (2002).

43 Kojève, *Introduction to the Reading of Hegel*.

44 See Daniel R. Headrick, *The Tools of Empire: Technology and European Imperialism in the Nineteenth Century* (New York: Oxford University Press, 1981).

45 On the township, see G. G. Maasdorp and A. S. B. Humphreys, eds., *From Shantytown to Township: An Economic Study of African Poverty and Rehousing in a South African City* (Cape Town: Juta, 1975).

46 Belinda Bozzoli, "Why Were the 1980s 'Millenarian'? Style, Repertoire, Space and Authority in South Africa's Black Cities," *Journal of Historical Sociology* 13 (2000): 79.

47 Bozzoli, "Why Were the 1980s 'Millenarian'?"

48 See Herman Giliomee, ed., *Up Against the Fences: Poverty, Passes and Privileges in South Africa* (Cape Town: David Philip, 1985); Francis Wilson, *Migrant Labour in South Africa* (Johannesburg: Christian Institute of Southern Africa, 1972).

49 Frantz Fanon, *The Wretched of the Earth*, trans. C. Farrington (New York: Grove Weidenfeld, 1991), 39.

50 Fanon, *Wretched of the Earth*, 37–39.

51 See Regina M. Schwartz, *The Curse of Cain: The Violent Legacy of Monotheism* (Chicago: University of Chicago Press, 1997).

52 See Lydia Flem, *L'Art et la mémoire des camps: Représenter exterminer*, ed. Jean-Luc Nancy (Paris: Seuil, 2001).

53 See Eyal Weizman, "The Politics of Verticality," *openDemocracy*, April 25, 2002, https://www.opendemocracy.net/ecology-politicsverticality/article_801.jsp.

54 See Stephen Graham and Simon Marvin, *Splintering Urbanism: Networked Infrastructures, Technological Mobility and the Urban Condition* (London: Routledge, 2001).

55 Weizman, "Politics of Verticality."

56 See Stephen Graham, "'Clean Territory': Urbicide in the West Bank," *openDemocracy*, August 7, 2002, https://www.opendemocracy.net/conflict-politics verticality/article_241.jsp.

57 Compare with the panoply of new bombs the United States deployed during the Gulf War and the war in Kosovo, most aimed at raining down graphite crystals to disable comprehensively electrical power and distribution stations. Michael Ignatieff, *Virtual War* (New York: Metropolitan Books, 2000).

58 See Michael Walzer, *Just and Unjust Wars: A Moral Argument with Historical Illustrations* (New York: Basic Books, 1977).

59 Benjamin Ederington and Michael J. Mazarr, eds., *Turning Point: The Gulf War and U. S. Military Strategy* (Boulder, CO: Westview, 1994).

60 Thomas W. Smith, "The New Law of War: Legitimizing Hi-Tech and Infrastructural Violence," *International Studies Quarterly* 46 (2002): 367. On Iraq, see G. L. Simons, *The Scourging of Iraq: Sanctions, Law and Natural Justice*, 2nd ed. (New York: St. Martin's, 1998); see also A. Shehabaldin and W. M. Laughlin Jr. , "Economic Sanctions against Iraq: Human and Economic Costs," *International Journal of Human Rights* 3, no. 4 (2000): 1–18.

61 Zygmunt Bauman, "Wars of the Globalization Era," *European Journal of Social Theory* 4, no. 1 (2001): 15. "Remote as they are from their 'targets,' scurrying over those they hit too fast to witness the devastation they cause and the blood they spill, the pilots-turned-computer-operators hardly ever have a chance of looking their victims in the face and to survey the human misery they have sowed," adds Bauman. "Military professionals of our time see no corpses and no wounds. They may sleep well; no pangs of conscience will keep them awake" (27). See also Zygmunt Bauman, "Penser la guerre aujourd'hui," *Cahiers de la Villa Gillet*, no. 16 (2002): 75–152.

62 Achille Mbembe, "At the Edge of the World: Boundaries, Territoriality, and Sovereignty in Africa," *Public Culture* 12 (2000): 259–84.

63 In international law, "privateers" are defined as "vessels belonging to private owners, and sailing under a commission of war empowering the person to whom it is granted to carry on all forms of hostility which are permissible at sea by the usages of war." I use the term here to mean armed formations acting in-

dependently of any politically organized society, in the pursuit of private interests, whether or not under the mask of the state. See Janice Thomson, *Mercenaries, Pirates, and Sovereigns* (Princeton: Princeton University Press, 1997), 21–22.

64 Gilles Deleuze and Félix Guattari, *A Thousand Plateaus: Capitalism and Schizophrenia, Vol. 2*, trans. and foreword by Brian Massumi (Minneapolis: University of Minnesota Press, 1987), 351–423.

65 Joseph C. Miller, *Way of Death: Merchant Capitalism and the Angolan Slave Trade, 1730–1830* (Madison: University of Wisconsin Press, 1988), especially chaps. 2 and 4.

66 See Jakkie Cilliers and Christian Dietrich, eds., *Angola's War Economy: The Role of Oil and Diamonds* (Pretoria: Institute for Security Studies, 2000).

67 See, for example, "Rapport du Groupe d'experts sur l'exploitation illégale des ressources naturelles et autres richesses de la République démocratique du Congo," United Nations Report No. 2/2001/357, submitted by the secretary-general to the Security Council, April 12, 2001. See also Richard Snyder, "Does Lootable Wealth Breed Disorder? States, Regimes, and the Political Economy of Extraction," unpublished manuscript.

68 See Loren B. Landau, "The Humanitarian Hangover: Transnationalization of Governmental Practice in Tanzania's Refugee-Populated Areas," *Refugee Survey Quarterly* 21, no. 1 (2002): 260–99, especially 281–87.

69 On *commandement*, see Achille Mbembe, *On the Postcolony* (Berkeley: University of California Press, 2001), chaps. 1–3.

70 See Leisel Talley, Paul B. Spiegel, and Mona Girgis, "An Investigation of Increasing Mortality among Congolese Refugees in Lugufu Camp, Tanzania, May–June 1999," *Journal of Refugee Studies* 14, no. 4 (2001): 412–27.

71 See Tony Hodges, *Angola: From Afro-Stalinism to Petro-Diamond Capitalism* (Oxford: James Currey, 2001), chap. 7; Stephen Ellis, *The Mask of Anarchy: The Destruction of Liberia and the Religious Dimension of an African Civil War* (London: Hurst, 1999).

72 See Elias Canetti, *Crowds and Power*, trans. C. Stewart (New York: Farrar, Straus and Giroux, 1984), 227–80.

73 Martin Heidegger, *Being and Time*, trans. Joan Stambaugh (Albany: State University of New York Press, 2010), 227–56.

74 Heidegger, *Being and Time*, 227–56.

75 Bataille, *Oeuvres complètes*, 336.

76 For what precedes, see Amira Hass, *Drinking the Sea at Gaza: Days and Nights in a Land under Siege* (New York: Henry Holt, 1996).

77 Gilroy, *Black Atlantic*, 63.

Four Viscerality

1 Martin Heidegger, *The Question concerning Technology and Other Essays*, trans. William Lovitt (New York: Harper and Row, 1977).

2 Heidegger, *The Question concerning Technology*, 4.

3 Heidegger, *The Question concerning Technology*, 25–26.

4 Lucien Lévy-Bruhl, *The Primitive Mentality*, trans. Lilian A. Clare (New York: Macmillan, 1966); André Leroi-Gourhan, *Gesture and Speech*, trans. Anna Bostock Berger (Cambridge, MA: MIT Press, 1993).

5 See S. A. Bedini, "The Role of Automata in the History of Technology," *Technology and Culture* 5, no. 1 (1964): 24–42.

6 See Gaby Wood, *Edison's Eve: A Magical History of the Quest for Mechanical Life* (New York: Anchor, 2002).

7 Matteo Pasquinelli, "Anomaly, Detection: The Mathematization of the Abnormal in Metadata Society," panel talk presented at Transmediale 2015, Berlin, https://transmediale.de/content/presentation-by-matteo-pasquinelli-all-watched-over-by-algorithms.

8 Margarida Mendes, "Molecular Colonialism," 2017, https://www.anthropocene-curriculum.org/files/partials/2413/Molecular%20Colonialism_%20Margarida%20Mendes.pdf.

9 See Jonathan F. Donges et al., "The Technosphere in Earth System Analysis: A Coevolutionary Perspective," *Anthropocene Review* 4, no. 1 (2017): 23–33.

10 See Bronislaw Szerszynski, "Viewing the Technosphere in an Interplanetary Light," *Anthropocene Review* 4, no. 2 (2017): 92–102.

11 For a recent reappraisal, see Gary Fields, *Enclosure: Palestinian Landscapes in a Historical Mirror* (Berkeley: University of California Press, 2017).

12 Marc Lamont Hill, *Nobody: Casualties of America's War on the Vulnerable, from Ferguson to Flint and Beyond* (New York: Atria Paperback, 2016).

13 Yves Winter, "The Siege of Gaza: Spatial Violence, Humanitarian Strategies, and the Biopolitics of Punishment," *Constellations* 23, no. 2 (2016): 308–19.

14 Marc Goodman, *Future Crimes: Everything Is Connected, Everyone Is Vulnerable and What We Can Do about It* (New York: Doubleday, 2015); Benjamin Wittes and Gabriella Blum, *The Future of Violence: Robots and Germs, Hackers and Drones—Confronting a New Age of Threat* (New York: Basic Books, 2015).

15 Elsa Dorlin, *Se défendre: Une philosophie de la violence* (Paris: La Découverte, 2017).

16 Grégoire Chamayou, *Manhunts: A Philosophical History*, trans. Steven Rendall (Princeton: Princeton University Press, 2012).

17 See Sam Frank, "Come with Us If You Want to Live," *Harper's Magazine*, January 2015.

18 See Corey Pein, "Mouthbreathing Machiavelli's Dream of a Silicon Reich," *The Baffler*, May 19, 2014, 13. https://thebaffler.com/latest/mouthbreathing-machiavellis.

19 Luciana Parisi, "Automated Thinking and the Limits of Reason," *Cultural Studies* 16, no. 5 (2016): 471–81.

20 Jean Comaroff, "Pentecostalism, Populism and the New Politics of Affect," in *Pentecostalism and Development: Churches, NGOs and Social Change in Africa*, ed. D. Freeman (London: Palgrave Macmillan, 2012).

21 Jacob Silverman, "Hotdogs in Zion," *The Baffler*, no. 31 (June 2016), https://thebaffler.com/salvos/hotdogs-zion-silverman.

22 Silverman, "Hotdogs in Zion."

23 Corey Pein, "Everybody Freeze," *The Baffler*, no. 30 (2016), https://thebaffler.com/salvos/everybody-freeze-pein.

24 Corinne Purtill, "Fifty Years Frozen: The World's First Cryonically Preserved Human's Disturbing Journey to Immortality," *Quartz*, January 12, 2017, https://qz.com/883524/fifty-years-frozen-the-worlds-first-cryonically-preserved-humans-disturbing-journey-to-immortality/.

25 Michael Hendricks, "The False Science of Cryonics," MIT *Technology Review*, September 15, 2015, https://www.technologyreview.com/s/541311/the-false-science-of-cryonics/.

26 Heather Havrilesky, "Apocalypse Soon," *The Baffler*, no. 28 (July 2015), https://thebaffler.com/salvos/apocalypse-soon.

27 Havrilesky, "Apocalypse Soon."

28 See Evan Osnos, "Survival of the Richest: Why Some of America's Wealthiest People Are Preparing for Disaster," *New Yorker*, January 22, 2017, 36.

29 Pasquinelli, "Anomaly, Detection."

30 See Aeron Davis and Karel Williams, introduction to "Special Issue: Elites and Power after Financialization," *Theory, Culture and Society* 34, nos. 5–6 (2017): 3–26.

31 Luciana Parisi, "Instrumentality, or the Time of Inhuman Thinking," *Technosphere*, April 15, 2017, https://technosphere-magazine.hkw.de/p/Instrumentality-or-the-Time-of-Inhuman-Thinking-5UvwaECXmmYev25GrmEBhX.

Five Fanon's Pharmacy

1 Sigmund Freud, "Thoughts for the Times on War and Death," in *The Complete Psychological Works of Sigmund Freud*, vol. 14 (1914–16), ed. James Strachey (New York: Norton, 1976), 3067.

2 Freud, "Thoughts for the Times on War and Death," 3070.

3 Sándor Ferenczi, "Two Types of War Neuroses" (1916), in *Further Contributions to the Theory and Technique of Psychoanalysis* (London: Karnac, 2002), 125.

4 Hugo Grotius, *The Rights of War and Peace* (1625), ed. Richard Tuck (Indianapolis: Liberty Fund, 2005), 250.

5 Ernst Jünger, *Storm of Steel* (1920), trans. Michael Hofmann (London: Penguin Classics, 2004).

6 Gerd Krumeich, "La place de la guerre de 1914–1918 dans l'histoire culturelle de l'Allemagne," *Vingtième siècle*, no. 41 (January–March 1994): 9–17.

7 See Sarah Everts, "When Chemicals Became Weapons of War," *Chemical and Engineering News*, February 23, 2015, http://chemicalweapons.cenmag.org.

8 Modris Eksteins, *Rites of Spring: The Great War and the Birth of the Modern Age* (Boston: Houghton Mifflin, 1989).

9 Sigmund Freud, *Reflections on War and Death*, vol. 1, trans. Abraham Arden Brill and Alfred Booth Kuttner (New York: Moffat, Yard, 1918), "The Disappointments of War," 4.

10 Freud, "The Disappointments of War," 4, 11, 17.

11 Freud, "The Disappointments of War," 17; Sigmund Freud, *Reflections on War and Death*, vol. 1, trans. Abraham Arden Brill and Alfred Booth Kuttner (New York: Moffat, Yard, 1918), "Our Attitude to Death," 48.

12 Freud, "Our Attitude to Death," 48; Freud, "The Disappointments of War," 32.

13 Sigmund Freud, "The Economic Problem of Masochism," in *The Standard Edition of the Complete Psychological Works of Sigmund Freud*, vol. 19, trans. and edited by James Strachey (London: The Hogarth Press, 1961), 169.

14 Hannah Arendt, *The Origins of Totalitarianism* (New York: Harvest, 1966).

15 Paul Valery, "A Crisis of the Mind," in *The Outlook for Intelligence*, trans. Denise Folliot and Jackson Matthews, with a preface by François Valéry (Princeton: Princeton University Press, 1989), 31.

16 See Federico Rahola, "La forme-camp: Pour une généalogie des lieux de transit et d'internement du présent," *Cultures et Conflits*, no. 68 (2007): 31–50.

17 Caroline Elkins, *Imperial Reckoning: The Untold Story of Britain's Gulag in Kenya* (New York: Henry Holt, 2005).

18 Paul Gilroy, "Fanon and Améry: Theory, Torture and the Prospect of Humanism," *Theory, Culture and Society* 27, nos. 7–8 (2007): 16–32.

19 Arendt, *Origins of Totalitarianism*; Michel Foucault, *Society Must Be Defended: Lectures at the Collège de France, 1975–1976*, ed. Mauro Bertani and Alessandro Fontano, trans. David Macey (New York: Picador, 2003).

20 Jonathan Hyslop, "The Invention of the Concentration Camp: Cuba, Southern Africa and the Philippines, 1896–1907," *South African Historical Journal* 63, no. 2 (2011): 251–76.

21 John Lawrence Tone, *War and Genocide in Cuba, 1895–1898* (Chapel Hill: University of North Carolina Press, 2006).

22 On these details, see the study by Richard Shelley Hartigan, *Lieber's Code and the Law of War* (New York: Transaction, 1983).

23 Brian McAllister Linn, *The Philippine War, 1899–1902* (Lawrence: University of Kansas Press, 2000).

24 Jean-François Bossy, *La Philosophie à l'épreuve d'Auschwitz: Les camps nazis, entre mémoire et histoire* (Paris: Ellipses, 2004), 32.

25 See Ralph Schor, *L'Opinion française et les étrangers, 1919–1939* (Paris: Publications de la Sorbonne, 1985).

26 See Bernard Laguerre, "Les dénaturalisés de Vichy, 1940–1944," *Vingtième Siècle* 20, no. 1 (1988): 3–15. See also Robert Paxton, *La France de Vichy, 1940–1944* (Paris: Seuil, 1974), 168–69.

27 Paul Armengaud, *Quelques enseignements des campagnes du Rif en matière d'aviation* (Paris: Berger-Levrault, 1928).

28 Claude Juin, *Des Soldats tortionnaires: Guerre d'Algérie. Des jeunes gens ordinaires confrontés à l'intolérable* (Paris: Robert Laffont, 2012).

29 Joseph-Simon Gallieni, *Rapport d'ensemble sur la pacification, l'organisation et la colonisation de Madagascar* (Paris: Charles-Lavauzelle, 1900); Hubert Lyautey, *Du Rôle colonial de l'armée* (Paris: Armand Colin, 1900).

30 Frantz Fanon, *The Wretched of the Earth*, trans. C. Farrington (New York: Grove Weidenfeld, 1991), 183.

31 Fanon, *Wretched of the Earth*, 183.

32 Frantz Fanon, "Racism and Culture," in *Towards the African Revolution*, trans. Haakon Chevalier (New York: Grove Press, 1988), 35.

33 Fanon, "Racism and Culture," 37.

34 Frantz Fanon, *Black Skin, White Masks*, trans. Richard Philcox (1952; New York: Grove Press, 2008), 142–43 [translation modified—SC].

35 Fanon, *Black Skin, White Masks*, 92, 89 [translation modified—SC].

36 Fanon, *Black Skin, White Masks*, 93.

37 Fanon, *Black Skin, White Masks*, 89, 96.

38 See Angelo Hesnard, *L'Univers morbide de la faute* (Paris: PUF, 1949).

39 Fanon, *Black Skin, White Masks*, 133.

40 See Charles Odier, *L'Angoisse et la pensée magique* (Neuchâtel: Delachaux et Niestlé, 1948).

41 Fanon, *Black Skin, White Masks*, 134.

42 [In colonial times, *petits blancs*, or "little whites," designated the white, non-plantation-owning underclass, who often reserved an intense hatred for the wealthier mulatto class. They contrasted with the *grands blancs*, or "big whites," the wealthy white upper class, comprising bureaucrats and planters. The term is used today to refer to the conservative right—SC].

43 Fanon, *Black Skin, White Masks*, 146.

44 Fanon, *Black Skin, White Masks*, 137.

45 Fanon, *Toward the African Revolution*, trans. Haakon Chevalier (1964; New York: Grove Press, 1967), 13.

46 Fanon, *Toward the African Revolution*, 14.

47 Fanon, *Toward the African Revolution*, 14.

48 Fanon, *Wretched of the Earth*, 10.

49 Frantz Fanon, *Alienation and Freedom*, trans. S. Corcoran (London: Bloomsbury, 2018), 224.

50 Fanon, *Alienation and Freedom*, 345, 346, 181, 322, 181.

51 Fanon, *Alienation and Freedom*, 234–35.

52 Fanon, *Alienation and Freedom*, 267.

53 Fanon, *Alienation and Freedom*, 304, 301, 304.

54 Fanon, *Alienation and Freedom*, 236.

55 Fanon, *Wretched of the Earth*, 197.

56 Fanon, *Wretched of the Earth*, 204–5.

57 Fanon, "Letter to the Resident Minister," in *Alienation and Freedom*, 434.

58 Fanon, "Letter to a Frenchman," in *Toward the African Revolution*, 49 [some translations modified—SC].

59 In *Toward the African Revolution*, 729–32 and 733–35. All subsequent citations are from these two texts.

60 Frantz Fanon, *A Dying Colonialism*, trans. Haakon Chevalier (1959; New York: Grove Press, 1965), 121.

61 Fanon, *Wretched of the Earth*, 181.

62 Fanon, *Wretched of the Earth*, 186.

63 Fanon, *Wretched of the Earth*, 188.

64 Fanon, *Wretched of the Earth*, 188, 189.

65 Fanon, *Wretched of the Earth*, 189.

66 Fanon, *Wretched of the Earth*, 190.

67 Fanon, *Wretched of the Earth*, 191.

68 Fanon, *Wretched of the Earth*, 191.

69 Fanon, *Wretched of the Earth*, 191.

70 Fanon, *Wretched of the Earth*, 192.

71 Fanon, *Wretched of the Earth*, 636 (subsequent citations are from the same page).

Six This Stifling Noonday

1 Frantz Fanon, "This Africa to Come," in *Towards the African Revolution*, trans. Haakon Chevalier (1964; New York: Grove Press, 1967), 177–78, 179, 178.

2 Andrews William, *To Tell a Free Story: The First Century of African American Autobiography, 1760–1865* (Urbana: University of Illinois Press, 1986).

3 John Ernest, *Liberation Historiography: African American Writers and the Challenge of History, 1794–1861* (Chapel Hill: University of North Carolina Press, 2004).

4 From this point of view, see Alexander Crummell, *Destiny and Race: Selected Writings, 1840–1898* (Amherst: University of Massachusetts Press, 1992); Edward W. Blyden, *Christianity, Islam and the Negro Race* (1887; Baltimore: Black Classic Press, 1978). See also Léopold Sédar Senghor, *Liberté I: Négritude et humanisme* (Paris: Seuil, 1964); Paul Gilroy, *Against Race: Imagining Political Culture beyond the Color Line* (Cambridge, MA: Harvard University Press, 1998); Fabien Eboussi-Boulaga, *La Crise du Muntu: Authenticité africaine et philosophie* (Paris: Présence africaine, 1981).

5 Fanon, "This Africa to Come," 177–78.

6 On the Atlantic side, see John Thornton, *Africa and Africans in the Making of the Atlantic World, 1400–1680* (Cambridge, UK: Cambridge University Press, 1992).

7 Ralph Ellison, *Invisible Man* (New York: Random House, 1952).

8 James Baldwin, *The Fire Next Time* (New York: Vintage Books, 1963).

9 Paul Gilroy, *The Black Atlantic: Modernity and Double Consciousness* (London: Verso, 1993).

10 See, for example, Sidney Mintz, *Sweetness and Power: The Place of Sugar in Modern History* (New York: Viking-Penguin, 1985); Seymour Shapiro, *Capital and the Cotton Industry in the Industrial Revolution* (Ithaca, NY: Cornell University Press, 1967); John Hebron Moore, *The Emergence of the Cotton Kingdom in the Old Southwest: Mississippi, 1770–1860* (Baton Rouge: University of Louisiana Press, 1988).

11 Marcus Rediker and Peter Linebaugh, *The Many-Headed Hydra: Sailors, Slaves, Commoners, and the Hidden History of the Revolutionary Atlantic* (Boston: Beacon Press, 2000).

12 See Peter Mark, *Portuguese Style and Luso-African Identity: Precolonial Senegambia, Sixteenth–Nineteenth Centuries* (Bloomington: Indiana University Press, 2002); J. Lorand Matory, *Black Atlantic Religion: Tradition, Transnationalism, and Matriarchy in the Afro-Brazilian Candomble* (Princeton: Princeton University Press, 2005); David Northrup, *Africa's Discovery of Europe, 1450–1850* (Oxford: Oxford University Press, 2009).

13 See "Conversation: Achille Mbembe and David Theo Goldberg of Critique of Black Reason," *Theory, Culture and Society*, July 3, 2018, https://www.theory culturesociety.org/conversation-achille-mbembe-and-david-theo-goldberg -on-critique-of-black-reason/.

14 Aimé Césaire, *Discourse on Colonialism*, trans. Joan Pinkham (1955; New York and London: Monthly Review Press, 1972).

15 See, from this point of view, Senghor, *Liberté I*; Édouard Glissant, *Traité du Tout-Monde* (Paris: Gallimard, 1997); Gilroy, *Against Race*.

16 David Scott, "The Re-enchantment of Humanism: An Interview of Sylvia Wynter," *Small Axe*, no. 8 (September 2000): 119–207; Sylvia Wynter, "Human Being as Noun? Or *Being Human* as Praxis? Towards the Autopoetic Turn/ Overturn: A Manifesto," *Slideshare*, August 25, 2007, http: //fr.slideshare.net.

17 Cheikh Anta Diop, *Nations nègres et culture* (Paris: Présence africaine, 1954).

18 Cheikh Anta Diop, *The African Origin of Civilization: Myth or Reality?* (1967; New York: Lawrence Hill & Co., 1974). See also Cheikh Anta Diop, *Civilization or Barbarism* (New York: Lawrence Hill Books, 1991).

19 See, for example, the works of science fiction by Samuel R. Delany and Octavia Butler. See also the paintings of Jean-Michel Basquiat and the photographs of Renée Cox and listen to the musical translations of extraterrestrial myths in the productions of Parliament-Funkadelic, Jonzun Crew, and Sun Ra. For a general

introduction, see Alondra Nelson, ed., "Afrofuturism: A Special Issue," *Social Text*, no. 71 (2002).

20 Kodwo Eshun, *More Brilliant Than the Sun: Adventures in Sonic Fiction* (London: Quartet Books, 1999).

21 See the works of authors as diverse as Alexander Weheliye, *Phonographies: Grooves in Sonic Afro-modernity* (Durham, NC: Duke University Press, 2005); Fred Moten, *In the Break: The Aesthetics of the Black Radical Tradition* (Minneapolis: University of Minnesota Press, 2003); Eshun, *More Brilliant Than the Sun*.

22 See in particular Nelson, "Afrofuturism"; Ytasha L. Womack, *Afrofuturism: The World of Black Science Fiction and Fantasy Culture* (Chicago: Chicago Review Press, 2013); Bill Campbell and Edward Austin Hall, *Mothership: Tales from Afrofuturism and Beyond* (Greenbelt, MD: Rosarium, 2013); Sheree R. Thomas, *Dark Matter: A Century of Speculative Fiction from the African Diaspora* (New York: Warner Books, 2000).

23 See Earl Gammon, "Nature as Adversary: The Rise of Modern Conceptions of Nature in Economic Thought," *Economy and Society* 38, no. 2 (2010): 218–46.

24 Marie-Noëlle Bourguet and Christophe Bonneuil, "De l'inventaire du globe à la 'mise en valeur' du monde: Botanique et colonisation (fin XVIIIeme siècle, début XXeme siècle)," *Revue française d'histoire d'Outre-mer* 86, nos. 322–23 (1999): 7–38.

25 For the colonial period, see for example Richard H. Grove, *Green Imperialism: Colonial Expansion, Tropical Islands, and the Origins of Environmentalism, 1660–1860* (Cambridge, UK: Cambridge University Press, 1995).

26 See Randy J. Sparks, *Where the Negroes Are Masters: An African Port in the Era of the Slave Trade* (Cambridge, MA: Harvard University Press, 2014).

27 Richard H. Steckel, "A Peculiar Population: The Nutrition, Health, and Mortality of U.S. Slaves from Childhood to Maturity," *Journal of Economic History* 46, no. 3 (1986): 721–41.

28 Michael Tadman, *Speculators and Slaves: Masters, Traders, and Slaves in the Old South* (Madison: University of Wisconsin Press, 1989); Laurence J. Kotlikoff, "Quantitative Description of the New Orleans Slave Market," in *Without Consent or Contract: The Rise and Fall of American Slavery*, ed. William Fogel and Stanley L. Engerman (New York: Norton, 1989); Maurie McInnis, *Slaves Waiting for Sale: Abolitionist Art and the American Slave Trade* (Chicago: University of Chicago Press, 2011).

29 Christopher Hager, *Word by Word: Emancipation and the Act of Writing* (Cambridge, MA: Harvard University Press, 2013).

30 Sharla M. Fett, *Working Cures: Healing, Health, and Power on Southern Slave Plantations* (Chapel Hill: University of North Carolina Press, 2002).

31 Edward E. Baptist, *The Half Has Never Been Told: Slavery and the Making of American Capitalism* (New York: Basic Books, 2014).

32 Caroline Oudin-Bastide and Philippe Steiner, *Calcul et morale: Coûts de l'es-clavage et valeur de l'émancipation (XVIIIe–XIXe siècle)* (Paris: Albin Michel, 2014).

33 Achille Mbembe, *Critique of Black Reason*, trans. Laurent Dubois (Durham, NC: Duke University Press, 2017).

34 Frantz Fanon, *Freedom and Alienation*, ed. Jean Khalfa and Robert Young, trans. Steven Corcoran (London: Bloomsbury, 2018), 219.

35 Fanon, *Freedom and Alienation*, 441, 442.

36 Consult the following two articles in particular: "On Some Cases Treated with the Bini Method" and "Indications of Electroconvulsive Therapy within Insti-tutional Therapies," in Fanon, *Freedom and Alienation*, 285–98.

37 Hito Steyerl, "A Thing Like You and Me," *e-flux*, no. 15 (2010).

38 Joseph Vogl, *Le Spectre du capital* (Paris: Diaphanes, 2013).

39 Saskia Sassen, *Expulsions: Brutality and Complexity in the Global Economy* (Cambridge, MA: Harvard University Press, 2014).

40 Mbembe, *Critique of Black Reason*.

41 Éric Sadin, *L'Humanité augmentée: L'administration numérique du monde* (Paris: L'Echappée, 2013).

42 Cedric J. Robinson, *Black Marxism: The Making of the Black Radical Tradition* (Chapel Hill: University of North Carolina Press, 1983).

Conclusion

1 Frantz Fanon, *Black Skin, White Masks*, trans. Richard Philcox (1952; New York: Grove Press, 2008), 206.

INDEX

enemy (*continued*)
120–21, 152; dehumanization of, 64,
65, 66, 126; internal versus external,
82, 129, 131
enmity, 2, 40–44, 141–55
Europe: borderization and, 99–100;
Fanon and, 5; fascism in, 121–22; and
migration, 12, 45, 98–99, 102–3; and
racism, 138, 147. *See also* colonialism

Fanon, Frantz, 2, 117–55, 156, 160, 185,
186, 187, 189; and colonialism, 4–8,
27, 79–81, 128–29; and creative violence, 118–30, 129; and decolonization, 6, 139–41; and humanism,
175–76; and racism, 130–39; relation
of care, 144, 176; and vulnerability,
175–76
fascism, 121, 122
Ferenczi, Sándor, 119
Foucault, Michel, 66, 70–74, 76, 92, 123
France, 12, 20, 22, 23, 73, 125, 192n21
Freud, Sigmund, 51, 56, 118–21, 195n1

Gilroy, Paul, 75, 91–92, 157, 160
Glissant, Édouard, 9, 160, 184, 188
Goldberg, David Theo, 200n36
governmentality, 86–87
Guattari, Félix, 85, 160

Hegel, G. W. F., 68–69, 74, 78, 91
Heidegger, Martin, 9, 28, 63, 64, 90,
93–94, 96
Hesnard, Angelo, 135
Holocaust, 38–39, 46, 63, 67, 120, 121,
123, 126
humanism, 157–61
humanity, 13–14, 29, 31–32

Israel, 43–45, 81

Jefferson, Thomas, 18–19, 20
Jews, 12, 112, 125, 130, 131; Holocaust and,

38–39, 46, 63, 67, 120, 121, 123, 126;
as Others, 6, 30, 43, 57, 59, 101
Jupiter (slave of Jefferson), 20

Kojève, Alexandre, 78

Lee, William, 20
"Letter to a Frenchman" (Fanon),
146
"Letter to the Resident Minister"
(Fanon), 146

messianism, 104–7
Mendes, Margarida, 95–96
migration: colonization and, 10–13, 45;
twenty-first-century, 98–99, 102–3
Montchrestien, Antoine de, 11
Muslims, 43, 112: as Others, 6, 30, 31, 38,
51, 59, 60, 115; and terrorism, 33
mythicoreligious reasoning, 49–52

Nazism, 71–72, 76, 121–22, 123, 125
necropower, 38–39, 78–83, 92, 200n36.
See also terror and terrorism
Negro/Negress: body of, 173–75; Fanon
and, 7; as Other, 30, 38, 43, 49–50,
132–38, 161–66; in the West, 156–57.
See also slavery

Other, 30, 38, 43, 49–50, 132–38, 161–66

Palestinian territories, 43–46, 80–82,
88–90, 97
Pasquinelli, Matteo, 109–10, 113
plantation, 10, 18–23, 74–76
political: idea of, 15, 50, 66–70; fantasy
of annihilation and, 63–64; Schmitt
and, 48–49
postcolony, 29–30

The Question Concerning Technology
(Heidegger), 93–94
quinine, 23–24